POLLING AND PRESIDENTIAL ELECTION COVERAGE

OTHER RECENT VOLUMES IN THE
SAGE FOCUS EDITIONS

POLLING AND PRESIDENTIAL ELECTION COVERAGE

Paul J. Lavrakas
Jack K. Holley

editors

SAGE PUBLICATIONS
The International Professional Publishers
Newbury Park   London   New Delhi

For information address:

SAGE Publications, Inc.
2455 Teller Road
Newbury Park, California 91320

SAGE Publications Ltd.
6 Bonhill Street
London EC2A 4PU
United Kingdom

SAGE Publications India Pvt. Ltd.
M-32 Market
Greater Kailash I
New Delhi 110 048 India

Printed in the United States of America

Library of Congress Cataloging-in-Publication Data

Polling and presidential election coverage / edited by Paul J.
Lavrakas and Jack K. Holley.
    p.   cm. —(Sage focus editions ; v 127)
Includes bibliographical references and index.
ISBN 0-8039-4073-4. — ISBN 0-8039-4074-2 (pbk.)
1. Public opinion—United States. 2. Public opinion polls.
3. Election forecasting—United States. 4. Press and politics—
United States.   I. Lavrakas, Paul J. II. Holley, Jack K.
HN90.P8P65 1991
303 .3'8—dc20   90-43950
                                                             CIP

RECEIVED

APR 2 9 1991

FIRST PRINTING, 1991

Kennedy School
Library

Sage Production Editor: Michelle R. Starika

Contents

This book is dedicated to I. W. "Bill" Cole, Dean of the
Medill School of Journalism, Northwestern University, 1957-1984,
without whose vision and support we would not have had
the opportunity to produce this book.

Preface

Our specific intention in this book is to improve the manner in which the news media use sample surveys, in particular, election polls, to cover important social issues.

We believe that, when properly disseminated, information gathered via high-quality surveys can educate the nation (both the general public and elites) and enhance our democratic processes. Unfortunately, too often we see an overuse and misuse of election survey findings by the news media.

Simply put, too few editors, producers, and reporters have the training and experience to be discriminating consumers of survey findings. Given this situation, it is hard to expect the public to do any better. The chapters in this book provide a great deal of information and suggestions for those in the media to consider as they continue to think about how to better incorporate survey findings into their coverage of elections and other important public policy issues.

The book also provides an "insider's" perspective, original research findings, and theoretical speculation on how polls, as measures of public opinion, may affect the public and certain elite groups (politicians, campaign workers and contributors, and the like). For this reason, pollsters, social scientists, and "politicos," as well as journalists, should find the chapters informative and provocative.

Work on this book, some of the original research we report here, and a symposium that brought together the chapter authors in January 1989 was made possible by the support of the former dean of the Medill School of Journalism, Dr. Edward P. Bassett. We appreciate his encouragement and the considerable financial support he provided to our efforts. We would also like to thank the Institute of Modern Communications; its director, Professor Peter V. Miller; and the Northwestern University Survey Laboratory for the support each provided. In addition, we appreciate the expert administrative assistance provided by J. Sophie Buchanan over the past two years in bringing this project to successful completion.

During the time this book was being put into its final form, one of our fellow contributors, I. A. "Bud" Lewis, died. We honor Bud's legacy to journalism and polling: He set an example of the highest quality not only for the polls he conducted but also in what he expected from the journalists who incorporated the poll results into their stories. Bud worked hard until the time of his death to achieve no less than the best from both.

—Paul J. Lavrakas
Jack K. Holley

1

Introduction

PAUL J. LAVRAKAS

As predictable as the rising of the sun, American journalists know which story they will be covering intensely every four years: the election campaign for the U.S. president. And just as reliably, many persons—including some journalists—complain that media coverage of presidential election campaigns is poorly executed and does more harm than good to the process whereby our nation chooses a president.

In the twentieth century, a prominent part of this coverage has included the use of sample surveys (polls) to generate "news" about the campaigns and elections. Especially since the 1950s, each decade has witnessed newspapers and other media organizations (television, in particular) develop an increasing capacity and willingness to use information generated by surveys as a prominent part of the campaign news they provide—from before the presidential primary season through the weeks following the November election.

This book was developed within this historical context. Specifically, it is an outgrowth of an ongoing program that I began in 1988 at Northwestern University to study the manner in which the American news media use results of polls in their coverage of election campaigns—in particular, presidential elections. The multiyear program has been jointly sponsored by Northwestern's Medill School of Journalism, the Institute of Modern Communications at Northwestern, and the Northwestern University Survey Laboratory.

As part of our efforts, a symposium was held at Northwestern in early 1989 to review and discuss (a) how the national news media used surveys in their coverage of the 1988 Bush-Dukakis election campaign, (b) what effect this type of news had on the public and others, including the candidates, their staff, and supporters, and (c) what should be done by the media with polls as a part of news coverage of future elections, in particular, the 1992 presidential campaign. Each of the contributors to this book participated in the 1989 symposium.

Several research projects also have been conducted at Northwestern. One was a large national research study to investigate public reactions to the ongoing media coverage of the 1988 presidential campaign. The findings of this unique study are reported in Chapter 7 of this book. Another study, reported in Chapter 10, was a 1989 national survey of daily newspapers about their use of polling for editorial and other purposes. Third, a large content analysis of the major American metropolitan dailies' use of polls to cover presidential elections is being conducted. Finally, experimental research studies to test the effects of various aspects of "polling news" on the public have been completed, with more in progress.

Some Perspectives from Contributors to This Book

As mentioned above, each of the expert contributors to this book participated in a symposium discussing the issues the book addresses. In addition to those from Northwestern University (Paul Lavrakas, Jack Holley, and Peter Miller), they included

- *Harrison Hickman*, president of Hickman-Maslin, a political consulting firm for Democratic incumbents and other political aspirants
- *Mike Kagay*, editor of news surveys at *The New York Times*
- *I. A. "Bud" Lewis*, director of the *Los Angeles Times* Poll
- *Frank McBride*, project director at Yankelovich, Clancey and Shulman, formerly with the election polling staff for George Bush's 1988 campaign at Market Opinion Research
- *Warren Mitofsky*, executive director of voter research & surveys, formerly director of the CBS Polling and Election Unit, and past president of the American Association for Public Opinion Research
- *Mike Traugott*, professor at the Institute for Social Research (University of Michigan) and study director for the 1988 Times-Mirror "The People, the Press, and the Public" project at Gallup

What follows are brief highlights of some of the information and opinion exchange from our two days of discussion in January 1989. The presentation of some of the verbal record from the symposium provides a brief historical and critical perspective for the chapters that follow.

Before the 1970s, the preelection poll results used by the news media in their coverage of presidential election campaigns almost always came from surveys conducted by outside firms, often hired by the media (e.g., Gallup and Harris). Apart from that source of polling information, reporters sometimes relied on the results of surveys conducted by private pollsters for political candidates.

As Mike Kagay observed, "When news organizations started their own polls in the 1970s, it could be seen as part of the movement toward more investigative reporting rather than merely reporting and/or reacting to polls done by others." According to Kagay, *The New York Times*, for example, developed its own polling capacity to "free" its reporters from dependence and thus from possible "victimization" by other poll sources, including from the results of private polls leaked by politicians. Furthermore, when media organizations do their own polls, their editors and reporters have the ability to ask their own questions and structure the data to meet their specific news interests rather than having to rely on the hope that some other pollster might ask the questions about which they want data. As Kagay also observed, this commitment by news organizations to doing their own polling has coincided with the "rise of 'public opinion' as a beat that deserves coverage like any other beat."

As the senior journalist participating in the symposium and a long-time observer of presidential election campaign news coverage, Bud Lewis chronicled the emergence of the television networks' dominance of election-eve news: first with live reporting in the 1950s of vote totals from "early precincts" through the now-common projections of election winners partially based on exit polls.

As noted by Warren Mitofsky, who has played a major role in the development of valid exit poll methodology, exit polls originally were used to gather detailed information to help understand the nature of the "mandate" of an election and *not* primarily to aid in the projecting of a winner. In fact, the first time a presidential winner was projected in part from exit poll data was in 1980. From Mitofsky's perspective, some print journalists have never forgiven the networks for "taking the story away" by being the first to proclaim the new president. To Mitofsky, this "sour grapes" behavior has contributed to the public's misunderstanding of valid exit polls, as many well-known political correspondenst at newspapers have done little to explain the proper use and value of exit polls.

Public complaints about polls (not just exit polls) and the news they generate may be partly explained by polls that are conducted and/or reported poorly. As Harrison Hickman observed, polling is "a business any fool can get into, and many have." Because of the importance of preelection polls to candidate viability, especially those conducted at the time of the primaries, our panelists agreed with Hickman that it is incumbent upon polling organizations and the media to conduct polls only when they are likely to be accurate and to report them accurately.

A related issue that was discussed, but of which few outside the survey field are likely to be aware, concerned various "technical" aspects of election surveys. For example, Bud Lewis suggested that "pollsters need to agree on standards [for measuring] a 'likely' voter or for how samples are weighted."

Frank McBride stressed the importance of not reporting or interpreting preelection polls out of context or of losing track of the lessons of history. For example, polls conducted early in a campaign that focus on which candidate is "winning," especially in off-year elections and for subpresidential races, may reflect "nothing more than [differences in] name recognition" in McBride's experience. Furthermore, Warren Mitofsky encouraged journalists to "compare change in [candidate] support *only* to [one's] own poll over time using similar methods."

Panelists also agreed with the call for much more creative use of polling data than merely focusing on the "horse race," although, as Mitofsky stressed, that aspect *is* still big news. For example, Mike Traugott suggested using data from preelection polls to help "define 'who' the candidate is in terms of political ideology" by using a profile of a candidate's supporters' positions on various issues.

As Peter Miller observed, "The rationale [for the media] to do polls needs to be more than just to counter what candidate polls [may say]—the rationale should be to help frame the editorial approach, to enlighten and [help the public to better] understand the election."

Yet, for this to happen, the capacity of journalists to use polls needs to improve. To this end, Jack Holley noted that "the sophistication that has developed in polling [methods] has not [yet] transferred to how reporters are trained to critically use surveys, especially at the nonnational level."

As a start in this direction, this book provides a good deal of information about what the media do with polls in covering presidential elections, what effects this type of news might have on the general public and other specific groups, and how the media might do things differently while preparing their coverage of future presidential and other nonpresidential elections.

Overview of the Book

The chapters that follow in this book were written by persons with special and extensive expertise on the subjects they have addressed. The structure that loosely organizes the book is as follows:

(1) What did the media do with polling in covering the 1988 Bush-Dukakis election campaign?

(2) What effect did this type of news have on various groups, including the public?

(3) What should be done by the media in using polling results as part of their coverage of future elections?

With few constraints from the editors, each contributor focused on what he judged was most significant to contribute. As such, there is some overlap of discussion of various topics by different authors. I believe that this is a definite strength of the book, as the careful reader can see where these experts agree (much more frequently), or disagree, on different aspects of the use of polling information by the media in covering presidential elections.

Chapters 2 to 4 provide information and comments about how the national media used polling to aid their coverage of the Bush-Dukakis race.

In Chapter 2, Mike Kagay provides in-depth insight on the yearlong election coverage program developed at *The New York Times*, focusing specifically on how polls were used as part of the coverage. The details here provide numerous examples and a model for other news organizations. As Kagay notes, *The Times*'s goal was to use "public opinion polling to aid both its reporters and its readers in understanding how the American electorate was reacting to the personalities, the issues, and the events of the [1988] presidential election campaign." Overall, *The Times* interviewed more than 80,000 Americans as part of 31 separate political polls in 1988, most of them conducted in partnership with CBS News but interpreted and reported independently. Of special value to journalists, media observers, and students of the media, Chapter 2 provides many specific examples of text and graphic uses of these 1988 poll results. Kagay also shares an insider's view of the dynamics of the 1988 election, that is, how the polling news documented the developing and changing attitudes that occurred in the electorate in 1988.

Addressing many of his and others' dissatisfaction with the reporting of elections, I. A. "Bud" Lewis brings over 40 years of experience as a journalist and 14 years as director of the *L.A. Times* Poll to the information he provides and suggestions he makes in Chapter 3. His considerable concern about the quality of today's reporting of election campaigns—in particular, the media's use of polls—shows throughout the chapter. Starting with a "report card on public polls," Chapter 3 clearly sets out what can and should be done better in future elections. Of value to all readers, but especially to those with an interest in historical perspectives, Bud Lewis's own experience, beginning in the 1940s, is used to illustrate his points. Also, in providing a case history of what the *Los Angeles Times* did in using polls as part of its 1988 election coverage, his insider's information complements that presented by Mike Kagay in the previous chapter. Lewis includes a section, "Some Lessons for 1992," noting that

> it is arguable that public opinion polls may have contributed to the [the public's political malaise] unintentionally, that they were often co-opted, made to be a tool of campaign manipulation rather than a mirror of public will. In 1992, it seems to me, media polls must be more sensitive to an exploration of the public agenda as opposed to the politicians' agenda.

In the past two decades, the projections made from exit polls, and thus the exit polls themselves, have developed a negative public image. But, as succinctly documented by Warren Mitofsky in Chapter 4, the image is not justified. As a leading figure in the development of exit poll methodology and as a rigorous survey research professional, Mitofsky provides a historical perspective on the development of exit polls in the United States and the controversy that has surrounded that development. "Since 1980, it is exit polling that has been attacked. Network critics now say that election conclusions based on actual [early] vote returns are acceptable, but it is exit polling that must be controlled," he observes. But despite the myriad claims that exit poll projections dampen voter turnout, especially in western states in presidential election years, Mitofsky finds no sound evidence that can document any such effects. In particular, he reviews those few studies that have been widely cited as showing an effect and clearly explains their methodological shortcomings. In addition to his review and discussion of these issues, the chapter provides a valuable summary of the procedures that are employed by those striving to conduct a valid exit poll.

Shifting focus from what the media did in 1988 with preelection surveys and exit polls, Chapters 5 to 8 address the issue of what effects this type of news coverage has on the general public, including voters and nonvoters, the campaigners, and other interested parties.

In Chapter 5, Harrison Hickman presents a detailed theoretical structure for understanding the possible effects of polling news on the public and elites, including candidates, their supporters, and their contributors. Based on his extensive work with the election campaigns of many political candidates and a deep understanding of survey research methodology and practice, Hickman argues that the impact of public polls is complex and nonstatic. Using carefully presented reasoning, he suggests

> that knowledge of poll standings is most likely to affect participants with strategic orientations who are unable to reliably predict the outcome of the contest from other information, feel great urgency to make a determination of candidate support, have little if any commitment to a particular candidate, have predispositions consistent with the direction of poll results, and trust the accuracy of polls.

In addition to his theorizing, Hickman shares much of his insider's knowledge of how polls were used in the 1988 presidential election, including an especially interesting analysis of the poll-related content of *Talking Points,* a daily fax sent to Democratic campaign professionals and opinion leaders around the country in 1988.

In Chapter 6, Mike Traugott presents and summarizes key findings about the electorates' attitudes toward the media and the news coverage of the 1988 election using his experience with the major study of the American electorate and the press in 1988—"The People, the Press, and Politics" project commissioned by Times Mirror and conducted through the Gallup organization. Overall, Traugott concludes that

> the Times Mirror surveys demonstrate the public's ambivalence toward the roles and influence of news organizations in the presidential selection process, with a healthy dose of skepticism about the appropriate role for polls as an element of campaign coverage.

Noted by Traugott and supported elsewhere in the book is the potential problem faced by news organizations due to

> the fact that those who are most likely to be concerned about the nature of contemporary political reporting, the role of polls in general, and the potential effects of network projections are the best educated, most politically sophisticated, and most active citizens. This means that they are also the most likely to make their views known to both the media and political elites and to demand change.

Consistent with many of Traugott's findings, Chapter 7 presents the results of the only large-scale national survey conducted in 1988 that focused specifically on the manner in which the public reacted to the polling news on the Bush-Dukakis election from early October through the week following the election. Here, Paul Lavrakas, Jack Holley, and Peter Miller present evidence—some of which is drawn from experimental methods incorporated into the overall survey design—from their preelection/postelection panel survey of 1,103 adults that (a) the vast majority of the public paid attention to the preelection poll stories, with nearly everyone knowing that Bush was consistently ahead and that the vast majority interviewed before the election expected a Bush victory; (b) most Americans thought preelection polling news was informative but few reportedly found it useful in helping them decide which candidate would get their vote, with the exception of those with relatively less formal education; (c) a large proportion of the population regarded these polls as harmful to the political process, especially the exit polls that were used by television networks to project George Bush as the winner on election eve; and (d) most important, knowing that the preelection polls had predicted a Bush victory was one of the primary reasons that some registered voters did not vote in the 1988 election. Chapter 7 concludes with a challenge to the media to seriously address their mandate to enhance, rather than impede, the democratic process through the responsible reporting of preelection and exit poll results.

Working at the time as an insider at Market Opinion Research, the firm that conducted George Bush's 1988 preelection polls, Frank McBride in Chapter 8 writes about the way the media use and misuse preelection polls. As he observes,

> the 1988 presidential election campaign confirmed two realities about preference polls and their use in the media. [First,] . . . there is no shortage of preelection pollings in a presidential election year [and] . . . the use of preference polls results by various media is a controversial practice.

McBride also "reconstructs the reality" of the 1988 Bush-Dukakis race using preelection poll results, which complement information about the evolution of preferences in 1988 presented in earlier chapters. Also complementing the insider's perspectives provided by Hickman in Chapter 5, McBride theorizes about the effects of preprimary and preelection polls on the electorate and the campaigns, at both presidential and subpresidential levels. He finishes his chapter with several specific suggestions for improving reporters' use of polling results in writing election campaign news stories, including the advice that

> pollsters have made a game effort to "scientifically" determine who will actually show up at the polls. . . . Regardless of the level of effort and good intentions, . . . primary polls often provide more embarrassment than information. For this reason, the use of primary polls is inherently dangerous and results should always be treated as very soft indicators of what will actually take place.

The final two chapters of the book address many important issues regarding what the media should consider doing differently in using polls as part of their election news coverage. In Chapter 9, Peter Miller, Daniel Merkle, and Paul Wang focus on the "uncomfortable relationship between the press and the polls [in] the way polling methods are described in poll stories." Although this may appear to be a narrow focus to some, it lies at the very heart of the concern about how the media use and report information from election polls. The authors observe

> that [survey] methodology is discussed at all is remarkable, because journalists rarely treat the process of news gathering as problematic. . . . It is a unique kind of journalism with "footnotes," wherein certain facts about polling methods are appended to a discussion of poll findings.

By reviewing the tensions inherent in these issues, Peter Miller and his colleagues illuminate the limitations of traditional efforts by the media to use polling news as part of their election coverage. They suggest, for example, "rather than a simple report of the percentages from a competitor's poll, the methodological and political context of the rival effort can be woven into the story." "The public at large [thus] can become involved in monitoring poll quality if journalists treat important methodological information as part of the poll story rather than as a technical appendix." Yet, for this to happen, "just as reporters become investigative experts, they must become polling experts. . . . They must understand the 'technical details' intimately, because they are not merely 'details' but journalism."

In the final chapter, Jack Holley, a 21-year newspaper veteran, begins with a review of past opinion on the shortcomings of "media polling" for the many readers of this book who are not likely to seek out those original sources. In this review, he addresses concerns about the "horse race" aspect of many preelection poll stories, "making" news rather than merely reporting it, the shift of "power" to the polls and away from political reporters, and the possibility of swaying voters with poll results. In addition to this review,

Chapter 10 also presents the findings of an original study Holley conducted in 1989 of a national sample of daily newspapers about their practices and standards regarding the use of polls and the reporting of poll results in news stories. Here, he reports that 40% of daily newspapers in 1989 were sponsoring/conducting their own political polls, yet hardly any had formal guidelines on survey quality or a rational structure for assigning reporters/ editors to survey stories. In his concluding comments, Holley notes findings and comments from several of the preceding chapters as they provide suggestions for the media to consider in rethinking their use of polls as part of election news coverage. Holley observes that "the media cannot and should not back away from using the relatively new and evolving technology of political polling, but clearly there are ways to handle the device better."

It is in this spirit that the chapters in this book have been written. Each of the authors sees the value that sample surveys can and do have both to enhance news coverage of elections (and other issues for that matter) and to educate the public and thus benefit our political processes. Yet, at the same time, each of the authors shows concern that too often survey techniques are not adequately understood by journalists and are thereby overused and/or misused. In an attempt to improve the current situation, the following chapters will offer information and suggestions to those who share these concerns.

2

The Use of Public Opinion Polls by
The New York Times

Some Examples from the 1988
Presidential Election

MICHAEL R. KAGAY

Throughout 1988, *The New York Times* used public opinion polling to aid both its reporters and its readers in understanding how the American electorate was reacting to the personalities, the issues, and the events of the Presidential election campaign. A total of 80,152 respondents were interviewed in 31 separate political polls, most conducted jointly with *The Times*'s polling partner, CBS News.

AUTHOR'S NOTE: I wish to acknowledge the signal contribution to all of the polls and analysis in this chapter of Adam Clymer, political editor of *The New York Times* in 1988, later senior editor, who oversaw all polling efforts at *The Times* from 1983 to early 1990. I also am indebted to the staff of the News Surveys Department at *The Times*, who originally computed, checked, and organized in scrupulous fashion most of the numerical data presented in this chapter: Marjorie Connelly, Janet Elder, and Deborah Hofmann. The correspondents and reporters who most frequently wrote the poll stories in 1988 also brought to the polling effort a seemingly endless supply of ideas, hypotheses, and interpretations: R. W. Apple, Jr., Michael Oreskes, and especially E. J. Dionne, Jr. Finally, many thanks to our partners in polling, our colleagues at CBS News: Warren Mitofsky, Kathleen Frankovic, and Keating Holland. None of the above individuals necessarily agrees with all the interpretations presented in this chapter. I also wish to thank Helmut Norpoth, with whom I collaborated on an extensive study of shifts in party identification in a paper delivered at the 1989 Annual Meeting of the American Political Science Association in Atlanta.

These polls included five major types:

(1) frequent national telephone polls to measure how voters' attitudes and perceptions shifted as the election year progressed, on a monthly basis early in the year and almost weekly toward the end;

(2) state and regional telephone polls in Iowa and the South early in the campaign cycle when those local electorates were "ahead" of the rest of the country by virtue of being subjected to much more intense campaign stimuli;

(3) statewide exit polls of voters leaving voting places on primary election day in states having major presidential primaries to interpret voter choices in the internal battle for each party's nomination;

(4) polls of delegates to the Democratic National Convention and the Republican National Convention to compare and contrast party activists with rank-and-file voters for each party; and

(5) a national exit poll of voters leaving voting stations across the country on Election Day in November to document the motivation and the demography of the electorate's final decision in 1988.

These polls were used in several ways. First, they formed the basis of 35 articles in *The Times* that relied heavily on polling data, often including graphic or tabular presentations of detailed analysis. Second, they were incorporated to a lesser extent into another 135 articles that cited one or more particular polling results. Third, they helped to inform reporting and editing during the election year by allowing reporters and editors to check hunches, to test the claims of candidates and their advisers, and to avoid being used by others trying to promote their own self-interested interpretations of what was happening in the electorate.

"These polls were not used to produce flashing maps to declare either a Dukakis victory in the spring or a Bush victory in the fall," points out Adam Clymer (1989, p. 1), political editor at *The Times* in 1988 (and later senior editor). "Such falsely predictive poll stories were the antithesis of *The Times'*s approach, which mined the data and found continual warning signs of fluidity and uncertainty. . . . We could usually find something more interesting than the horse race for a lead."

The Times has been involved in directly conducting its own public opinion polls since 1975. Most of these polls have been conducted jointly with CBS News. In 1988, as in previous years, the questionnaires were developed jointly. On telephone polls, the nighttime and weekend interviewing took place at *The New York Times*, while daytime interviewing on weekdays took place at CBS News. On exit polls, interviewing was done by an outside firm. CBS drew the samples and took responsibility for the data processing. Once the data were ready, each news organization had independent access to the data sets, and each news organization interpreted and reported its findings independently. The polls of delegates to the Democratic and Republican conventions, reported in this chapter, were conducted by *The New York Times* alone; CBS News did similar delegate surveys also on its own. The actual data sets of all these polls have been archived both in the Roper Center for Public Opinion Research at the University of Connecticut and in the Inter-university Consortium for Political and Social Research at the University of Michigan.

In 1988, *The Times* conducted a planned program of polling research designed to cover public reactions to the campaign. We viewed the campaign as a yearlong process in which the public could take the measure of those who would lead, and our polls were designed to find out what the public learned and concluded. Drawing on selected examples from the 31 political polls, the sections below discuss many of our major goals in this program, many of the particular devices we used to try to accomplish our objectives, and many of our findings about the public's reaction to the 1988 campaign. The chapter is organized into six sections, according to the type of use we made of polls.

Charting the Dynamics of the Campaign Year

When a presidential election year is viewed as a yearlong cycle of events, with key aspects rising or falling at different points in the cycle, the research imperative becomes the designing of a program of research that can chart the cycle's course. In 1988, *The Times* and CBS News planned a series of frequent national telephone polls containing certain key trend questions that were to be asked again and again to capture the dynamics of the election year. Chief examples are (a) public interest in the campaign from month to month, (b) the impression of George Bush formed by the electorate over the months, and (c) the impression of Michael Dukakis formed by voters over the course of the election year.

Public attention to the campaign. From the Iowa caucuses in early February 1988 to Election Day in early November, the campaign for nomination and election formally took nine months. The actual process, of course, extended over an even longer period of time, as potential candidates tested the waters, assembled campaign staffs, and plotted strategies sometimes

TABLE 2.1 Registered Voters Paying "a Lot of Attention" to the Campaign

Dates of Poll (in 1988)	Percentage Paying "a Lot of Attention" to the Campaign	Number of Registered Voters in Poll
January 17-21	15	1,287
February 17-21	27	2,077
March 19-22	34	1,271
May 9-12	30	1,056
July 5-8	24	947
July 31 to August 3	26	941
August 19-21	33	1,282
September 8-11	29	1,159
September 21-23	32	883
October 1-3	34	1,136
October 8-10	39	1,115
October 21-24	31	1,391
November 2-4	45	1,542

SOURCE: Based on registered voters in 12 *New York Times*/CBS News polls and one CBS News poll (August 19-21).
NOTE: Question: "How much attention have you been able to pay to the 1988 presidential campaign— a lot, some, not much, or no attention so far?"

years in advance. But, from the perspective of the electorate, the period from February to November was when they were invited to get involved—by appeals from the candidates and through increased coverage by news-gathering organizations.

But the audience for this drama of personalities, issues, and events was not static. It was much greater at some points in the year than others. Table 2.1 shows the percentage of registered voters, in 13 national polls by *The Times* and CBS News, who said they were paying "a lot of attention" to the 1988 presidential campaign.

Public attention tripled between January and November, but not at a steady rate. It jumped dramatically—nearly doubling from 15% to 27%—between the beginning of the year and the time of the Iowa caucuses and the New Hampshire primary in February. Attention rose even further—to 34% after the Super Tuesday group of primaries in the South and border states in March, which essentially settled the Republican nomination and served to prolong the race for the nomination on the Democratic side. The levels of public attention in the winter and spring were presented in a May 16, 1988, story in *The Times* by Michael Oreskes under the headline "In a Surprise, Voters Say They're Watching a Lot."

During the summer months between the primaries and the party conventions, public interest declined somewhat to about the level it had been in February. But public attention increased again around the Democratic convention in July and especially around the Republican convention in August, when the 33% paying "a lot of attention" rivaled the level registered at the peak of the primary season. Except for a temporary dip right after Labor Day in early September, public attention then stayed at this substantial level into early October as the campaigns got into high gear and the TV debates took place.

Attention rose again to 39% paying "a lot" of attention just before the second presidential debate in mid-October. Curiously, it then dipped to 31% in late October, after the final debate when the drama of one-on-one confrontation between the presidential candidates was ended. This period was also the aftermath of Governor Dukakis's lackluster performance in the second debate. At this time, some widely publicized polls showed Vice President Bush with a large lead and appeared to "give" the election to Bush, making the contest seem over and temporarily demoralizing many Dukakis supporters.

Finally, public attention rose again—to the year's high point of 45%—in the last week before Election Day, as the denouement of the yearlong contest approached and as the Dukakis campaign adopted a more populist spirit and seemed to be reinvigorated.

It is useful for both campaigners and journalists to realize that the audience for election-year messages rises and falls over the course of the year rather than being uniformly high or constantly building. Indeed, many registered voters clearly weren't paying much attention until the last few weeks before the election—and, even at the peak of attention, a majority were still paying less than "a lot" of attention. Thus appeals from the candidates made earlier—even repeatedly—in the campaign may not have reached some voters until the final moments of the yearlong process. And the audience for coverage by journalists expands enormously as Election Day approaches to include many voters who are innocent of most of the previous news coverage.

Voters' shifting opinion of George Bush. Another device we used to capture the dynamics of the election cycle was to ask registered voters whether their opinion of each of the major candidates was favorable, not favorable, undecided, or if they hadn't heard enough about particular candidates yet to form an opinion. This device also required repeating an identical question on a frequent basis throughout the year. *The Times* and CBS News registered 14 readings on this question for George Bush and 13 for Michael Dukakis and somewhat fewer readings for other presidential candidates in the spring and for the vice presidential candidates in the fall.

These findings enable the reader to stand back from the multiplicity of individual events of the election year and to view the net outcome or impact of those events—the personalities, the issues, the strategies of each campaign, the primary victories, the convention speeches, the advertisements and campaign propaganda, the TV debates, and the news coverage. Another useful feature of this question format is that voters are not required to choose between the candidates; voters are free to like all, some, or none of the candidates. Each candidate, in effect, runs mainly against himself. Our findings were twice published as time-series charts: first in *The Times* of July 12, 1988, with a page-one story by E. J. Dionne, Jr., under the headline "Poll Finds Public Is Wary of Both Bush and Dukakis," and a second time in the early editions of the paper of November 9, 1988, on a half-page of election graphics under the overall heading "The Candidates on the Trail and in the Minds of the Voters."

Table 2.2 shows the voters' shifting opinion of George Bush. By spring 1988, George Bush, in a race against himself, seemed to be losing. Although he started out a year before Election Day with a quite positive balance of voter opinion—a 20-point excess of favorable impressions over unfavorable impressions—that advantage melted away during late 1987 and early 1988 as the vice president was challenged for the Republican nomination by Senate Minority Leader Robert Dole and other Republican candidates.

After Bush's initial defeat in the Iowa caucuses, he rebounded to win the New Hampshire primary, and he effectively put the nomination away with his Super Tuesday primary victories in March. Even so, by that time, the balance of voter sentiment concerning Bush had become evenly split, and it then turned slightly negative throughout the rest of the spring and summer into August.

But the Republican National Convention in mid-August propelled Bush to a dramatic turnaround in the public's view. After the convention, favorable impressions of Bush shot up by 12 percentage points and unfavorable sentiment dropped by 8 percentage points. Most candidates traditionally enjoy a postconvention bounce in the polls; Bush badly needed such a bounce. After his rebound in August, the balance of public sentiment regarding Bush remained fairly constant—and positive—for the rest of the campaign.

Some observers have speculated that this reversal was so sudden—and perhaps so delayed—because Vice President Bush had been out of the limelight once the Republican nomination was essentially decided in March. After March, attention in news coverage shifted toward the continuing contest among Democratic candidates for their party's nomination, as Bush no longer had any Republican to beat in the remaining Republican primaries. Partly in

TABLE 2.2 Registered Voters' Shifting Opinion of George Bush

Dates of Poll	Favorable Opinion (percentage)	Not Favorable Opinion (percentage)	Balance: Favorable Minus Not Favorable
October 18-22, 1987	45	25	+20
November 20-24, 1987	38	27	+11
January 30-31, 1988	31	28	+ 3
March 19-22	34	35	− 1
May 9-12	33	35	− 2
July 5-8	26	31	− 5
July 31 to August 3	27	33	− 6
August 19-21	39	25	+14
September 8-11	39	27	+12
September 21-23	37	30	+ 7
October 1-3	38	30	+ 8
October 8-10	41	31	+10
October 21-24	45	30	+15
November 2-4	44	34	+10

SOURCE: Based on registered voters interviewed in 12 *New York Times*/CBS News polls, one *New York Times* poll (January 30-31), and one CBS News poll (August 19-21). Not shown are those who said they were undecided or had not yet heard enough about the candidate. The October 1987 poll was based on 1,058 registered voters; the November 1987 poll was based on 1,227 registered voters; the poll taken January 30-31, 1988, was based on 912 registered voters.
NOTE: Question: "Is your opinion of George Bush favorable, not favorable, undecided, or haven't you heard enough about George Bush yet to have an opinion?"

response, the Bush campaign went on the attack during the summer, criticizing Dukakis with the Pledge of Allegiance to the flag issue. But the Republican National Convention was Bush's next major opportunity to regain the limelight for himself, and he had every reason to try to use it well.

Voters' shifting opinion of Michael Dukakis. Table 2.3 displays the dynamics of voter reactions to Michael Dukakis over the course of the long election cycle. In the first half of the time period, the figures trace a classic pattern: a little-known candidate starting out with a core of partisans and then growing dramatically in recognition—and support—by winning key primary contests.

By late March, Dukakis was beginning to be perceived by Democrats as having the best chance of achieving victory for their party in November. Although the battle for the Democratic nomination was not settled until June, the contest after March narrowed to Dukakis and Jesse Jackson—whom Dukakis was seen beating Tuesday after Tuesday.

TABLE 2.3 Registered Voters' Shifting Opinion of Michael Dukakis

Dates of Poll	Favorable Opinion (percentage)	Not Favorable Opinion (percentage)	Balance: Favorable Minus Not Favorable
October 18-22, 1987	15	10	+ 5
November 20-24, 1987	13	10	+ 3
March 19-22, 1988	29	17	+12
May 9-12	38	14	+24
July 5-8	28	21	+ 7
July 31 to August 3	38	19	+19
August 19-21	32	25	+ 7
September 8-11	28	31	− 3
September 21-23	29	31	− 2
October 1-3	32	33	− 1
October 8-10	29	38	− 9
October 21-24	31	42	−11
November 2-4	32	40	− 8

SOURCE: Based on registered voters interviewed in 12 *New York Times*/CBS News polls and one CBS News poll (August 19-21). Opinion of Dukakis was not asked in a *New York Times* poll of January 30-31. Not shown are those who said they were undecided or had not yet heard enough about the candidate.
NOTE: Question: "Is your opinion of Michael Dukakis favorable, not favorable, undecided, or haven't you heard enough about Michael Dukakis yet to have an opinion?"

Once the primary season was over, Dukakis suffered a dip in voter sentiment. This may have occurred in part because, after early June, Dukakis was out of the limelight, just as George Bush had been for a longer period of time. But, during the summer, the Bush campaign also launched a series of attacks on Dukakis, aiming to convince voters that many of Dukakis's "values" were out of the mainstream, and this assault began to take a toll on Dukakis's image.

After the Democratic National Convention in July, Dukakis rebounded in voter sentiment, enjoying his own version of the traditional postconvention bounce. But, by late August, after the Republican National Convention, the balance of opinion concerning Dukakis was back roughly to what it had been in July. And, by the second week of September—after weeks of ineffectively answering the attacks from the Bush campaign—Dukakis experienced a fateful reversal in the public's impression of him. The public became seriously split on Michael Dukakis, a balance of sentiment that was initially only slightly negative but that later turned decidedly negative.

It is tempting to argue that the period of late August and early September was the watershed of the 1988 campaign. We examined each candidate's turnaround in public esteem in our early September poll, reported by E. J. Dionne, Jr., on page one in *The Times* of September 14, 1988, under the headline "Poll Shows Bush Sets Agenda for Principal Election Issues." But matters got even worse for Dukakis; by early October, voter sentiment regarding Dukakis became approximately 10 points more negative than positive.

Putting Major Campaign Events into Perspective

Another principal use of public opinion polls by *The Times* during 1988 was to put into perspective some major event or series of events in the election cycle by summarizing and highlighting their underlying features. Two examples are cited here: (a) summarizing the voting patterns of all the Democratic primaries by constructing a composite of the nationwide Democratic primary electorate, and (b) highlighting the spectrum of American political views in 1988 by comparing the ideological differences among Republican convention delegates, Democratic convention delegates, and the rank-and-file voters of their respective parties.

A composite national Democratic Party primary electorate. During 1988, *The Times* and CBS News analyzed voting patterns in many individual state primaries, using exit polls of voters leaving voting stations on primary election day. Inevitably, however, certain patterns were more evident in some state primaries than in others, and reporters and editors were necessarily as interested in the unique features of individual contests as they were in the underlying commonalities. By the end of the primary season it seemed useful to summarize for reporters as well as readers the overall voting patterns that had been most persistent across both time and geography in the Democratic primary battles.

Therefore, *The Times* constructed a composite Democratic primary electorate for the nation, a device originated by political editor Adam Clymer in 1984. To synthesize a national Democratic primary electorate for 1988, Table 2.4 combines vote totals and exit-poll percentages from 33 primary states where delegates were selected from February to June. The polls covered 30 of the 33 states; the popular vote count is based on all 33 states. A graphic that presented these results ran in *The Times* of June 13, 1988, with a story by E. J. Dionne, Jr., under the headline "Jackson Share of Votes by Whites Triples in '88."

TABLE 2.4 The Primaries Seen as a Whole: How the Democrats Voted

Voting Group	Percentage of All Democratic Primary Votes Cast by Each Group	Percentage of Each Group Voting for		
		Dukakis	Jackson	Others
Total votes (percentage)	100	43	29	28
Men	47	41	29	30
Women	53	43	30	26
White	75	54	12	35
Black	21	4	92	4
Hispanic	3	48	30	20
18-29 years	14	35	38	27
30-44	31	37	36	26
45-59	25	42	30	28
60 and older	30	53	19	29
Liberal	27	41	41	19
Moderate	47	47	25	28
Conservative	22	38	23	38
Democrat	72	43	33	24
Independent	20	44	20	34
Catholic	30	60	18	22
White Protestant	36	43	10	47
Jewish	7	75	8	17
Total votes (in millions)	(22.7)	(9.7)	(6.6)	(6.4)

NOTE : This table, which constructs a composite Democratic primary electorate for the nation, combines vote totals and exit poll percentages from 33 primary states where delegates were selected from February to June. Vote totals are from secretaries of state. Sources of exit poll percentages: 10 frrom *New York Times* /CBS News, 14 from CBS News alone, 5 from ABC news, and 1 from NBC News. No exit polls were available in Montanta, Oregon, or Washington, D.C.

The most striking feature was the impressive achievement of Reverend Jesse Jackson, who came in second overall to Dukakis, winning 29% of all votes cast in Democratic primaries in 1988. He accomplished that by drawing 92% of the Black vote and 12% of the White vote.

For Jackson, this represented an improvement among both races since 1984, when he had taken only 5% of the White vote and 77% of the Black vote. But, even with this breakthrough, the level of White support was clearly insufficient for Jackson to accomplish the primary-election victories he sought. Even in his best states—Wisconsin and California— Jackson took only about a quarter of the White vote. (No exit polls were available from Oregon, where his share may have reached as high as 35% of Whites, but even that would have raised Jackson's overall support among White Democrats nationally less than one percentage point.)

Perhaps the most important finding, however, was that Michael Dukakis was the candidate favored by moderate Democrats. Dukakis had to split liberal Democrats with Jackson, and he had to split conservative Democrats with other candidates such as Senator Albert Gore and, earlier, Congressman Richard Gephardt. But Dukakis dominated among moderates.

This may be partly because, in the later primaries, Dukakis was Jackson's main opponent. Throughout the spring and early summer, Dukakis successfully presented himself as a nonideological moderate, and this image was particularly credible so long as he had Jackson so visible to his left.

Indeed, some observers contend that Dukakis's troubles began with the end of the primary season, when he no longer enjoyed the advantage of being seen defeating the very liberal Black leader week after week. It was then that Dukakis became increasingly vulnerable to attacks from the Bush campaign, which aimed to paint Dukakis as the liberal pariah for the fall general election campaign in order to attract some moderate voters away from Dukakis and into the Bush camp.

The spectrum of political choice. The quadrennial gathering of party activists in the Democratic and Republican national conventions provided an opportunity to examine the spectrum of political views in American politics—at least that part of the spectrum contained within the two major party coalitions. Candidates may sometimes try to hide their ideology or their policy views on certain issues; party activists as represented by convention delegates, however, do not.

The Times conducted separate polls of Democratic convention delegates and Republican delegates in the weeks preceding each party's gathering. The delegates were asked many of the same questions that had already been asked of rank-and-file voters across the country in *Times*/CBS News national polls during the spring and summer. These ranged from the ideological labels used to describe themselves, to the preferred size of government, to federal spending in areas such as defense, education, and day care, to their positions on abortion, and to the degree of attention they wanted to be given to the needs of Blacks.

Table 2.5 compares and contrasts the party activists and the public on these issues. A graphic with these findings was published in *The Times* on

TABLE 2.5 A Spectrum of Political Views: Party Convention Delegates and the Public on the Issues

	Democratic Convention Delegates (percentage)	Democratic Voters (percentage)	The Public Total Adults (percentage)	Republican Voters (percentage)	Republican Convention Delegates (percentage)
Political Philosophy:					
Describe own political views as conservative	5	22	30	43	60
Describe own political views as liberal	39	25	20	12	1
Size of government:					
Prefer smaller government providing fewer services	16	33	43	59	87
Prefer bigger government providing more services	58	56	44	30	3
Domestic policy:					
Favor increased federal spending on education programs	90	76	71	67	41
Favor increased federal spending on day care and after-school care for children	87	56	52	44	36
Say abortion should be legal, as it is now	72	43	40	39	29
Say government is paying too little attention to the needs of Blacks	68	45	34	19	14

Foreign and military issues:

Favor keeping spending on military and defense programs at least at current level	32	59	66	73	84
Are more worried about Communist takeover in Central America than about U.S. involvement in a war there	12	25	37	55	80
Support use of military to stop inflow of drugs	54	61	61	63	67

NOTE: Delegates' views are based on *New York Times* polls of 1,059 delegates to the Democratic National Convention, conducted June 20 to July 12, 1988, and with 739 delegates to the Republican Convention, conducted July 22 to August 4, 1988. Views of total adults and each party's registered voters are based on *New York Times*/CBS News polls of March, May, July, and August 1988.

August 14, 1988, with a story interpreting the two delegate polls by Michael Oreskes under the headline "Convention a Conservative Gathering."

A remarkable clarity is evident in these results. On item after item, the two political party coalitions in 1988 had clearly distinct policy positions—with the Democrats expressing more liberal views and the Republicans taking more conservative positions. The contrast is strongest between the two sets of convention delegates; there often was a 50-percentage-point spread between the views of Democratic activists on the one hand and Republican activists on the other. But even rank-and-file Democratic and Republican voters clearly differed from each other on most of the issues examined; there was frequently a 25-percentage-point spread separating the views of the two coalitions of voters.

Policy choices existed in 1988 for anyone who cared to see them. As Michael Oreskes put it in his story, the two sets of party activists were "separated by a vast ideological chasm." Table 2.5 reveals in a particularly succinct way the issue stakes of the 1988 presidential election. The table also updates some patterns first revealed by Herbert McClosky in his surveys of voters and party convention delegates in the late 1950s.

Analyzing Key Factors
Affecting the Campaign

During 1988, *The Times* frequently used polling to give its reporters and readers insights into the campaign, helping to explain *why* the election was developing as it did. We viewed the electorate as being influenced by numerous forces—some of long duration, some of middling permanence, and many of short-lived intensity—and we made efforts to study each type.

The selected examples below include (a) the long-term trend in party identification in the electorate; (b) a middle-term factor, the effect of the condition of the national economy; and (c) a shorter-term phenomenon, the effect of the Bush campaign's effort to paint Dukakis as too soft on crime and criminals, part of the larger effort to label Dukakis as a "liberal" of a stigmatized sort.

Party identification. "Party identification" expresses the electorate's underlying party loyalty or proclivity. It normally changes only slowly as generations gradually enter or depart the population or as long-term secular trends such as industrialization, suburbanization, or population migration work their social and political consequences. Only rarely does party identification undergo more rapid shifts, accompanying historic junctures like the Civil War or the Great Depression.

Therefore, the balance of party loyalty, including any recent shifts, operates as a long-term force affecting any given election. Typically, it gives one party a starting advantage, which it must work to keep or expand, while it gives the other party an initial disadvantage that it must work to overcome.

The Times and CBS News measure party identification in every poll they conduct. Tables 2.6 and 2.7 present the division in party loyalty during the decade of the 1980s, as registered in 76 separate *Times*/CBS News polls and *New York Times* polls, based on a total of more than 110,000 interviews.

A chart based on a briefer version of this table was published in *The Times* on October 31, 1988, with a page-one story by E. J. Dionne, Jr., under the headline "G.O.P. Makes Reagan Lure of Young a Long-Term Asset." It highlighted the findings for just the presidential election years of 1980, 1984, and 1988. The version in Table 2.6 adds all the intervening years for a more complete time trend, and it also combines those who say they think of themselves as a Democrat or Republican and those who say they "lean" toward one party or the other. A chart based on this expanded version was published in the paper of April 20, 1989, in a story by R. W. Apple, Jr., headlined "Public Rates Bush Highly But Sees Mostly Style."

During the decade that led up to the 1988 election, the Republicans—initially disadvantaged in party identification—had been closing the gap between themselves and the Democrats. The Democratic advantage among adults—which was 19 points in 1980 and averaged about 13 points during the first four years of the Reagan administration—declined by half during the second Reagan administration, when Democrats averaged only about a 6-point advantage in public loyalty.

But among the newest generation in the electorate—the 18- to 29-year-old age group, who are normally most open or vulnerable to the changing tides of politics—the trend has been even more dramatic. The Democratic advantage in this age group—which was 21 points in 1980 and averaged about 7 points during the first four years of the Reagan administration—completely dissolved during the second Reagan administration when it turned into an average deficit of 4 points for the Democrats. Beginning around 1985, the Republicans took a slight advantage in the political loyalties of 18- to 29-year-old Americans.

Tables 2.6 and 2.7 also contain data from the first three months of the Bush administration in 1989. This helps to make clearer a pattern of surge and partial decline that seems to have occurred after each of the last three presidential elections. In 1981, 1985, and 1989, the Republican share of party

TABLE 2.6 Shifts in Party Identification in the 1980s: All Adults

Year	Percentage of All Adults Identifying with Each Party		Democratic Advantage
	Republican or Leaning Republican	Democratic or Leaning Democratic	
1980	34	53	+19
1981	39	49	+10
1982	35	52	+17
1983	35	53	+18
1984	40	48	+ 8
1985	43	47	+ 4
1986	42	47	+ 5
1987	41	49	+ 8
1988	40	47	+ 7
1989 (first quarter)	44	46	+ 2

SOURCE: Based on 76 *New York Times*/CBS News polls and *New York Times* polls, which have been pooled for each year. They include 9,908 respondents in 1980; 7,330 in 1981; 7,749 in 1982; 7,183 in 1983; 19,427 in 1984; 9,639 in 1985; 11,824 in 1986; 14,152 in 1987; 18,979 in 1988; and 4,178 in the first quarter of 1989.
NOTE: Question: "Generally speaking, do you usually consider yourself a Republican, a Democrat, an independent, or what?" (If independent or don't know: "Do you think of yourself as closer to the Republican party or to the Democratic party?")

loyalists surged—perhaps in response to the party's victory in the preceding year's contest for the presidency—only to sag a bit in the following years until another White House victory reenergized it. On each occasion, however, the sag was only partial, resulting in a series of two-steps-forward-one-step-back motions for the Republicans.

The latest surge in the year following the 1988 campaign is visible in polls taken during the first quarter of 1989, when Republican identification rose by four points among all adults and by eight points among the 18- to 29-year-old group. In the first quarter of 1989, the Democrats clung to a two-point advantage among all adults, but the Republicans enjoyed a four-teen-point advantage in the newest generation of adults.

The division of party loyalty in the nation served as a backdrop to the 1988 election campaign. As the election approached, the Democrats still had a marginal advantage in this long-term force of party loyalty, but it was a considerably reduced advantage. And the momentum seemed to be working against the Democrats and in favor of the Republicans. The battle for victory by a minority party is by nature an uphill fight; but, for the Republicans in

TABLE 2.7 Shifts in Party Identification in the 1980s:
The 18- to 29-Year-Old Age Group

	Percentage of 18- to 29-Year-Olds Identifying with Each Party		
	---	---	---
Year	Republican or Leaning Republican	Democratic or Leaning Democratic	Democratic Advantage
1980	33	54	+21
1981	42	47	+ 5
1982	39	49	+10
1983	37	50	+13
1984	45	44	− 1
1985	48	42	− 6
1986	47	41	− 6
1987	47	43	− 4
1988	44	43	− 1
1989 (first quarter)	52	38	−14

NOTE: See the notes for Table 2.6 for source information and the question asked.

1988, that hill was not nearly so steep as it had been in the past. Their task, therefore, was to be easier than it otherwise might have been.

The economy and the candidates. The link between the national economy and the election is an example of a middle-term factor that *The Times* and CBS News sought to analyze. *Middle-term* seems an appropriate designation, for the economy changes more rapidly than does a long-term factor like party identification, but not nearly so fast as some of the truly short-term factors in the campaign, such as issue appeals and candidate images, to be discussed later.

Analysts were puzzled in the spring and early summer as to why Bush failed to gain greater benefit from what appeared to be a generally favorable economic climate. But, by the end of the summer and the beginning of fall, that benefit was clearly demonstrable. Table 2.8 presents the strong link between the economy and the candidates as registered in a September poll. A chart presenting essentially these same findings ran in *The Times* with the September 14, 1988, page-one story by E. J. Dionne, Jr.

Voters seemed to reward or punish the incumbent Republicans according to the voters' view of the national economy. Voters who perceived that the economy was getting *better* split for Bush over Dukakis by a ratio of 69 to 19, but they were a fairly small group—just 15% of all voters. Likewise, voters who perceived that the economy was getting *worse* split in favor of

TABLE 2.8 The Economy and the Candidates

Percentage of All Registered Voters who Fall into Each Category		Percentage of Registered Voters in Each Category Who:	
		Prefer Michael Dukakis	Prefer George Bush
15	Those who say the economy is getting *better*	19	69
42	Those who say the economy is staying about the *same* and is *good*	30	56
14	Those who say the economy is staying about the *same* and is *bad*	49	30
27	Those who say the economy is getting *worse*	58	27

SOURCE: Based on a *New York Times*/CBS News poll conducted September 8-11. Those with no opinion on economic change are not shown. Figures above are percentage of registered voters; figures originally published were percentage of "probable electorate."
NOTE: Questions: "How would you rate the condition of the national economy these days? Is it very good, fairly good, fairly bad, or very bad?" *and* "Do you think the economy is getting better, getting worse, or staying about the same?"

Dukakis over Bush by a ratio of 58 to 27. They were a somewhat larger group, comprising 27% of all voters.

The majority of voters, however, perceived that the economy was staying about the *same*, and the way they split between the candidates also seemed to reward or punish the incumbent Republicans according to views of whether that stable economic condition was good or bad. Those who saw the economy staying the same and who pronounced it *good* split in favor of Bush over Dukakis by 56 to 30. Those who saw the economy staying the same and who judged it *bad* divided in favor of Dukakis over Bush by 49 to 30. But the key fact was that the size of the former group—the group satisfied with the economic situation—was three times the size of the latter group (42% of all registered voters compared with 14%), enough to give Bush a slight advantage overall.

Thus, if the election were seen as a referendum on the nation's economic situation—produced in part by the policies and stewardship of the incumbent

Republicans—then each candidate was drawing heavily from the economic constituencies he naturally "ought" to attract. Incumbent Vice President Bush was getting the larger share of the economic optimists and the satisfied; the challenger Dukakis was attracting the bulk of the economic pessimists and the dissatisfied.

Due to economic conditions, there simply were more economic optimists and economically satisfied voters by fall 1988. Thus this middle-term force of the economy worked to the Republicans' advantage. However, it is also apparent from Table 2.8 that Bush was having slightly greater success in attracting his natural economic constituencies than Dukakis was having in harvesting his, underlining the obvious fact that factors in addition to the economy also were at work.

Tough enough on crime and criminals. Much of the activity in election polling concentrates—perhaps too much so—on measuring the effects of shorter-term phenomena that occur during any election campaign. These include the propaganda and advertising strategies of each side, major speeches and issue appeals by the candidates, dramatic performances in TV debates, or particular events that occur on the campaign trail. These shorter-term factors occupy such attention, of course, because they are new since the last poll, because they are most likely to account for month-to-month fluctuations in the fortunes of the candidates, and because they determine the what-might-have-beens of any election year.

The matters that any campaign organization has the most control over are also—necessarily—the shorter-term aspects. A campaign organization cannot do much about either the long-term forces it faces or the middle-term conditions it has to contend with, except to try to exploit them when favorable and to distract people's attention to other topics when unfavorable.

Of the numerous short-term factors analyzed by *The Times* and CBS News during 1988, the example below examines the outcome of the Bush campaign's attempt to paint Bush as sufficiently tough on crime and criminals and to paint Dukakis as overly soft. Table 2.9 shows the images that voters held of Bush and Dukakis in early July as compared with late October. A chart presenting these findings ran in *The Times* on October 26, 1988, with a page-one story by E. J. Dionne, Jr., under the headline "New Poll Shows Attacks by Bush Are Building Lead."

In July, the preponderance of voters—49%—perceived Bush as not sufficiently tough on crime and criminals. In that period, he was still suffering from the "wimp" image that had dogged him throughout the winter and spring. But, by October, a clear majority—61%—said Bush was tough enough.

TABLE 2.9 Tough Enough on Crime? Images of the Candidates in July and October

| Candidate | Dates of Polls | Percent of Registered Voters Calling Candidate | | |
		Tough Enough	Not Tough Enough	Don't Know
George Bush	July 5-8, 1988	23	49	28
	October 21-24	61	25	14
Michael Dukakis	July 5-8, 1988	20	36	44
	October 21-24	36	49	15

SOURCE: Based on registered voters in *New York Times*/CBS News polls of July 5-8 and October 21-24, 1988.
NOTE: Question: (in July) "Do you think (George Bush/Michael Dukakis) has been tough enough in dealing with crime and criminals, or don't you think so?" (in October) "Do you think (George Bush/Michael Dukakis) would be tough enough in dealing with crime and criminals, or don't you think so?"

For Dukakis's part, in July, the preponderence of voters—44% said they didn't know whether or not he was tough enough on crime and criminals. By October, the "don't knows" had dropped by two-thirds, but the preponderence of voters—49%—had come to view Dukakis as insufficiently tough.

This shift in the images of the candidates over less than four months was no doubt influenced enormously by the Bush campaign's attack on Dukakis over issues such as the death penalty, the prisoner furlough program in Massachusetts, and the infamous case of Black murderer-rapist Willie Horton. But the shift also was abetted by Dukakis's seeming inability to parry or disarm such an attack, much less to defend or promote his own views convincingly. This inability was symbolized by Dukakis's ineffectual handling of a question at the beginning of the second presidential debate on TV about whether he would favor the death penalty if his wife were raped and murdered.

His inability was even more curious because many other Democratic and liberal politicians had learned years ago how to finesse this style of attack and to protect themselves from being perceived as too "soft." It has been more than two decades since the "social issues" first arose as a potent political force—a force consisting of such law-and-order themes as crime and violence in the streets, such moral issues as the death penalty, such cultural-value issues as alternate life-styles and flag-burning protest, and some of the more threatening or disruptive aspects of race relations and civil rights. Because the public tends to take a "tough" line on many such social issues,

Republicans and conservatives have at times enjoyed considerable profit when they could succeed in painting Democrats and liberals as too "soft" or "permissive" on such issues.

It was, therefore, a fateful weakness of the Dukakis campaign that, as revealed in polling data, it proved to be so vulnerable to such familiar tactics from the Republican camp and turned out to be unable to blunt or counter the attack. Much the same is true when it came to the success of the Bush campaign in expropriating for its own purpose such powerful national symbols as the flag—an even older ploy among politicians—and the inability of the Dukakis campaign to neutralize that gambit.

Some observers have said that the Dukakis camp simply refused to believe that voters would take such "issues" seriously in 1988 and that it underestimated the importance of emphasizing the proper "values" in contemporary campaigning. Others have suggested that Dukakis, a politician whose electoral career was largely confined to the state level in one of the liberal Democratic stronghold states, had limited experience campaigning against strong Republican opponents, giving him less opportunity to develop the type of defense and counterthrust needed against the campaign mounted by the national Republicans in 1988.

Of course, Republicans and conservatives have their own image vulnerabilities—particularly their image of favoring economic elites rather than the common people—which Democrats and liberals have often managed to exploit for their own electoral profit over the years. Dukakis pursued such a populist counterattack only during the final two to three weeks of his campaign, however.

Dukakis's image as a "liberal." The effort of the Bush campaign to paint Dukakis as too soft on crime and criminals was part of a larger strategy to try to define Dukakis in voters' minds as a "liberal" of the soft-headed variety. That was a tempting strategy because being a liberal was out of fashion in 1988. The percentage of Americans describing their own views as liberal reached the lowest point in the 12-year history of *Times*/CBS News polls during 1988 when it hit 15% in early September and again in early November.

Such a strategy also was made possible for the Republicans because, even by midsummer, voters' impressions of Dukakis still were not very well formed. For most voters, Dukakis had emerged from the obscurity of the pack of Democratic hopefuls only recently and rapidly. He was perceived to be a winner because of his victories in the primary season, but many voters had not yet formed detailed impressions about his competence, character, or issue positions. As shown in Table 2.3, discussed earlier,

TABLE 2.10 Percentage of Registered Voters Perceiving Michael Dukakis as a "Liberal"

| | *Percentage Perceiving Michael Dukakis as* | | | |
Dates of Poll	Liberal	Moderate	Conservative	Don't Know
March 19-22, 1988	30	26	11	33
May 9-12	27	34	14	25
July 5-8	28	34	17	21
July 31 to August 3	34	32	13	21
August 19-21	35	27	16	22
September 8-11	35	31	13	21
September 21-23	34	29	20	17
October 1-3	42	26	14	18
November 2-4	53	24	9	14

SOURCE: Based on registered voters in eight *New York Times*/CBS News polls and one CBS News poll (August 19-21).
NOTE: Question: "In politics, do you think of Michael Dukakis as a liberal, a moderate, or a conservative?" The question in the March poll was worded slightly differently: "In politics, do you think of Michael Dukakis as more of a liberal, a moderate, or a conservative?"

until early August a majority of voters were still saying they were undecided in their opinion of Michael Dukakis or had not yet heard enough about him to have an opinion.

Table 2.10 reveals the extent to which this larger Republican strategy succeeded. *Times*/CBS News polls measured the ideological image that voters held of Dukakis on nine separate occasions during 1988 but registered little movement in this measure until the beginning of October. Only then did the proportion seeing Dukakis as a liberal begin to rise, reaching majority proportions by the week before the election.

Of course, late in the campaign, Dukakis himself publicly declared that he was a liberal in the tradition of Franklin Roosevelt, Harry Truman, and John Kennedy. He launched a last-minute, populist-flavored counterattack, with the theme "I'm on your side," that emphasized the more popular helping and caring aspects of the liberal political tradition. Several of the findings in Table 2.10 were presented in *The Times* on October 31, 1988, in a page-one story by Robin Toner under the headline "Dukakis Asserts He Is a 'Liberal,' But in Old Tradition of His Party."

Documenting the Outcome
of the Election

At the end of the 1988 presidential campaign cycle, *The Times* used public opinion polling to document and interpret the outcome of the election. We sought to measure how the public evaluated the campaign, how they finally divided in their choice of candidates, and why many decided to stay away and not vote at all. To accomplish this, we relied on a combination of preelection telephone polls, Election Day exit polling, and a postelection panel-back survey in which every respondent in the final preelection poll who could be reached again was reinterviewed after the election was over.

The examples below include (a) the negative judgment rendered by many voters on the content and tone of the 1988 campaign, (b) the head-to-head trial heats from March until the weekend before Election Day, (c) the detailed "Portrait of the Electorate" who turned out on Election Day, and (d) a comparison of the voting public with the other half of the adult population who stayed away on Election Day 1988.

A campaign the public disliked. The style and content of the 1988 campaign drew criticism from many voters. As shown in Table 2.11, majorities of registered voters criticized the dullness of the 1988 campaign, the perceived low level of issue discussion, and the negative tone and said they wished there were choices other than Bush and Dukakis. The Times and CBS News tried to measure this mood, track its development and its consequences, and compare it with other campaign years.

For instance, by late October 1988, 64% of registered voters said they wished there were choices other than Bush and Dukakis. This compares with only 48% in fall 1984 who said they wished there were choices other than Reagan and Mondale, and only 45% in fall 1980 who said they wished there were choices other than Reagan, Carter, and Anderson. As another example, by late October, 47% of registered voters had come to view the 1988 campaign as more negative than past campaigns. That level of dissatisfaction grew to a substantial majority of 61% by the week before Election Day.

In addition, 46% of registered voters said there had been less discussion of issues in 1988 than in past campaigns. A majority (53%) said that neither candidate had talked enough about the particular issue that respondents said should be the most important. A majority (52%) described the 1988 campaign as "dull" rather than as "interesting."

Bush received somewhat more criticism than did Dukakis for the nasty tone of the 1988 campaign. Voters were half again more likely to blame Bush

TABLE 2.11 Registered Voters Evaluate the 1988 Campaign

Registered Voters Who:	*Percentage*
From a September 1980 poll:	
Say they wish there were choices other than Reagan, Carter, and Anderson	45
From a September 1984 poll:	
Say they wish there were choices other than Reagan and Mondale	48
From the October 21-24, 1988, poll:	
Say they wish there were choices other than Bush and Dukakis	64
Describe the 1988 campaign as dull	52
Say there has been less discussion of the issues this year than in past campaigns	46
Say neither candidate is talking enough about the particular issue the voter says should be the most important	53
Say this year's campaign has been more negative than past campaigns	
From the November 2-4, 1988, poll:	
Say this year's campaign has been more negative than past campaigns	61
Say Bush is more responsible for the negative campaigning	33
Say Dukakis is more responsible for the negative campaigning	21

SOURCE: Based on registered voters in four *New York Times*/CBS News polls, two in the fall of 1988 and one each in the fall of 1980 and 1984.

(33%) for negative campaigning than they were to blame Dukakis (21%). But many others blamed both candidates.

These findings were presented in several stories in *The Times*, often accompanied by detailed graphic presentations. Examples are a page-one story by E. J. Dionne, Jr., on September 25, 1988, under the headline "A Third of Voters Remain Uncertain on Eve of Debate," and the page-one story by Mr. Dionne on October 26, 1988.

Trial heats and final preelection poll. The measurement of the "horse race" has always been viewed as a decidedly secondary objective in polls sponsored by The Times, which are designed to explore public reactions to political issues, personalities, and events. However, trial heats between Bush and Dukakis were included in 11 of the polls beginning in March.

From March through early July, the results were based on all registered voters in each poll. From early August through November, the results were weighted to reflect a "probable electorate." As explained in the "Method Box" that accompanied most major poll stories, this technique uses responses to questions dealing with voter registration, past voting history, and the likelihood of voting in 1988 as a measure of the probability of particular respondents voting in the presidential election. The technique weighted registered respondents from 0.05 to 0.90, according to their likelihood, attempting to represent the views of the approximately one-half of the voting age population who turn out on Election Day.

When *The Times* reported trial heat results, it made a deliberate practice of *not* allocating undecided voters who, in answers to a subsequent question, said they "leaned" toward one candidate or the other. When CBS News reported trial heats, they often allocated the leaners. Table 2.12 shows that the preference of voters in the trial heats from March to November broke into three distinct time periods.

In the earliest head-to-head trial heat in March, at a time when Bush and Dukakis had each emerged as a front-runner within his own party, the two candidates stood in a virtual tie, dividing the voters almost evenly between them. In the next three readings from May through early August, Dukakis enjoyed an advantage that averaged at first about nine points and that temporarily swelled in the afterglow of the Democratic National Convention. Then, in the third period, beginning after the Republican National Convention in late August and lasting into early November, Bush gained an advantage that averaged about seven points, which seemed to narrow slightly in early October and to enlarge slightly in late October.

But the most striking feature of Table 2.12 is the relative stability of the standings across the entire autumn campaign, a stability that seemed to set in once the political conventions were over and each party had put forward its official ticket. Although individual voters may have switched back and forth or wavered to some extent, and although many voters said they might yet change their minds, the net outcome of all the individual voter decisions resulted in very stable aggregate standings for the two presidential candidates

TABLE 2.12 Voters' Preference Between George Bush and
Michael Dukakis

Dates of Polls	Prefer George Bush	Prefer Michael Dukakis	Bush Advantage
March 19-22, 1988	46	45	+ 1
May 9-12	39	49	−10
July 5-8	39	47	− 8
July 31 to August 3	34	50	−16
August 19-21	47	40	+ 7
September 8-11	47	39	+ 8
September 21-23	46	40	+ 6
October 1-3	45	43	+ 2
October 8-10	47	42	+ 5
October 21-24	51	38	+13
November 2-4	48	40	+ 8

SOURCE: Based on registered voters in 10 *New York Times*/CBS News polls and one CBS News poll (August 19-21). Beginning with the poll of July 31 to August 3, the respondents were weighted to reflect a "probable electorate." This technique uses responses to questions dealing with voter registration, past voting history, and the likelihood of voting in 1988 as a measure of the probability of particular respondents voting in November 1988. Not shown are those who were undecided, some of whom, in answer to a subsequent question, said that they currently leaned toward one candidate or the other.

NOTE: Question (beginning with the August 19-21 poll): "If the 1988 presidential election were being held today, would you vote for George Bush for president and Dan Quayle for vice president, the Republican candidates, or for Michael Dukakis for president and Lloyd Bentsen for vice president, the Democratic candidates?" Question (prior to the August 19-21 poll): "If the 1988 presidential election were being held today, and the candidates were George Bush, the Republican, and Michael Dukakis, the Democrat, would you vote for George Bush or for Michael Dukakis?"

throughout the fall. In seven successive polls over an 11-week period, the preference of the "probable electorate" for George Bush stood within plus or minus three points of 48%. In the same seven polls, the preference of the "probable electorate" for Michael Dukakis was within plus or minus three points of 40%.

Such relatively minor fluctuations were within the sampling error of most of these polls. Although the slight jiggles measured in the support for Bush and Dukakis were probably real, one cannot rule out the statistical possibility that there was no movement at all in the standings of the two candidates during the fall campaign.

In the final preelection poll conducted by *The Times* and CBS News November 2 to 4, the candidates stood at 48% of the "probable electorate" preferring Bush and 40% of the "probable electorate" preferring Dukakis, with the rest undecided. These were the final figures reported by *The Times* in the paper of November 6, 1988, on the Sunday before the election in a page-one story by E. J. Dionne, Jr., under the headline "Bush Still Ahead as End Nears But Dukakis Gains in Survey."

When respondents who said they leaned toward one candidate or the other were allocated, the figures for the probable electorate became 52% for Bush to 43% for Dukakis with the rest undecided; these were the numbers reported by CBS News on its evening broadcast November 5, 1988. CBS News also continued by itself to do tracking polls even closer to Election Day.

Thus the signs in the final joint *Times*/CBS News poll pointed to a victory in the popular vote by George Bush that would be substantial—about an eight-point margin—but short of the overwhelming landslide proportions experienced by Reagan in 1984. On Election Day, November 8, 1988, the actual outcome of the balloting across the country was an almost eight-point margin for Bush. According to official returns compiled by Associated Press, the outcome was 53.37% of the popular vote for Bush compared with 45.67% for Dukakis, or a margin of 7.7 percentage points.

Throughout the election year, *The Times* usually did find something more interesting than the horse race to put in the lead of its poll stories, but, at the end of the contest, when the actual finish of the horse race finally became the story and legitimately came to lead the news, the poll numbers were solidly there.

The degree of closeness of final preelection poll estimates to the actual outcome of an election constitutes a natural "acid test" of the methods used in opinion polls and creates a very visible and built-in incentive for constant refinement and improvement in techniques. The 1988 election year was a fairly good year for the polls in the United States. The results of major polls tightly bracketed the true outcome of the election—some right on, some slightly high, some slightly low—just as they should if their methods were adequate to the task.

"Portrait of the electorate." Use of polling data by *The Times* in 1988 culminated on the Thursday morning after Election Day when it printed a "Supertable" that was a half-page wide and a full page deep, showing how 102 subgroups of the population had voted in the presidential elections of 1988, 1984, and 1980. It helped to inform the page-one story on November 10, 1988, by E. J. Dionne, Jr., under the headline "Voters Delay Republican Hopes of Dominance in Post-Reagan Era." Table 2.13 presents the contents of that "Supertable."

A major motive for preparing and publishing the Supertable is to share with readers some of the rich data obtained through the Election Day exit

TABLE 2.13 Portrait of the Electorate

Percentage of 1988 Total		Percentage Who Voted in 1980			Percentage Who Voted in 1984		Percentage Who Voted in 1988	
		Reagan	Carter	Anderson	Reagan	Mondale	Bush	Dukakis
—	Total	51	41	7	59	40	53	45
48	Men	55	36	7	62	37	57	41
52	Women	47	45	7	56	44	50	49
85	Whites	55	36	7	64	35	59	40
10	Blacks	11	85	3	9	89	12	86
3	Hispanics	35	56	8	37	61	30	69
69	Married	—	—	—	62	38	57	42
31	Not married	—	—	—	52	46	46	53
20	18-29 years old	43	44	11	59	40	52	47
35	30-44 years old	54	36	8	57	42	54	45
22	45-59 years old	55	39	5	59	39	57	42
22	60 and older	54	41	4	60	39	50	49
8	Not a high school graduate	46	51	2	49	50	43	56
27	High school graduate	51	43	4	60	39	50	49
30	Some college education	55	35	8	61	37	57	42
35	College graduate or more	52	35	11	58	41	56	43
19	College graduate	—	—	—	—	—	62	37
16	Postgraduate education	—	—	—	—	—	50	48
48	White Protestant	63	31	6	72	27	66	33
28	Catholic	49	42	7	54	45	52	47
4	Jewish	39	45	15	31	67	35	64
9	White Fundamentalist or evangelical Christian	63	33	3	78	22	81	18
25	Union household	43	48	6	46	53	42	57
12	Family income under $12,500	42	51	6	45	54	37	62
20	$12,500-$24,999	44	46	7	57	42	49	50
20	$25,000-$34,999	52	39	7	59	40	56	44
20	$35,000-$49,999	59	32	8	66	33	56	42
24	$50,000 and over	63	26	9	69	30	62	37
19	$50,000-$100,000	—	—	—	—	—	61	38
5	Over $100,000	—	—	—	—	—	65	32
25	From the East	47	42	9	52	47	50	49
28	From the Midwest	51	40	7	58	40	52	47
28	From the South	52	44	3	64	36	58	41

Percentage of 1988 Total		Percentage Who Voted in 1980			Percentage Who Voted in 1984		Percentage Who Voted in 1988	
		Reagan	Carter	Anderson	Reagan	Mondale	Bush	Dukakis
19	From the West	53	34	10	61	38	52	46
35	Republicans	86	8	4	93	6	91	8
37	Democrats	26	67	6	24	75	17	82
26	Independents	55	30	12	63	35	55	43
18	Liberals	25	60	11	28	70	18	81
45	Moderates	48	42	8	53	47	49	50
33	Conservatives	72	23	4	82	17	80	19
31	Professional or manager	57	32	9	62	37	59	40
11	White-collar worker	50	41	8	59	40	57	42
13	Blue-collar worker	47	46	5	54	45	49	50
4	Full-time student	—	—	—	52	47	44	54
5	Teacher	46	42	10	51	48	47	51
5	Unemployed	39	51	8	32	67	37	62
10	Homemaker	—	—	—	61	38	58	41
2	Agricultural worker	36	59	4	—	—	55	44
16	Retired	—	—	—	60	40	50	49
56	1984 Reagan voters	75	9	2	100	0	80	19
9	1984 Democratic Reagan voters	57	23	2	100	0	48	51
28	1984 Mondale voters	14	63	8	0	100	7	92
23	Democratic primary voters	—	—	—	—	—	21	78
18	Republican primary voters	—	—	—	—	—	87	11
7	First-time voters	—	—	—	61	38	51	47
41	White men	59	32	7	67	32	63	36
44	White women	52	39	8	62	38	56	43
5	Black men	14	82	3	12	84	15	81
5	Black women	9	88	3	7	93	9	90
10	Men, 18-29 years old	47	39	11	63	36	55	43
11	Women, 18-29 years old	39	49	10	55	44	49	50
17	Men, 30-44 years old	59	31	8	61	38	58	40
19	Women, 30-44 years old	50	41	8	54	45	50	49
11	Men, 45-59 years old	60	34	5	62	36	62	36
12	Women, 45-59 years old	50	44	5	57	42	52	48

continued

(Table 2.13 continued)

Percentage of 1988 Total		*Percentage Who Voted in 1980* Reagan	Carter	Anderson	*Percentage Who Voted in 1984* Reagan	Mondale	*Percentage Who Voted in 1988* Bush	Dukakis
11	Men, 60 and older	56	40	3	62	37	53	46
11	Women, 60 and older	52	43	4	58	42	48	52
16	Whites, 18-29 years old	48	38	12	68	31	60	39
3	Blacks, 18-29 years old	7	89	3	6	94	12	86
30	Whites, 30-44 years old	59	31	8	63	36	60	39
4	Blacks, 30-44 years old	12	84	3	10	89	13	85
19	Whites, 45-59 years old	59	34	5	65	34	63	36
2	Blacks, 45-59 years old	13	84	3	10	86	10	86
20	Whites, 60 and older	56	39	4	63	37	54	45
2	Blacks; 60 and older	20	77	3	15	81	9	90
34	Married men	—	—	—	64	35	60	39
35	Married women	—	—	—	59	41	54	46
14	Unmarried men	—	—	—	55	42	51	47
17	Unmarried women	—	—	—	49	50	42	57
18	Republican men	87	8	4	94	5	91	8
17	Republican women	85	10	5	93	7	90	9
16	Democratic men	29	63	6	27	72	18	80
21	Democratic women	23	71	5	21	78	16	84
13	Independent men	60	27	10	66	32	58	40
13	Independent women	49	34	13	59	39	52	46
27	White Democrats	30	62	6	29	70	21	79
7	Black Democrats	4	94	2	3	96	4	95
4	Men with less than high school education	51	47	2	52	47	49	50
4	Women with less than high school education	41	55	2	46	52	38	62
12	Male high school graduates	53	42	3	62	37	50	49
15	Female high school graduates	50	44	5	58	41	50	50
13	Men with some college	59	31	8	65	33	60	38
17	Women with some college	52	39	8	58	41	54	45
19	Male college graduates	58	28	11	63	36	63	36
16	Female college graduates	42	44	12	52	47	49	51
21	Whites in the East	51	38	10	57	42	54	45
2	Blacks in the East	12	85	3	7	90	12	85
25	Whites in the Midwest	55	37	7	64	35	57	42

Percentage of 1988 Total		Percentage Who Voted in 1980 Reagan Carter Anderson			Percentage Who Voted in 1984 Reagan Mondale		Percentage Who Voted in 1988 Bush Dukakis	
2	Blacks in the Midwest	11	84	4	6	92	8	91
23	Whites in the South	61	35	3	71	28	67	32
4	Blacks in the South	9	89	2	10	89	12	86
15	Whites in the West	55	32	10	66	33	58	41
2	Blacks in the West	Insufficient data available					13	83

SOURCE: Based on *New York Times*/CBS News exit polls of voters leaving polling places around the nation on election day. 1988 data based on questionnaires completed by 11,645 voters; 1984 data based on questionnaires from 9,174 voters; 1980 data based on questionnaires from 15,201 voters. Those who gave no answer are not shown. Dashes indicate that a question was not asked in a particular year.
NOTE: Family income categories in 1980: Under $10,000, $10,000-14,999, $15,000-24,999, $25,000-49,999, and $50,000 and over. "Fundamentalist or evangelical Christian" was labeled "born-again Christian" in 1980 and 1984.

poll of voters leaving polling places across the country. The national exit polls conducted by *The Times* and CBS News in presidential elections include such large samples—11,645 in the case of the 1988 exit poll—that results can be determined much more precisely than is the case with the much smaller samples used in normal polls conducted by telephone. Results from a large exit poll can be reliably reported for smaller groups—such as Jews, Hispanics, and people with over $100,000 income—who do not have sufficient respondents for analysis in ordinary polls. Results also can be shown for groups defined by multiple criteria—such as Black Southerners, or men aged 18-29 years, or female college graduates.

These are the kind of data that analysts at the news polls study closely on election night and in the days afterward. But, in the ordinary course of assembling a news story, relatively little of the material can actually make it into print or onto the air. Publishing it systematically as a Supertable assures that these data can be utilized by a much wider audience.

The Supertable also invites the reader to do his or her own analysis of the demography of the vote. One can compare groups with one another within a given election year or compare individual categories of voters over time. For instance, when comparing the votes of men and women, one can discern both that a "gender gap" of seven points existed in the 1988 vote and that such a gap between the sexes of six to eight points has persisted across the past three presidential elections. As another example, in comparing how party identification translated into votes, one notices that, although George Bush in 1988 did about as well among Republican identifiers as Ronald Reagan had in 1980 and 1984, Bush managed to attract fewer Democratic identifiers into his camp in 1988 than Reagan had in the previous two elections.

One can also discern in the demography of the 1988 vote the continuing outlines of the New Deal coalition. Dukakis did best among Blacks, Hispanics, Jews, the unemployed, those with less income and lower education, and liberals. Alternately, the persistent outlines of the traditional Republican coalition are also still apparent. Bush did especially well among White Protestants, the professional and managerial classes, people with income over $50,000, those with four-year college degrees, and conservatives.

But it also is apparent from the table that the party coalitions are not what they once were. Although Dukakis took a majority of the vote of union households, he could do no better than run evenly with Bush among blue-collar workers as a whole, and Bush actually took a majority of Catholics. All were once mainstays of the New Deal coalition. Moreover, White Southerners—formerly a key element in the Roosevelt coalition—have defected in large numbers to the Republicans in recent presidential elections, a shift that has been under way for decades.

The device of the Supertable was originated by Edward Tufte of Yale University in 1980, when he was a consultant for *The Times* poll. It was expanded and made a fixture of *The Times*'s political coverage in 1984. It requires weeks of preparation and checking of past data in advance of the election and a furious amount of calculating and checking of the new data on the day after the election. Its very existence expresses our faith that there are "political junkies" among *Times* readers who want their political numbers, and know what to do with them, just as much as do readers of the paper's financial section or the sports pages regarding the numbers relevant to their own particular passions.

What about the nonvoters? But, in 1988, the Supertable tells the story of only half the voting age population. The other half of that population stayed away and did not cast any vote on Election Day. Their story also is relevant in a year that saw the lowest rate of voter turnout since the 1920s—when women first entered the electorate and temporarily lowered the turnout rate.

A final polling device used by *The Times* and CBS News was a post-election panel-back survey in which every respondent in the final pre-election poll who could be reached again was reinterviewed after the election was over. The purpose of this survey was to compare voters with nonvoters, to investigate the reasons for nonvoting, and to check whether

TABLE 2.14 Who Were the Voters and Nonvoters?

	Percentage of Voters Who:	*Percentage of non-Voters Who:*
Demographic characteristics		
Were under 30 years of age	24	42
Reported annual household income under $25,000	38	49
Have not attended college	58	75
Are Black	11	11
Moved in the last two years	16	35
Partisanship and candidate preference		
Preferred Bush for President	53	50
Preferred Dukakis for President	45	34
Have a favorable opinion now of at least one of the presidential candidates	83	64 √
Say there are important differences in what the Democratic and Republican parties stand for	64	44
Identify strongly with a party	39	20
Describe selves as independent or decline to identify with a party	27	50 ∨
Civic attitudes		
Say things go on as before no matter who is elected	23	31
Trust government in Washington to do what is right always or most of the time	45	41
Say people in the government waste a lot of the money paid in taxes	73	67
Say government is run by a few big interests looking out for themselves	57	59
Paid a lot of attention to campaign	50	26 ✓
Say they cared a good deal who would win this year	83	57

SOURCE: Based on a *New York Times*/CBS News panel survey of 1,627 respondents conducted November 10-16, 1988. Respondents were also interviewed November 2-4, just before the election.

people acted on Election Day as they had told us they intended—or, if not, why not.

Table 2.14 compares voters and nonvoters on their demographic characteristics, their partisanship and candidate preferences, and their civic attitudes. Nonvoters tended to be younger and to be less well off in terms of income and education. They also were more mobile, being twice as likely as voters to have moved in the past two years and thus to have been required to take the extra step of reregistering to vote at their new address. When asked about their reasons for not voting, nonvoters most frequently cited their lack of registration; 37% of the nonvoters cited their being unregistered as the chief reason for their not voting.

Nonvoters were much less connected with the political system than were voters. They were less partisan and more independent of the parties. Fewer nonvoters said they saw much difference between the political parties. Fewer nonvoters had a favorable opinion of at least one of the two presidential candidates.

Nonvoters' levels of cynicism and distrust of politics and government were about the same as those of voters. But nonvoters were only half as likely to pay a lot of attention to the campaign, and they were much less likely than voters to say they cared who would win in 1988.

But when asked before the election which candidate they preferred, and again after the election which candidate they would have voted for, the nonvoters split in the same direction as voters did, favoring George Bush over Michael Dukakis. If everyone had turned out to vote in 1988, then Bush's margin of victory, according to the poll, would have been at least as large as it was, probably even slightly larger. All these comparisons of voters and nonvoters were presented in *The Times* on November 21, 1988, in a story by E. J. Dionne, Jr., under the headline "If Nonvoters Had Voted: Same Winner, But Bigger."

Testing Hunches and Claims

The introduction to this chapter mentioned that, in addition to contributing to stories in major ways, the 31 polls we conducted during 1988 helped in other ways to inform reporting and editing at *The Times* throughout the election year. They did this on a week-in/week-out basis by allowing reporters and editors to check hunches, to test claims, and to avoid being manipulated. Using the growing body of polling data that accumulated throughout 1988, we tested a large number of hypotheses—many suggested by our own reporters and editors, some originated by outside political pundits, scholars, or other pollsters, and even a few advanced by interested parties, such as spokespersons for the individual campaigns.

Described briefly below are just two examples of the many interesting questions we were able to answer during 1988 because we had available the resource that polling data provided: (a) How much did Jesse Jackson's prominent role at the Democratic National Convention hurt Michael Dukakis? (b) How much did having Dan Quayle on the Republican national ticket hurt George Bush?

Jackson's impact on Dukakis. In a September 1, 1988, column in *The Times*, William Safire aired his suspicion that "the Democratic Convention came across on television as dominated night after night by Jesse Jackson and his legions of admirers, while the Republican Convention was vanilla ice cream on white bread—culturally majoritarian and non-threatening." To the viewer at home, Safire conjectured, the picture on the tube was saying for the Democrats that "we are not you" and for the Republicans that "we are you and not them." Potentially, this could have been one major explanation for the dramatic reversal in the public's opinion of Michael Dukakis between July and September.

By using the *Times*/CBS News poll, we were able to test this hypothesis but found little support for it. For instance, in the poll taken from July 31 to August 3, soon after the Democratic National Convention, 56% of registered voters said they approved of the role that Jesse Jackson had in the convention, while only 27% said they disapproved and 18% had no opinion. Moreover, when asked what impressed them most about the Democratic convention, more registered voters cited Jackson (19%) than cited Dukakis (14%). In a later poll, taken October 21 to 24, Jackson actually achieved a higher favorability rating with the public than Dukakis did at that time. These findings, which were not at all consistent with Safire's suspicions, waved us away from putting much weight on Jackson's role in Dukakis's reverses.

Public reactions to the Republican National Convention in August clearly did have a payoff for Bush and negative implications for Dukakis, but it does not seem fair to single out Jesse Jackson and his followers as the public's main point of comparison between the two party gatherings. Rather, as E. J. Dionne, Jr., concluded in his page-one story in *The Times* on September 14, 1988,

> Mr. Dukakis's situation is a textbook case of an increasingly common phenomenon: the politician who is virtually unknown, wins primaries and with them a vaguely favorable image and then suffers a sharp decline in his standing as voters—getting much of their new information from the opposition—study him more closely and have second thoughts.

Quayle's impact on Bush. George Bush's selection of Senator Dan Quayle as the Republican nominee for vice president also raised widespread speculation as to how much the presidential nominee would be hurt. It was widely assumed that Quayle was a major liability who would cost Bush considerably in the final vote, even if this did not preclude eventual victory for the Republican ticket. Using both preelection telephone polls and the Election Day exit poll of actual voters, we were able to test this hypothesis, and—once again—we found little support for it.

Quayle was clearly the least popular of the four major party nominees. As the campaign wore on, the public had an increasingly unfavorable balance of opinion about Dan Quayle and an increasingly favorable balance of opinion about Senator Lloyd Bentsen, the Democratic vice presidential nominee. But the voters seemed to be making up their minds much more on the basis of the presidential nominees than on the basis of their vice presidential running mates.

Our telephone poll taken October 8 to 10 showed that the two vice presidential nominees together—that is, the contrast between Quayle and Bentsen—might be cutting the Republican ticket's margin by about four percentage points. That was because, when respondents were asked about a hypothetical contest with only the two presidential candidates, Bush led Dukakis by nine percentage points; but, when the full party tickets were brought into the picture, Bush-Quayle led Dukakis-Bentsen by only five percentage points—a four-point difference. This finding was mentioned briefly in a page-one story on October 13, 1988, by E. J. Dionne, Jr., headlined "Poll Shows U.S. Voter Optimism Is Helping Bush in the Campaign."

However, the Election Day exit poll of actual voters leaving polling stations across the country showed even less damage from the "Quayle factor." Analysis of the exit poll showed that the two vice presidential nominations together—that is, the contrast between Bentsen and Quayle—had cost the Republicans perhaps one percentage point in the national vote. That was because, when voters were asked about a hypothetical contest with only the two presidential candidates, Bush led Dukakis by nine percentage points; but, when the full party tickets were introduced into the picture, Bush-Quayle still led Dukakis-Bentsen by eight percentage points—just one percentage-point shift. Although the exit poll could not rule out the possibility that damage to the Republicans from the "Quayle factor" had been greater, one percentage point was all that could be demonstrated using the data from actual voters.

This finding was mentioned in a page-one story on November 9, 1988—the morning after the election—by E. J. Dionne, Jr., headlined "Bush Is

Elected by a 6-5 Margin with Solid G.O.P. Base in South; Democrats Hold Both Houses." Together, these findings from two different types of polls convinced us not to put much emphasis on the conventional wisdom about Quayle's damage to the Republican ticket.

Conclusion

In *The Times*'s experience, the major polling lesson learned or confirmed in 1988 is that any program of political research must be designed to be appropriate to its task. Because the election is a yearlong process, it is necessary to design a series of polls with the cycle of political events in mind. Because long-term, middle-term, and short-term forces can each affect the outcome to some extent, it is important to study all three types of factors. Because public reactions to personalities, issues, and events can change during the year, it is important to repeat many trend questions to capture the dynamics of the campaign. Because voter turnout can be critical, it is important to develop ways to estimate the likelihood that individuals will vote. Because last minute shifts in voter preference can and sometimes do occur, it is important to poll as close as is practical to Election Day and then to call back the same respondents afterward with additional questions. Because nonvoters are now about half of the voting age population, it is important to find ways to hear their voices too. And because the quality of the polling data is crucial to all subsequent interpretation and reporting, it is important to invest in properly drawn samples, high-quality interviewing, and an experienced staff for question writing and data analysis. Finally, when it comes to the reporting of the results, it certainly helps to have some fine correspondents, editors, and graphics artists on your team!

References

Apple, R. W., Jr. (1989, April 20). Public rates Bush highly but sees mostly style. *The New York Times*, p. B12.

Clymer, A. (1989, January 24). [Internal *New York Times* memorandum.] New York. *The New York Times*.

Dionne, E. J., Jr. (1988, June 13). Jackson share of votes by Whites triples in '88. *The New York Times*, p. B7.

Dionne, E. J., Jr. (1988, July 12). Poll finds public is wary of both Bush and Dukakis. *The New York Times*, p. 1.

Dionne, E. J., Jr. (1988, September 14). Poll shows Bush sets agenda for principal election issues. *The New York Times*, p. 1.

Dionne, E. J., Jr. (1988, September 25). A third of voters remain uncertain on eve of debate. *The New York Times*, p. 1.

Dionne, E. J., Jr. (1988, October 13). Poll shows U.S. voter optimism is helping Bush in the campaign. *The New York Times*, p. 1.

Dionne, E. J., Jr. (1988, October 26). New poll shows attacks by Bush are building lead. *The New York Times*, p. 1.

Dionne, E. J., Jr. (1988, October 31). G.O.P. makes Reagan lure of young a long-term asset. *The New York Times*, p. 1.

Dionne, E. J., Jr. (1988, November 6). Bush still ahead as end nears but Dukakis gains in survey. *The New York Times*, p. 1.

Dionne, E. J., Jr. (1988, November 9). Bush is elected by a 6-5 margin with solid G.O.P. base in South; Democrats hold both houses. *The New York Times*, p. 1.

Dionne, E. J., Jr. (1988, November 10). Voters delay Republican hopes of dominance in post-Reagan era. *The New York Times*, p. 1.

Dionne, E. J., Jr. (1988, November 21). If nonvoters had voted: Same winner but bigger. *The New York Times*, p. B16.

Oreskes, M. (1988, May 16). In a surprise, voters say they're watching a lot. *The New York Times*, p. A15.

Oreskes, M. (1988, August 14). Convention a conservative gathering. *The New York Times*, p. A32.

Safire, W. (1988, September 1). Bush the front runner. [Column.] *The New York Times*, p. A25.

Toner, R. (1988, October 31). Dukakis asserts he is a "liberal," but in old tradition of his party. *The New York Times*, p. 1.

3

Media Polls, the Los Angeles Times *Poll, and the* 1988 Presidential Election

I. A. (BUD) LEWIS

The votes in the 1988 presidential election had hardly been counted before the criticism began. People of every political persuasion seemed to be saying, "Isn't there a better way to run an election?" People found fault with registration, with turnout, with the electoral college. They felt the primaries were too stretched out, threw too much emphasis on small groups of voters, took decisions out of the hands of professionals, and, what's more, had destroyed any southern candidate on Super Tuesday. The media had become players; they should have covered more issues; and, of course, TV was too expensive. But, more than anything else, there were complaints about ethics—that negative campaigning was trashing the political system. A clear-cut electoral outcome had left behind uncertainty and anxiety.

Perhaps that was because the presidential campaign of 1988 had demonstrated more convincingly than ever before how completely an election could be "managed." How else could the Republican candidate, who was 17 percentage points behind at the start, have swept to victory in 16 short weeks? And did not the Democrat lose because he conducted an inept campaign?

Indeed, public opinion manipulation (or the bungling of it) seemed a major theme running through much of the dismay about the campaign, often coupled with a fresh probing of the messenger role played by the press and especially by the public, or media, polls. Said Marvin Kalb[1]:

There is no escape from the conclusion that the press is now part of the political process. We are in a loop without exit signs. We influence politicians. We are influenced by polls. The American people are polled. They provide answers based upon what they have read or seen or heard. Politicians set their agendas on the basis of what tracking polls tell them. It's conceivable that this loop is destructive to the continuation of a vibrant and free democracy. (personal communication, n.d.)

To what extent is criticism of media polls justified? This chapter is an effort to address that question by first assessing the performance of public polls in 1988. After that, I attempt to retrace the development of media polls in an effort to explain how they got to be the way they are. Then follows a description of current public polling practice calling mainly upon my own experience at the *Los Angeles Times* Poll. Then I offer a few suggestions about how things might be done differently in 1992 and end with a few conjectures about the future direction of media polls.

I have always taken great pride in my profession but, upon rereading this chapter, it seems to me that some of what I have to say may appear negative. That has not been my intention. I have spent much of my life defending the press and public polls. As a journalist for more than 40 years and a pollster for more than 25, I hope I can be considered one of the family and, as such, may be permitted a certain amount of criticism.

I also believe that public opinion research has, within my lifetime, become an inextricable part of journalism. So, although my focus is on media public opinion polling, general comments about the press will inevitably creep into the discussion from time to time.

A Report Card on Public Polls

There were more polls in 1988, and that was a good thing. Certainly the degree and extent of survey research in 1988 far exceeded that of previous elections. The *Los Angeles Times* Poll, for example, conducted more than twice as many polls in 1988 as it did in 1984 and interviewed 88% more respondents. To a considerable extent, the nationwide increase in polling activity had a salutary effect. A large number of polls—even though some might be of questionable quality—more often than not produce reasonable estimates about reality. And the echo effect, the media reverberation of isolated polling factoids, is, of course, reduced. Moreover, the trend toward use of newer quantitative methods of analysis, as opposed to "inside dopester" gossip, which used to be the rule, must be considered an improvement.

Fairness is, of course, a subjective criterion, but it seemed to me that almost all the public polls were neutral and objective. It would be difficult to ascribe a Republican or Democratic bias to the results of any of the nationally recognized polls.

I would say that the quality of public polls was generally of higher standards than before. Most polls sponsored by the larger media organizations conformed to recognized practices. Of course, there were the occasional lapses: call-in polls,[2] for example, conducted by some second-rank newspapers and, surprisingly, by CNN, among others. But most public polls followed well-tested standards and benefited from reliable results. It would seem that appropriate methodologies for conducting political polls are today widely accepted and generally adhered to by most national polls.

The accuracy of media polling throughout the campaign was never seriously questioned.[3] To a certain extent, the public polls were lucky in 1988 because, at least toward the end, the outcome was not close. If there was a general practice that might have contributed to inaccuracy, it had to do with voter screens I suspect were inadequate as well as the reluctance of most pollsters to reveal their methods for determining "likely voters." Still, the public generally received a continuing stream of polling assessments that were overwhelmingly accurate. Very few were surprised by the presidential outcome or by the results of most statewide races.

There were, as usual, complaints about the emphasis on candidate horse races[4] by media polls and little appreciation of their function. Few people remember an early experiment by the CBS News/*New York Times* Poll when an excess of good intentions led the two partners to refrain from any mention of the presidential standings throughout the entire 1976 campaign.

The results were sometimes inscrutable. More often than not, what was reported was how much of a candidate's support came from various voting blocs: perhaps 60% from Whites and 25% from Blacks, and so on—the profile of the vote. Occasionally, there were even examples of how far ahead a candidate was among selected subgroups of the electorate: Among Blacks, say, he might have been ahead 85% to 15%—but the standings were never given for all voters. This curious practice, of course, excited the puzzle-fanciers and, to be sure, it was never very difficult to deduce the national standings when one knew the standings for both men and women. But, in the long run, a great deal was missing in this experiment. An election is certainly about, among other things, who will win, and an analysis lacking that dimension does not fully explain the situation.

As for relevance, I would have to rate the 1988 public polls undistinguished at best—but perhaps this is a failure of the process itself. Granted, the polls were usually able to describe political maneuvers and to offer useful explanations for campaign strategies. But the opinion research technique also has a way of dredging up secondhand residue that has been cast off first by the campaign and then by the media. If they are not careful, media polls can be a bizarre set of fun-house mirrors. Poll findings about issue positions and candidate impressions are often reflections in a mirror casting back an image from the media themselves, which, like another mirror, had reflected nothing more than a view projected by campaign machinery.

For example, the media polls did a fairly good job of explaining issues like Willie Horton's prison furlough and the Pledge of Allegiance (one was condemned, the other applauded). But media polls had a hard time coming to grips with Nicaragua, the savings and loan crisis, nuclear disarmament, and, above all, the federal budget deficit simply because these were issues that were seldom discussed by either party campaign and, therefore, they did not pop up in the public polls. In a way, the polling process excluded these issues from the agenda of the so-called agenda-setting media.

As far as influence is concerned, I believe that media polls were very influential in the 1988 election—but not in the way most people think. Critics of public polls usually claim they sway many voters. However, the literature on this subject is not only extensive but also innocent of evidence that media polls have ever influenced an election.

But this is not to say that media polls have no effect. In the first place, they do exert enormous influence on *politicians*. In studies for the *Los Angeles Times* in California, the evidence shows that political activists are more aware of political polls than the average voter and are clearly encouraged or discouraged by them. Moreover, there is considerable anecdotal evidence confirming this finding. Politicians have often described the devastating psychological effect that negative poll results have had on campaign workers. And there are campaign managers who refuse to show poll results to the candidate.

There is also evidence to show that campaign contributors are even more avid readers of political polls than party activists. This is, of course, to be expected. If one assumes even the smallest connection between campaign contributions and future comforts, one would not anticipate large expenditures devoted to losers if that could be avoided by studying poll results.

But perhaps the most profound influence of media polls, in my opinion, is on neither political activists nor campaign contributors but on the media themselves. It has been my experience that some journalists—and not all of them in the boondocks, either—have a tendency to make as much as possible out of horse race figures. The inclination is understandable. News, by one definition, is what is *unexpected*, and the search for variation urges some reporters to play up what to survey researchers would be considered insignificant or inconsistent distinctions. This impulse, often the result of inexperience, can sometimes produce unintentionally slanted stories, stories that seek to explain the successes of presumed winners and that emphasize the failings of expected losers. In such cases, the influence of polls on the press is a communicable disease; it spreads to everyone.

As an example, consider an ABC/Washington Post poll published two days before the Bush-Dukakis second debate.[5] The poll, in my opinion, represented a commendable effort to show the electoral implications of the popular vote. Moreover, the subsequent *Post* story dealt with the findings conservatively. But most of the media drew another conclusion: Only a decisive win in the second debate could revive an obviously faltering Dukakis campaign. Dukakis, though, was generally not credited with having accomplishing such a knockout blow (although polls at the time indicated he made a creditable showing), and the second debate proved to have a negative influence on the Dukakis candidacy, in part because of the impact this poll had had on the media.

It is unnecessary to belabor the point. My experience is that polls often reflect but seldom directly influence public opinion. But polls do have an important influence on special elites like political activists, campaign contributors, and, especially, journalists. And it is the journalists who, I believe, convey a poll-inspired feedback to public opinion. The impact of media polls upon the media themselves cannot be overestimated.

To sum up, the report card for public polls in the 1988 election shows good grades. I should think there is little here for which the media need apologize. But if I were permitted a comment at the bottom, it might read: "Capable of doing much better."

The Historical Context

It is probably impossible to date the beginning of public opinion research because—a great deal depends on how *polling* is defined. But survey research surely came into its own in the 1930s. It is interesting that the occasion was a presidential campaign (1936, between Roosevelt and Landon) and the agency (indeed, in the case of *The Literary Digest*, the victim) was the press.

Since that time when George Gallup and Archibald Crossley made a name for themselves by contradicting *The Literary Digest*'s prediction of a Landon victory, politics and polling have never been very far apart. To this day, survey research firms—which make most of their income from custom polls for private clients—sometimes feel the need to indulge in politics to keep their names before the public.

Indeed, the media and the pollsters became fast friends. Elmo Roper began a highly successful survey operation for *Fortune* magazine; Crossley began to rate radio listeners; and Gallup began a syndicated newspaper column that continues to this day.

There is no doubt that the relationship between political campaigns and the polls became firmly fixed in the public mind, so that interest in one profited from interest in the other. The interest was stimulated by a Gallup invention soon afterward, which found a convenient way to create a simulated election by means of the job-rating question.[6] By this simple device, pollsters no longer needed to languish between elections. Was a pseudoelection required years before the next campaign? Simply ask the job-rating question and an attention-getting popular referendum could be conducted on demand. Indeed, George Gallup always believed that he had contributed to the democratic process by providing a way to construct periodic referenda on the people's representatives.

The next great media contribution to the political process occurred in the early 1960s. Broadcasters discovered that television audiences flipped channels on election night until they came to rest on the one displaying the highest vote—presumably, the channel with the largest totals knew the most. Election coverage quickly became a contest to determine which broadcaster could collect the most votes (or, to be more accurate, *display* the most votes: Rival broadcasters carefully monitored each other and often suspected that the competition copied vote totals and amplified the returns a bit before displaying them as their own).

At NBC in 1960, Elmer Lower, then vice president in charge of election coverage, devised what he called the Distant Early Warning Line.[7] This "DEW Line" consisted of a large number of precincts scattered across the country each of which had only one characteristic: It reported its vote quickly. These precinct results could be tabulated and posted long before results were available from the slower-counting county clerks across the nation. Thus, in 1960, NBC was able to report early vote totals far larger than those of the competition.

But the DEW Line was self-destroying. As other broadcasters began to copy the procedure, competition demanded higher and higher vote totals.

And that meant "stringing" more and more precincts, which meant spending more and more money. Soon, all of the networks were staffing thousands of precincts. The time was fast approaching when this kind of expenditure was no longer cost-effective.

In the 1964 California primary, the whole system came crashing to the ground. In those days, there were about 30,000 precincts in the state, and precinct reporters were paid about $10 apiece. On the night of June 2, each of the three networks staffed every precinct, a total expenditure of nearly $1 million for a single state primary.

The following day, the network presidents of ABC, CBS, and NBC met and agreed to sponsor the News Election Service.[8] The networks were to share the costs of the vote collection process, and each agreed not to use different vote totals. The agreement immediately spelled the end of the struggle to collect more votes than the opposition.

The network rivalry remained; it only took on another form. Where the networks once competed to gather faster vote returns, they now scrambled to collect "Key"[9] Precinct returns, which could be used to make faster predictions about who had won the election.

Soon even larger amounts of money—millions of dollars at each network—were being spent on vote projection models. At NBC, for example, a seven-computer configuration was devised in 1964 to make Key Precinct estimates of election outcomes.[10] In subsequent years, each network became proficient at predicting election results on the basis of minute fractions of the expected vote. Rival network teams began to record the exact minute and second of every network projection to prove who had been first in announcing a winner. More often than not, the winning network was the one that wasn't making a commercial announcement at the time. Other networks might have been ready to project a winner, but, of course, they could never be expected to break into a commercial.

At about the same time, NBC discovered ways to put their precinct returns to further use. "Tag"[11] Precincts were selected to track the voting characteristics of various voting blocs. Black Tag Precincts, for example, could be shown to be 90% Black. Catholic precincts, on the other hand, could never approach such purity except perhaps in Louisiana's Plaquemines Parish, nor could Jewish precincts be so consistent, not even in Beverly Hills, California, or Scarsdale, New York. Moreover, Catholic voters in South Boston or Los Angeles's Boyle Heights often did not vote the way Catholics did in Nassau County, New York, or Stearns County, Minnesota. Voters in these precincts were often "ghettoized" and exhibited different characteristics than their counterparts elsewhere.

Network researchers soon became implacable enemies of the secret ballot, attempting to devise ways of determining the nature and motivation behind each individual ballot cast. Stemming from this desire to explain elections more completely, the exit poll was invented about this time.

The earliest recorded exit poll was conducted in California on June 2, 1964, the same night that was responsible for the creation of the News Election Service. A number of California election officials had refused to cooperate with NBC precinct stringers and this caused NBC to devise a sample of 21 precincts statewide, all of them staffed by college students.[12] The students were instructed to stop voters leaving their respective precincts and to ask them how they voted in the Nelson Rockefeller-Barry Goldwater Republican presidential primary as well as the Pierre Salinger-Alan Cranston Democratic Senate race and the George Murphy-Leland Kaiser Republican Senate contest. Ballots were deposited in "ballot boxes" marked "secret" and five times during the day each stringer called in partial and then final results. These were tabulated on six hand-operated calculators at KNBC, the NBC television station in Burbank, California; the results then were phoned to the RCA "Operation Ballot" computer center in Cherry Hill, New Jersey.[13]

It is interesting to note that CBS, using 18 Key Precincts statewide and a preelection survey by Lou Harris, called Barry Goldwater the winner 22 minutes after the polls had closed in Los Angeles (but 38 minutes before the polls closed in the Rockefeller strongholds of San Francisco and Northern California). Far from contributing to a quick call, however, the first exit poll was partly responsible for the fact that NBC withheld its projection until 12:51 a.m., eastern time (Gould, 1964). In point of fact, the "raw" vote, the vote tabulated from the returns of the 30,000 precinct stringers, did not indicate a clear winner until the following morning, when it was possible to say that Barry Goldwater had prevailed by only the narrowest of margins.

More conventional polling seems to have begun at the networks some time later. Oliver Quayle was conducting surveys for NBC at least as early as 1969 during the New York City Republican mayoral primary between John Lindsay and John Marchi. But network polling efforts began in earnest after the 1972 presidential campaign. Every Wednesday morning following each Democratic primary, Pat Caddell[14] would gather network reporters to disclose that George McGovern had once again captured the blue-collar vote.[15] The press, of course, had no way to verify these findings or any of the others that were frequently made available to the press. As a result of the 1972 experience, the networks resolved to conduct their own polls so they would never again be vulnerable to exaggerated poll findings or selective survey disclosures. Moreover, they wanted to be better able to explain the effectiveness of issues, candidate images, and campaign strategies. It was during the off years, from 1973 to 1975, that most of the networks began to develop an in-house capability to conduct survey research.

In one way or another, all of the national public polling operations derive from these beginnings and still use many of the procedures developed during those years. But today, new methods, changing circumstances, and a number of new media demands have expanded the range of public polling and extended its involvement in the journalistic process.

Public Polls Today: Some Complexities

The general public is often surprised to learn how few individuals are involved in the actual production of public polls. There is a certain amount of expansion over time (especially in presidential election years), but the basic staff is small.

At the *Los Angeles Times*, for example, there are seven permanent employees in the polling unit (not counting about 250 part-time interviewers). At ABC, there is an equal number (not counting the employees of Chilton Research Services—an ABC subsidiary that staffs all exit poll precincts, draws telephone samples, recruits, interviews, and builds files of final poll data—and the employees of International Communications Research, a private polling firm). Until recently, the NBC polling unit never had more than 25 permanent employees, and the staff at the CBS Elections and Polling Unit is roughly comparable in size. The roster at Gallup and Harris is perhaps larger, but only because both firms conduct a considerable number of custom polls for private clients; the number of employees engaged exclusively in public polls is small.

But the investment in these public polling organizations is quite substantial. The annual public polls budget for all but a few of these national organizations is easily in six figures. Partly, this is because of sizable telephone toll charges, large payrolls, and a heavy commitment to computers. But mostly it is because of the variety and complexity of the tasks that media pollsters are called upon to perform. Each kind of poll requires different techniques and each kind has become more and more difficult to conduct.

In the 1988 presidential campaign year, most public polling organizations were called upon to conduct most, if not all, of the following kinds of polls.

Preprimary polls. Polling before a primary election or a caucus is without doubt riskier than any other political poll. Several reasons are frequently mentioned: Because all candidates in a primary belong to the same party, the candidate's party affiliation cannot anchor voters, who are thus more volatile. Moreover, turnout is typically lower than in a general election, requiring carefully constructed voter screens. Also, voter attention is not firmly directed to early political events like these and so convictions or impressions are likely to be more unstable.

Another preprimary polling handicap that is not so often mentioned is the frivolous quality of the primary vote decision. Voters know the vote that counts is cast in November, so they often consider their primary vote a demonstration of their personalities or of their stands on particular issues. It is almost as if the voter were saying, "I will vote for this minority candidate (about whom, it is true, I have some reservations) because that will show I am a liberal," or "I despise that candidate, but my primary vote will send a message about taxes (or whatever)."

Also, because the primary period is short, new contests follow one another rapidly and opinions can change overnight. Moreover, primaries, which are mostly multicandidate elections, promote viability strategies in the mind of the voter. The last primary or the latest poll gives rise to new "expectations" and requires modifications of voting tactics concerning lesser evils and wasted votes. All of these factors contribute to fickle voter attitudes that may or not translate into predictable voting behavior.

Preelection polls. A commercial pollster is free to tell a client that his or her new toothpaste tube should be green, because he knows he can never be proved wrong. (Even if the product flops, that can be blamed on advertising, merchandising, production, and so on.) But a media pollster who says Flomnoddy will win with 56% of the vote very definitely can be proved wrong and, sadly, sometimes is. There is a correct answer to a political poll.

Or, at least, the public expects one. Opinion researchers may insist that they are only taking a snapshot in time or merely using a helpful tool for exploring collective attitudes. But that does no good. The public continues to believe that survey research can predict the future. And, of course, no one—not even pollsters—can do that.

The trouble is not that the polls fail so often but that they succeed "only" 70%, 80%, 90% of the time. Social scientists have discovered a research technique that is not only reproducible but reasonably accurate and the public has come to depend on it. When polls occasionally miss the mark (whether because of slipshod methods or misinterpretation of the findings or maybe just sampling error), the public, which has bestowed upon them such faith, reacts with bitter resentment.

One of the reasons polls cannot always predict the future accurately is, quite simply, that human beings' opinion does not always shape events. Primitive magic assumes that special words or procedures can force nature into compliance, but most people today, no matter how egocentric, are willing to admit that external forces can also shape eventualities, political or otherwise.

But perhaps a more important limitation of political polls is the fact that attitudes do not always simulate behaviors. People say they will vote for Flomnoddy, but then they don't. What's a poor pollster to do?

Often, it is useful to know how people mislead themselves. For example, name recognition, early on, may be a major component of any well-known candidate's advantage (which will evaporate when his or her opponent becomes better known). Frequently, voters mislead themselves according to Lewis's Law.[16] Sometimes a question about typical behavior is the best indicator of what people think. The sad truth is that respondents are sometimes the last people to ask directly for an opinion about themselves.

By far the most important question to be answered in a preelection poll is this: "Are you going to vote?" Typically, most adults say *yes*. But for at least half of all respondents, the answer is really *no*.

At the *Los Angeles Times* Poll, this quandary results in an especially extensive voter screen (consisting of 12 separate questions concerning qualifications, intentions, past behaviors, and present attitudes about voting) that is used to create Paul Perry's[17] classic scale of likely voters. Some media pollsters—Warren Mitosfky[18] is one—use a slight modification that substitutes respondent voting probabilities for scalar quantities. Only Mervin Field,[19] to my knowledge, weights respondent vote likelihood according to past turnout among various demographic variables. One suspects that, all too often, media pollsters simply take the word of respondents themselves when they are asked how likely they are to vote (an obviously unreliable criterion).

The media pollsters who pay more attention to this vital subject usually sort respondents from the most likely to vote down to the least likely and then determine what proportion of these must be excluded to arrive at an expected turnout ratio. Unfortunately, relative voter turnout ratios are very difficult to estimate and account for much of the variability in candidate preference. Sadly, most pollsters have no rigorous procedure for deriving these important parameters. They are usually approximated by holding a damp finger to the wind while casting a dubious eye toward past voter turnout.

Convention surveys. For the past three presidential elections, the *Los Angeles Times* has conducted surveys of delegates to the Democratic and Republican national conventions.[20] A questionnaire is mailed to each delegate as soon as he or she has been selected by a primary or convention. The schedule consists of approximately 100 questions dealing with commitment to presidential candidates; 30 or 40 questions concerning opinions about political issues and personalities, demographic information and certain housekeeping questions like party and local status and where they can be reached; and so on. Usually about 50% of the delegates respond to the mail questionnaire; all but about 5% are recovered through telephone callbacks.

These files prove extremely useful (even more so if convention activity is predictable or uneventful). The questionnaire provides enough material for at least two preconvention weekend stories. Moreover, the data base has proved helpful to reporters who are covering specific stories. In 1988, these convention surveys also provided the basis for focus group discussion sessions out of which developed three newspaper stories at each convention and an equal number of television stories aired by Cable News Network.

Debate polls. Conventions and debates are often important turning points in presidential campaigns and, for that reason, most public polls pay them special attention. A number of media polls compete to be the first to disclose national debate reaction.[21]

Debate polls present a challenge for at least two reasons. What is wanted, of course, is some measure of effect. But merely asking respondents whether this or that part of the debate changed their minds always raises complex problems regarding memory recall, and it often elicits a defensive reaction to an implied inconsistency. Both in 1984 and 1988, the *Los Angeles Times* polled about 2,000 respondents immediately before important debates and another 2,000 immediately afterward with identical questions regarding candidates, events, and important issues. The assumption is that any difference of opinion between the two poll findings would have to be regarded as the result of the debate itself and of its influence on the public.

Also, various public opinion surveys have shown marked differences of opinion between polls taken immediately after a debate and others taken hours or even days later, at which time respondents, presumably, had had an opportunity to discuss reactions with others and to absorb commentary from the media. In 1988, therefore, the *Times* polled an additional 2,000 respondents four days following the debate.

One would like to be able to say that this elaborate—and expensive— research design discovered many hidden insights, but unfortunately that was not the case. In 1988, the debates did not prove to be important turning points in the campaign, and the three successive callback waves produced few significant trends. Nevertheless, I believe the technique was appropriate and I would try it again, should the occasion warrant.

Exit polls. There is little doubt that exit polls have contributed immeasurably to our understanding of voting behavior in the United States. At the *Los Angeles Times*, we routinely conduct exit polls, which produce next-morning analysis of important elections. In 1988, the *Times* conducted exit polls in 12 states[22] as well as one national exit poll in November. Exit polls are not used to project election outcomes, partly because, as a morning newspaper, there is no such necessity, but also because exit polls are not extremely accurate, being subject to fairly large confidence limits and many uncertainties.

A Case History: What the Los Angeles Times *Did in 1988*

In a number of ways, the *Los Angeles Times* Poll methodology is similar to other national media polling organizations. Where there are distinctions, they are mainly in matters of size, perhaps, and variety.

For example, the sample size for routine national telephone surveys is usually somewhat more than 2,000 responses. The effort here is not just to be more certain about results but also to permit analysis of smaller subsamples. In addition, study instruments tend to be longer than most, typically 75 to 100 substantive questions.

In addition to news-related subjects, which are often determined by late-breaking events, *Los Angeles Times* polls often are devoted to more detailed research organized around a single theme (some recent national studies have concerned older Americans, abortion, American Jews and the Palestinian Problem, and so on) that are conducted five or six times a year and produce anywhere from one to four separate stories of considerable length.

The *Los Angeles Times* Poll does not limit itself only to conventional survey sampling. Non-sampling projects consume a substantial portion of our activities. The poll has, from the beginning, experimented with a number of ways to make social science techniques more available to journalism.

As an example, for the last seven years, the *Times* has been building a computer file of political campaign contributions in California. Data are abstracted from the public record (currently, more than 65,000 contributions have been entered) and are then supplemented by interviews with each of the more than 30,000 contributors involved. The donors are

asked, among other things, whether they do business with the government, their contribution objectives, their attitudes on political issues,
and also a number of questions regarding demographic variables. This
file has proved important in developing a number of newspaper stories
linking campaign contributions to political developments (for example, in
the current investigation of Mayor Tom Bradley over conflict of interest
charges involving sums he collected from Los Angeles businesses).

For several years, the *Times* has also computerized hospital mortality rates
to determine the best and worst places to be treated for the five most common
causes of death. The polling unit has also conducted elite polls of California
administrators to determine their reactions to the state's Proposition 13 ten
years later and has conducted probation studies ten years apart to measure
changes in crime patterns as well as a number of other nonsampling computerized data projects.

As mentioned before, every four years, the *Los Angeles Times* Poll updates
its files of delegates to the Republican and Democratic national presidential
nominating conventions. Also, there is a consistent effort to conduct polls
abroad (recent polls in England, Israel, Japan, Mexico, and West Germany),
some of which are matched by identical questionnaires conducted in the
United States.

There is another important difference: The entire polling procedure, from
sample generation to final analysis, is conducted in-house rather than being
farmed out to existing polling firms or handled by paid consultants.

There is a procedure concerning timing political coverage that is different
from most national polls. For at least ten years, it has been my practice to
refrain from polling later than two weeks before an election. This point of
view arises out of a number of considerations, foremost of which refers to
the original intention of political polling. It has seemed to me that the purpose
behind political polling is to illustrate more accurately the true factors playing
upon the electoral process so that the voter may understand the reasons
behind political events and strategies and also appreciate more completely
the personality and character of the candidates.

How well the candidate is faring (the horse race) is a substantial part of
the explanation of the forces at play during the campaign and, therefore, must
be detailed but never by obscuring the underlying issues, the personalities
involved, or the actions and reactions of the various camps. During a political
campaign, I believe the press has a compelling responsibility to illuminate
all of these aspects of the process.

But once the campaign has come down to the final moments, and the
candidates and the issues have been described, in my opinion, no further

purpose is served by horse racing except to add to the decibel level of the campaign and, perhaps, to contribute to possible bandwagon or underdog impulses on the part of the voter. The argument made here is that the true function of the press has been fulfilled and no public or journalistic purpose is further served by the "numbers game."

Moreover, there is always the opportunity to misinform or mislead. In a typical national media poll, candidate standings seldom are claimed to be accurate more than nineteen times out of twenty—and then only within a two- to three-point error range. Put another way, this means that political stories based on close horse races will be off the mark 5% of the time. No self-respecting journalist will knowingly accept that degree of error, I believe, especially when—as is claimed here—little valid purpose is served.

But public polling organizations can be described in more ways than by a list of projects or principles. Media polls, of course, operate within newsrooms and their clients and consumers have special requirements. They have to deal with public issues in a newsworthy manner and they must communicate fairly complex ideas to a wide and unsophisticated audience. All of which means that public pollsters must pay careful attention to how findings will fit into a story and how that story is told. Getting the story right on the air or in the newspaper is one of my main concerns and is easily the hardest part of my job.

At the *Los Angeles Times*, I try to remind writers and editors of my first rule of poll usage: A number is not a lead and a lead is not a number. Numbers can never appear in the lead except for the most compelling reasons (like, "the editor made me put it in"). What I think should be in the lead is the significance of a number or, better still, the significance of a combination of numbers. Furthermore, I think that numbers also are not analysis; they are things that have to be explained, not reported. In fact, there are far too many numbers in a poll. A poll is a tool, not a fact; a poll is an insight, not a prediction.

But this is not to say that numbers should be avoided. By far the best place for them, I think, is in high-data density graphics with a minimum of cute gimmicks that hide numbers inside pictures. I don't think graphics should "Mickey Mouse" the story (rehash numbers with which the text has already dealt). Graphics should clarify numbers and amplify their meanings in ways that cannot be handled as well in copy. They should be like box scores for baseball enthusiasts who cannot get enough numbers.

Closely connected to my first rule for poll writers is the second: Don't be a pointer. The writer should avoid that majestic march through the marginals that declares Democrats prefer so-and-so by 68% to 27% whereas women prefer such-and-such by 72% to 20% and Blacks and so on.

I also believe that a poll should never be allowed to become the sole ingredient of a story. One can always find quotes or background description or references to other developments to enhance the survey findings. Better still, a poll might well be the stepping off point for further reporting. Four years ago, the *Los Angeles Times* conducted a national poll on the subject of poverty that included a large oversample of poor people. A team of reporters then spent months in the field learning how the opinions expressed in the poll compared with reality. In this case, the poll formed the framework for a story but it certainly did not tell the whole story; neither had that been the plan.

I believe it is important to train the writers, not the public. I think it is the journalist's job to learn the intricacies of his or her specialty and then explain it in terms that are understandable to a layperson without doing violence to the essential truthfulness of the story. When a writer reports a finding, the reader has a right to expect that it is statistically significant and should not have to puzzle over confidence limits or sampling error. In fact, polls on polling indicate that most readers do not fully understand the meaning of confidence limits when they are included in poll stories.[23]

It is sadly true that some writers never do get a feel for writing poll stories even though they may be good writers in their specialties. My third rule: Never assign a writer to a poll only because he or she is an expert on the subject of the poll. Poor poll writers can easily jeopardize newsworthy findings by writing a clumsy or, worse, a confusing poll story. In my opinion, it is far better to train a good poll writer who will produce a readable, interesting story on almost any subject the poll can investigate.

Because polling is every day becoming a more and more important part of journalism, I would advocate that journalism schools place additional emphasis on the social science research techniques that Philip Meyers[24] has so well described as "Precision Journalism." Years ago, a reporter who had interviewed 15 people felt himself well prepared to write a story about what had taken place. Out of force of habit, I think, that same reporter was also ready to generalize about what people thought or did, with little concern for the dangers of a 15-person sample. Qualitative methods die hard.

This is especially true about political reporting. In the old days, political writers were essentially gossip collectors who relied on well-placed sources to explain political developments. These writers had convinced themselves and their readers that there was an "inside story" behind every political development. But, when polling irrevocably changed the nature of political reporting, it introduced another kind of expert, one who dealt with computers, random samples, and aggregate numbers. These new purveyors of revealed truth cared little or nothing about deals, scandals, or influence; all they needed were computer printouts. The inside dopester story suddenly got harder to write.

Nowadays, the old-style political reporter is the one who calls to ask, "What have you got that shows such-and-such?" Most media pollsters would recoil at such a request, seeing little point in fortifying cocktail party chatter with selective poll data that more often than not had to be taken out of context. I would prefer the question, "Does what you've got confirm or deny what I heard?"

Of course, the coming of the pollsters did not always represent progress. For one thing, they created an insatiable appetite among reporters for more polls under any circumstance or pretext and regardless of how inconsequential or distant an election might be. This, despite the fact that, in my opinion, any poll taken earlier than five weeks before an election may be useless for judging images, issues, or outcomes.

A Few Disquieting Developments

I should point out some of the things the *Los Angeles Times* didn't do in 1988.

In the first place, the *Times* did not use exit polls to project elections. Doing so is, at best, a dubious procedure—both as a statistical exercise and as a public relations gesture.

Most people are not aware how many voters leaving their polling places fail to cooperate with exit poll interviewers. The refusal rate is often dangerously high: between 25% and 45% of all voters approached. Moreover, these refusals produce a nonrepresentative set of responses because more old people, Blacks, and women decline to participate. While there are methods for correcting this bias, the fact remains that exit polls are unsatisfactory when used as the only basis for election projection.

There is, of course, one other reason the *Times* does not project outcomes from exit polls. Because the public believes so strongly that exit polls affect the outcome of elections (no matter how mistakenly), it seems somehow contemptuous of voters' wishes to persist in using exit polls for projections.

Fortunately, there is a remedy at hand. Many people believe that this Congress will legislate some form of uniform poll-closing time. This will minimize the importance of individual statewide projections and their cumulative effect as the electoral vote count mounts beyond 270, ensuring a presidential victory before many polls have closed.

The *Los Angeles Times* Poll did not, in 1988, conduct any "unscientific" polls. It is difficult to understand the value of the polls that are readily admitted to be unscientific. My suggestion would be to substitute the word *inaccurate* for the word *unscientific*. Then announcers would have to say, "Of course, this is an inaccurate poll, but. . . ."

In the same category, the *Los Angeles Times* Poll does not report call-in polls. Like most self-selected samples (letters to the editor are another example), this gimmick is overloaded with special pleaders who seldom represent an accurate profile of the public.

Focus groups have already shown themselves to be helpful for a special kind of qualitative research. The *Times* uses them cautiously: for pretesting questionnaire ideas before they are submitted to quantitative disciplines or for demonstrating poll findings, allowing readers and viewers to see in personal terms the meaning of the dry statistics. But the *Times* has never used focus groups to indicate, on the basis of eight to fifteen participants, what any larger population is thinking or doing.

The *Los Angeles Times* Poll employs "instant"[25] polls sparingly, being careful to remember that immediate public reaction to events is often later tempered by contact with peers and with the media. When immediate reaction is what is desired, instant polls are appropriate. A better method might be to do two polls, one immediately following the event and another a little while later.[26]

Of a similar nature are "tracking polls," a string of instant polls usually taken daily and analyzed sometimes separately but often using some form of floating average of the most recent two or three or more polls. Tracking polls have all of the drawbacks of instant polls plus a few more of their own. Because tracking polls call for a commitment over an extended period of time—sometimes several weeks, sometimes throughout an entire campaign—costs can be enormous and the need to shave costs imperative. This is usually accomplished by minimizing sample size (perhaps 100 to 300 completed interviews a night) and questionnaire length (often little more than a candidate preference and several demographic variables). The inevitable result of all of this is to focus attention on the horse race—indeed, there is little else on which to focus.

Moreover, politicians and reporters who are not familiar with the swings often observed between successive nights of polling results must be prepared for the sickening experience associated with roller coaster rides. For, even though one appreciates that each day may represent a sampling error of plus or minus seven (sometimes more than plus or minus twelve), it is almost impossible to disregard one single night's findings and not read some significance into the results. How many times have we heard it said that so-and-so's tracking poll picked up the sudden plunge after such-and-such an event or caught the upsurge of the last day's commercial blitz? A tracking poll is a poor use of resources.

And, finally, the *Los Angeles Times* poll does not use people meters, devices that measure second-by-second group reactions to different stimuli, including questions. Putting aside the various difficulties associated with small samples, immediate reactions, and a certain degree of frivolity, there still remains the unsolved problem of how they could be useful effectively by the media. If people meters are the answer, what is the question?

Some Lessons for 1992

The 1988 presidential campaign seems to have left behind a deep and widely noted sense of malaise. One explanation was suggested at the beginning of this chapter: a growing suspicion that people were losing their supposedly dominant role in the democratic process. The public had been *managed* more completely than ever before.

If such is the case, it is arguable that public opinion polls may have contributed to the process unintentionally, that they were often co-opted, made to be a tool of campaign manipulation rather than a mirror of the public will.

In 1992, it seems to me, media polls must be more sensitive to an exploration of the public agenda as opposed to the politicians' agenda.

During the last presidential campaign, I think the media were unprepared for the extent and efficiency of political exploitation. And when the most egregious examples were encountered, the media hastily concocted only ineffectual responses.

When George Bush, for example, held a press conference at a flag factory to defend the Pledge of Allegiance, the press gave the event full play, expecting, I assume, that a faithful description would betray its essential demagoguery. My guess is that the publicity only reinforced the vice president's message.

At other times, the media exposed the "spin doctors."[27] Following the presidential debates, for example, there was a mad rush of television correspondents and newspaper reporters to interview a waiting group of pundits, not all of whom could be described as objective. A number of reporters described the freakishness of the scene and the blatant efforts at manipulation. But, instead of holding them up to ridicule, in my opinion, the press merely gave publicity to the spin doctors and their points of view.

Afterward, the media polls reinforced the message. Instead of testing the public's opinion, the public polls tested the assertions of their manipulators. And, once again—the media having set the agenda—the media polls detected what they themselves had publicized.

Throughout 1988, it seemed to me that the media—and the media polls— took their marching orders from the campaign, reacting almost exclusively to developments. There was little emphasis on electoral consequences: What might be expected from the next Congress following the indicated election results? What was the public reaction to the Bush agenda beyond prison furloughs and pledges of allegiance? Did the public approve of the Dukakis foreign policy objectives? What was the public attitude about the savings and loan crisis, about the environment (beyond Boston Harbor), about foreign trade, and, above all, about what should be done about the federal budget deficit? Public opinion polls must have asked thousands of different questions in 1988 but not many of them, it seemed, were like those above.

The media, we are told, are agenda-setters. But do the *media* have an agenda? Should they have one? It's a delicate subject. Journalists, and I believe rightly so, feel an obligation to report the news without becoming unduly involved in the news, to be passive and objective observers, not participants. But what is to be done when the media are excluded from the news except for carefully contrived "opportunities," when self-serving but exclusive information is leaked to them, when striking visual settings (with appropriate promotional messages) are arranged for the television cameras, when, in simple language, the media have been manipulated?

I suggest that there is a middle way that very much involves public polls. Cannot enterprising reporters and inquisitive media pollsters question the public concerning government policy, and, if some measures are found to be important and popular, cannot these issues be raised justifiably in the media? It seems to me that such an approach is fully consistent with the long-standing obligation of the press to better inform the American public.

I am not proposing any withholding of information—far from it—or that the media should set themselves up as judge and jury. Political managers have a right to set forth their particular points of view and the media have an obligation to report it. I only suggest that the public polls also have a duty to represent popular alternatives in the interests of fair discussion.

Another suggestion: Nobody seems satisfied with the way media polls cover early presidential primaries—and perhaps with good reason. Somehow, I think, the focus ought to be more balanced between "who's ahead?" and other important questions, for example, "Who are these people and what do they stand for?" or "What would be the consequences of their election?" Nearly half of all news stories during the primaries are about the Iowa caucuses and the New Hampshire primaries. This overbalance might be sanctioned if the media—and media polls—saw the coverage more often as an opportunity to educate voters.

By the same token, I think there ought to be an effort to *back-load* media coverage (if that is the antonym for the *front-loading* of news coverage early in the campaign). I have been involved in eight presidential campaigns, and, it seems to me that, in every one of them, political editors have scheduled in-depth biographical and long pieces on the issue stands of the candidates. The stories usually run in December or January, when few people are ready for them; but, in September or October (when the public is starting to get interested), the same ideas are killed because they have been done already. The media—and media polls, as well—spend, I think, far too much time covering political events before the public is curious and in effect ignoring the public when the same information is most needed.

How does all this add up? I think media should conduct fewer polls with larger samples and longer questionnaires. During political campaigns, the media polls seem to fall all over themselves to repeat the same studies everybody else is conducting. The result is reiterated job ratings, continuous measures of name recognition, and incessant vote preferences. Each succeeding poll adds hardly anything new to the one that went before. What if the media polls, each following its own bent, were to explore the more subtle complexities of the campaign? Taken together, such results could lead to a far richer body of information and a much greater public understanding of our presidential selection process—what some have called the most important scheduled news event in the "free world."

Media polls also have a responsibility, I think, to explain the crucial differences between voting in early, multicandidate primaries and in one-on-one general elections. Media polls should make an effort to explain the mechanics of momentum, name recognition, candidate viability, electoral voting strategies—and even the possible effects of media polling.

I also think that the media could have made a greater effort to explain the impact of the winner-take-all electoral college voting process. ABC News made a commendable effort but unfortunately spread its resources thinly throughout 50 states;[28] I would rather media pollsters concentrate on crucial swing states. Everybody should have known that Idaho, for example, would go Republican. But how about Michigan, or New York, or California? The media could have done a great deal more to explain the electoral college by concentrated polling in crucial swing states.

Media pollsters should have revealed their voter methodologies long before now. It is an unconscionable act, bordering on chicanery, for pollsters to hide their methods of determining that most mysterious of respondents, the "likely voter." Surely the secret weights assigned to screening variables and the assumptions made about turnout render a poll's estimated outcome very close to a magical performance. Does the public wish to know how media polls can be so different? If so, they must pay special attention to these "scientific" procedures.

Unfortunately, the media themselves sometimes understand these matters imperfectly. Perhaps there should be a greater effort to train journalists in how to find out what a poll tells us. More often than not, well-meaning seminars on polling for journalists end up explaining how to go about conducting polls (who cares?) with a few bewildering statistics thrown in to *épater les bourgeois*.

The public would also be better served, I think, by fewer preprimary polls and more analytical primary exit polls. Those of us who helped develop exit polls, and who have sustained a great deal of criticism for it, were amused by an apparent change in attitude after the Michigan caucuses in 1988 were swept by Jesse Jackson. Most commentators criticized the media for *not* having conducted an exit poll, leaving the public ignorant of whether Jackson's victory depended on White or Black votes.

Finally, one other suggestion for 1992: This past presidential campaign saw the emergence of the "usual suspects."[29] I suspect that their real function is to provide whatever conclusions are not easily expressed by a simple statement of the available facts and figures. They exist, I think, because of a media hang-up about polls: Most journalists consider a poll to be a conglomeration of facts instead of research on which analysis is possible. If the data imply the truth of the matter but do not say it outright in so many words and numbers, then the point must be made by quoting somebody who will say as much. How much easier to label a media poll *public opinion analysis*—which, of course, it is—and then write the story so that it says what the poll means in a forthright manner.

The Future of Media Political Polls

The casual viewer or reader will have noticed a marked increase in the usage of media polls over the past decade. This is especially true in the case

TABLE 3.1 *Los Angeles Times* Polling Activity

Year	Surveys	Interviews
1977	1	1,000
1978	12	18,577
1979	8	10,793
1980	17	37,767
1981	10	34,623
1982	15	42,163
1983	11	19,569
1984	16	46,872
1985	9	23,203
1986	19	50,630
1987	17	21,050
1988	34	88,190

of political polls. At the *Los Angeles Times*, the recent growth of polling activity has been explosive, as can be seen in Table 3.1. Many other media outlets demonstrate the same expanded attention to public opinion research. Where once media polling was the exclusive domain of Gallup and Harris, who syndicated columns of survey information, most self-respecting newspapers and television stations today have custom polls conducted by outside firms. Some of the larger organizations (TV networks, a few newspapers) have their own in-house operations.

Over the last decade, media polls have become an increasingly useful reporting tool and have added an extra dimension to journalism. They have replaced the old roundup survey of correspondents on topics of the day, they have added a more solid mathematical basis for the usual sweeping generalities, and, without doubt, they have revolutionized political reporting. Today, it is difficult to imagine a major media organization that could adequately serve its viewers or readers without using public opinion surveys. And there seems to be no letup in the trend.

But even as that trend continues, viewers and readers are becoming more sophisticated. They are less satisfied with the dreary procession of presidential job ratings and are, I believe, more receptive to inventive applications of the polling art.

The future of media polling, it seems, lies along the road of "theme" polls: studies that probe for greater extent and finer subtleties, stories developing from longer questionnaires that often generate two or three related stories in a series.

In the specific area of politics, two anticipated developments forecast important changes in election coverage. First, a nearly uniform poll-closing bill, one of which may be enacted by Congress before 1992, would have the effect of downplaying the importance of election night projections. With the vast majority of polls closing at the same sidereal time, all but a handful of votes from the 50 states and the District of Columbia would be immediately available to all concerned and would diminish the competitive advantage of that information.

Second, the enormous costs involved in projecting winners on election night[30] are forcing broadcasters and wire services to consider cooperative efforts to project election outcomes. Should such a consortium emerge,[31] producing only one election estimate for all subscribers, then competition over projections would immediately disappear (as would the need for haste, incidentally). The media might have to fall back on a more complete and well-organized explanation of what had happened; in other words, projection might give way to analysis. For this purpose, election day precinct interviews are ideal and I feel sure that we can expect to hear much more about exit polls in the future.

There is another important advantage of public opinion surveys that has hardly been tapped so far by media polls: social and economic indicator surveys. Quite aside from detailing the opinions of the American people, polls have the ability to explore the history of our time and to describe what we do and how it feels to be alive today. Public opinion studies concerned with questions describing our social structure can be repeated periodically to show how our concerns and occupations have changed and why. Excellent work along these lines has, of course, been conducted by the General Social Surveys of the National Opinion Research Center and by the University of Michigan. And, of course, Gallup, Roper, Harris, and others repeat questions of this nature periodically. But the press is perhaps the only institution capable of maintaining large yearly public opinion trend studies that would permit cross-tabulation between social, economic, and demographic indicators.

By the same token, the media have a responsibility to conduct more survey research on public policy. Media polls rarely fulfill their promise as a periodic referendum. Quite probably, media polls have an obligation to explore more frequently what the country wants as a national agenda.

Finally, and perhaps most important, media polls will expand their services in the future as they continue to develop a higher sense of profession-alism. Public opinion research needs fewer reporters and editors and pollsters seeking news beats. Within the ranks of the media polls, we need more students who want to know what the people truly do and think and who want to communicate that knowledge to inform others.

Notes

1. He is long-time NBC correspondent and currently director of the Joan Shorensten Barone Center of the Press, Politics and Public Policy at Harvard University.

2. This kind of poll offers several 900 area code telephone numbers, one usually for *yes*, the other for *no*, which the respondent may call to register an opinion. Most authorities consider these polls flawed because they represent a self-selected sample.

3. The exception is, perhaps, the New Hampshire primaries, when Gallup and others had the wrong Republican winner.

4. To *horse race*, in polling terms, may be defined as placing undue emphasis on the contest standings to the near exclusion of other aspects of the campaign such as candidate image, issue positions, campaign strategy, and political developments.

5. Among 10,018 likely voters polled in 50 states, with the poll published in the *Washington Post* on October 13th, 1989: The research was conducted over a three-week period (during which time opinions might have been changing) and produced estimates of electoral college winners for almost every state based on samples that, in some cases, were very small.

6. "As of today, do you approve or disapprove of the job that so-in-so is doing as president (or governor, senator, or the like)?"

7. The name was lifted from an intercontinental defense system then under construction across Canada.

8. This was originally called the Network Election Service until the two wire services were included, thus necessitating the change in name.

9. "So-called" because they provided important data for election projections. Early Key Precincts were selected because they were "barometric," that is, their final vote percentages were similar to the percentage of the vote in their state. Later, Key Precincts were "swingometric," their percentage change from an earlier base race was similar to the change experienced by the whole state. In the end, Key Precincts were selected at random and often doubled as exit poll precincts.

10. It never produced any meaningful output on election night. Fortunately, Lyndon Johnson had a landslide victory that year and Richard Scammon had no difficulty making speedy projections.

11. "So-called" because they could be tagged as having a high degree of homogeneity as far as certain important characteristics were concerned.

12. Eleven precincts were later eliminated because they had changed from the base race in voter composition, in boundary lines, or in major new construction.

13. I am indebted to Bert Ivry, former field supervisor for NBC News Elections, who has authenticated the date and details of this first exit poll and has provided me with copies of his 25-year-old notes.

14. He was, at the time, a Harvard undergraduate wunderkind, who, as George McGovern's pollster, preached the doctrine of voter anomie.

15. In point of fact, McGovern was much more likely to have won the vote of suburban Jewish housewives and their college-educated children.

16. Lewis's Law says that if you don't know much about a candidate, you like him.

17. He is former president of the Gallup organization and is responsible for seminal experiments in vote measurement and turnout.

18. He is former director of the CBS News Elections and Polling Unit.

19. He is chairman of Field Research Corporation and founder of the California Poll.

20. CBS News has done the same for the last five presidential campaigns. Other organizations, for example, the *Washington Post*, have sampled delegates rather than conducting a full census.

21. ABC News, to gain a time advantage, even begins polling the nation before the debate is finished.

22. The states were California, Florida, Georgia, Illinois, Iowa, Kentucky, Mississippi, New Hampshire, New York, North Carolina, Pennsylvania, and Texas.

23. Unfortunately, I have not been able to convince my editors to accept this point of view.

24. Professor Meyers, a longtime Knight-Ridder newsman, now teaches at the University of North Carolina at Chapel Hill.

25. These are sometimes called "hot" or "quickie" polls.

26. See the section of presidential debates above.

27. "Spin doctors" are political professionals who are called upon to put a desired interpretation, or "spin," on campaign developments—especially any that might seem ambiguous. Bob Drogin, a reporter for the *Los Angeles Times*, recalls being told that, if they missed each other after the debate, Drogin could say that the spin doctor was very impressed with his candidate's performance.

28. See "*A Report Card on Public Polls*" above.

29. This small group of media experts can usually be depended upon for an instant opinion by deadline. The name derives from the scene in the movie *Casablanca* after Ingrid Bergman and Paul Henreid have escaped and Claude Rains turn to his lieutenant and says, "Round up the usual suspects."

30. One estimate claims that the three U.S. television networks together spent in excess of $50 million to determine election winners in 1988.

31. *Editor's Note*: Such a consortium, Voter Research & Surveys, was formed by ABC, NBC, CBS, and CNN in 1990.

Reference

Gould, J. (1964, June 4). N.B.C. wisely waits out primary; resists pressure to pick coast winner. *The New York Times*.

4

A Short History of Exit Polls

WARREN J. MITOFSKY

Shortly after 9 p.m. in the East, the CBS News anchorman told the nation whom it had elected as its next president. The public uproar over those early projections led to congressional hearings to see what could be done about it. The president of CBS urged Congress to adapt the nation's voting hours to the new vote counting technology. He said, if all voting ended at the same time nationwide, all projections would be made after the last vote was cast. The year was 1964. Lyndon Johnson was elected in a landslide. There were no exit polls.

Civic-minded Americans have been bothered ever since. They believe that Westerners who haven't yet voted hear projections from eastern states, which causes them to change their vote or not vote at all. Democrats have charged that the early projection of Ronald Reagan's 1980 victory caused two representatives and a senator to lose their seats.

Yet, broadcasters have resisted the call to delay these projections. They say they are announcing results only in states that have closed their polls, not in states in which they are open. They only add together the electoral votes from the states that are closed. They say it is good journalism to report the

AUTHOR'S NOTE: The development of exit polls was started by the author when CBS News asked him to head the statistical research effort for its first in-house election unit in 1967. At that time, Richard Maisel was the director. Almost from the beginning, Murray Edelman participated in the development of the techniques with both skill and imagination. The field procedures were designed by both CBS News and Michael Fine. Fine's meticulous planning produced the logistical know-how to make the field effort possible.

news in those states where the polls are closed and public officials are making the returns publicly available. Rather than broadcasters withholding news about states that have finished voting, they say the problem can be solved by closing all the polls across the country at the same time.

Since 1980, it is exit polling that has been attacked. Network critics now say that election conclusions based on actual vote returns are acceptable, but it is exit polling that must be controlled. Exit polls have become the primary focus of editorials, legislation, and public indignation. Even though the controversy started long before there were exit polls, critics say that exit polls could defeat the purpose of uniform poll closing if the networks use them to broadcast results before the polls close. However, the network news presidents gave their assurance to Congress that they would not broadcast exit polls until a state closes its polls. The networks never have announced the winner in any state before its polls closed. (In states with multiple poll closing times, such as Indiana, they wait until the vast majority of polls are closed.) The network assurances suggest they also won't do any analysis from the exit polls that might imply who the winner would be.

At the heart of this controversy is the belief that projections affect voter turnout. The stories about voters leaving the voting lines after the network projections are apocryphal. It never happens. The stories about lower turnout or switching from the losing candidate to the winner after the network projections are not supported by the myriad academic studies. Nonetheless, Westerners believe projections of eastern states diminish the importance of their votes. Some argue that that alone is sufficient reason for Congress to act.

This chapter will provide background about the uses of exit polls and why they are important to broadcasters for their election coverage. It also will trace the course of the controversy, the legislation, and the lawsuits that accompanied the networks' use of exit polls. To conclude the topic, there is a technical description of some of the methods used for conducting exit polls.

Exit polls, as they have come to be known,[1] are sample surveys conducted on election days at polling places while voting is in progress. They have become an invaluable tool for election analysis. No longer do scholars and journalists have to wonder about the shape of an election mandate. Exit polls make it possible to correlate votes for a presidential candidate with votes for other candidates in his or her party or a voter's position on abortion with his or her vote for a candidate. Exit polls also have become increasingly expensive and highly competitive tools for both broadcast and print journalists.

The First Uses of Exit Polls

The dominance of television networks over newspapers in election night news coverage began in 1956, the second Eisenhower-Stevenson election. [2] The networks' election coverage continued until the presidential outcome seemed certain. What was new was the use of computers to project the outcome. That early model, put together by Max Woodbury of the University of Pennsylvania, used incomplete county data in what now seems to be a crude attempt to project the national popular vote. It was not until 1962 that CBS News and Louis Harris used quota samples, or a "recipe" (as he called it), of precincts within states to project the winning candidates in 13 contests for senator and governor.

The networks were not satisfied to tell who won without explaining something about why and how it happened. To do this, they needed data. At the time, there were two apparent sources known to the networks' researchers for this information: It could come either from preelection polls or from the analysis of precinct returns.

Preelection polls have been a source of information about the the electorate since George Gallup, Elmo Roper, and Archibald Crossley started conducting their polls in the 1930s. But there were problems for the broadcasters in using these data. First, and most important, the results of the preelection polls might vary too much from the outcome on election night for a live broadcast to depend on this as *the* source of analytical information. Between the preelection poll and election day, campaigns progressed, trying to change voters' minds. Some voters could switch their candidate preferences, and others might switch their intention to go to the polls and decide to stay home.

Preelection polls presented another problem to networks for use on election night. They required much larger sample sizes for adequate analysis than are usually used in most preelection polls. A typical preelection sample of 1,500 adults may yield about 1,000 registered voters, not all of whom go to the polls on election day. The breakdown of voters into meaningful subgroups results in sample sizes that are too small to be very reliable.

For example, newly registered first-time voters have been of interest in the 1980s due to appeals to them by both Ronald Reagan and Jesse Jackson, each with a different agenda for attracting them to his respective party. Most preelection polls of 1,500 people would produce fewer than 100 of these new voters. Anyone wanting to study Catholic women under 30, middle-class Blacks, Jews, or similar groups would find fewer than 50 voters in a national sample of 1,500. All these subgroups are much too small to provide reliable and thus meaningful data for analysis. These problems are common enough that preelection polls are too risky to be counted upon for a live television broadcast on election night.

Rather than basing their analyses on the preelection polls, the networks, instead used a by-product of the information from certain precincts for their election projections. They did this by classifying precincts into analytical categories. There were urban precincts and rural precincts, Black precincts and White precincts, rich precincts and poor precincts, and many other types. Louis Harris had a type he called "polyglot" precincts, ones that had a mixture of races and/or ethnicity. In the 1960s, when this type of analysis took place, the dependent variable was the vote in each analytical group of precincts.

The weakness of these data soon became apparent. Most Blacks did not live in Black precincts, neither did most rich people live only in high-income precincts, neither did Jews live only in Jewish precincts, and so on. Precincts, as a source of data, were fine for geographic categorization, such as "urban" or "rural," but were misleading for representing personal characteristics.

As an example of an erroneous conclusion from precinct data, consider the following: CBS News collected both exit poll data and vote returns in predominantly "Black" precincts nationwide in 1972. However, only about a third of Blacks live in clustered inner-city areas, according to a Census Bureau study of neighborhood living patterns, and the Blacks living in the "Black" precincts that make up these areas do not vote the same way as other Blacks. The vote for Nixon from predominantly Black sample precincts was 13%, which was significantly less than the 17% recorded in the exit poll from all Blacks regardless of where they lived. The precinct analysis also failed to show the diversity of Black votes for Nixon, from 6% in the inner cities to 34% in the more affluent suburbs (see Table 4.1).

In 1967, a new research team, which I directed, was started at CBS News and was determined to solve these analytical problems. CBS News also wanted a means for making estimates of the election outcome prior to the time when real votes were available. Again, preelection polls were a possibility. If there was a prior estimate, the reasoning went, then it could be used as a composite including actual returns and it would provide a second source to help guard against mistakes.

The first opportunity for the new group to try different election analysis approaches was the Kentucky gubernatorial election in November 1967. Several techniques were tested in that election, including the exit poll, which was used only to make an estimate of the outcome. However, at that time, it was not used as the only source of information for a projection. Actual vote

TABLE 4.1 1972 Exit Poll Results

	Blacks Voting for	
Where Blacks Live	Nixon (percentage)	McGovern (percentage)
Mostly Black city neighborhoods	6	93
Integrated city neighborhoods	18	81
Suburbs	34	66
Rural/small towns	31	67
Overall Black vote	17	82

returns from sample precincts were available shortly after the polls closed, as were county returns somewhat later. The first on-air projection that was permitted was from a combined estimate based on both the actual precinct returns and the exit poll. The two together were used for projections. The closer the contest, the more data were required for a reliable projection.

The actual vote in the sample precincts (and not the exit poll responses) was used to describe the electorate. The precincts had been classified by geographic section of the state, the type of locale (urban, suburban, rural) from which they came, and whether they had voters who were predominately from an ethnic or racial group, who had voted mostly for Republicans or Democrats, or who were middle-of-the-road voters. In addition, there was an attempt to classify precincts based on a dominant characteristic of the voters who lived there, such as high-income precincts, blue-collar precincts, and so on.

However, on the same day as the Kentucky gubernatorial election, it also was decided to experiment with election day telephone polls of voters in three cities having mayoral elections. These polls proved to be unworkable. It was not possible to interview a probability sample of voters on the day of the election. The sample that was interviewed was badly skewed in terms of both the characteristics of the people in the sample and the measure of the election outcome.

That 1967 Kentucky exit poll, on the other hand, was quite accurate. The technique was used repeatedly throughout the 1968 primaries and for the general election. On election night that year, exit polls were conducted in 20 states. The results were used as prior estimates for the presidential, senatorial, and gubernatorial contests in those states. New estimates were formed by combining the exit poll estimates with those based on actual returns in the sample precincts. The combining of the two estimates was done by averaging them in a way that gave a proportionally greater weight to the estimate with smaller sampling error.

Data on voters' sex and race also were collected in the 1968 polls. However, the logistical problems of conducting interviews in remote precincts around the country and getting detailed data into a central computer had not yet been solved. A cross-tabulation of the data would involve putting the individual responses of each respondent to each question into the computer. Instead, in 1968, the cross-tabulation of sex and race with vote was done manually at the polling place by the interviewer.

The first significant analytical use of exit polls occurred in the 1969 New York City mayoral race. The science reporter for WCBS-TV, Earl Ubell, developed a lengthy questionnaire about issues in the campaign to go along with the vote question. This breakthrough made it possible to present a detailed analysis on election night based on the exit poll.

Between 1970 and 1980, CBS News used exit polls in its broadcasts *only for analysis*. It was not until 1982 that CBS News used exit polls for projections.

During the preparation of this chapter, I have learned about what appears to be an even earlier experiment with exit polls. During the 1964 Maryland presidential primary, an associate of the Louis Harris company, Ruth Clark, was sent to Baltimore on election day by Harris to talk to voters in their homes. Clark said she got tired of climbing to the fifth floor of apartment buildings to find voters, so she went to the neighborhood public school where the voting was taking place. With the officials' permission, she interviewed voters as they left the polling place.

When Clark told Harris what she had done, he liked the idea and adapted it for use in the 1964 California Republican primary. For an extensive statewide sample, he had interviewers ask voters for whom they had cast their ballots. This was the source of the early projection that showed Barry Goldwater beating Nelson Rockefeller.

ABC News did its first exit polls of any type in 1980. By 1982, ABC News too was making exit poll *projections*.

Several NBC News staffers said NBC did its first real exit poll in 1973 for a mayoral election, using it only for analysis and not for projections. No one was able to remember which year NBC made its first exit poll *projection*, only that it was sometime in the mid-1970s.

NBC had people at precincts for the 1964 Goldwater-Rockefeller California presidential primary. It sent students to 10 precincts to ask voters how they voted, much the way news organizations have sent reporters to polling places for many years to make election inquiries. There was nothing systematic about the approach. The 10 precincts were among the 19 originally selected by analyst Richard Scammon, but they were not a random sample of the state. The students were sponsored by local television stations and not NBC. The data did not find their way into a computer, and there was no projection based on them. They were looked at by election analysts for "guidance," said Burton Ivry, then manager of Election Operations. I. A. Lewis, an NBC election analyst at the time and later its election director, said the results made them "not call" a winner in that primary until sometime later than they might have without it. None of the half dozen people queried who had worked on elections at NBC between the mid-1960s and 1973 said he or she did anything remotely resembling an exit poll following that initial experience until 1973, the year Roy Wetzel, subsequently director of the unit, insists NBC did its first exit poll.

The Controversy

It was the 1980 NBC News projection of Ronald Reagan's victory over Jimmy Carter at 8:15 p.m., eastern standard time, that sparked the "exit poll controversy." NBC News had projected Reagan's victory by accumulating 270 electoral votes for him in 22 states, all of which had closed their polls. Ten of those state projections were made precisely at poll closing time in the states and were based on exit polls. Projections in the other states, where there were no exit polls, were made sufficiently after poll closing time and probably were based on actual vote returns.

CBS News and ABC News made their projections that night only from actual vote returns. There were no exit polls used for projections by either network. Even so, both networks counted an electoral vote majority for Reagan before the West Coast polls closed at 11 p.m., eastern time. In the controversy that followed, all three networks drew public wrath, and exit polls were identified as the culprit. Perhaps the controversy should have focused on all projections, but it did not. Over and over during the next few years, exit polls were the target of criticism. The election in 1980 was the first for which exit polls were identified as a source of projections.

As mentioned earlier, when Lyndon Johnson defeated Barry Goldwater in 1964, there was a similar public outcry with the same charges directed at the networks. However, there were no exit polls in 1964. The criticism was just about projections, which were based on *actual vote returns* in sample precincts. That was the first presidential election for which there was a state-by-state projection of electoral votes. Shortly after 9 p.m., eastern time,

CBS News had reached the magic number of electoral votes Johnson needed to win. In the months that followed, Senator John Pastore (Democrat, Rhode Island) held congressional hearings to let the networks know of public displeasure over the use of this new technology. No legislation to curb the networks came out of the hearings.

It was at those same 1964-1965 hearings, however, that Frank Stanton, then president of the Columbia Broadcasting System, proposed that Congress deal with the problem not by interfering with the networks' First Amendment right to broadcast news but by closing the polls at a uniform time across the nation. It was not until 1985 that this legislation got a serious hearing and was approved by the House of Representatives. The House passed the same legislation in the next two sessions of Congress, but it never came up for a vote in the Senate. However, the Senate seems likely to act in time for the 1992 presidential election. In May 1989, the Senate Rules Committee approved a uniform poll-closing bill, slightly different than the House version.

The day after the 1980 election, newspapers were filled with apocryphal stories about large numbers of voters leaving waiting lines outside polling places all across the West without having voted. The defeat of longtime representatives Al Ullman (Democrat, Oregon) and James Corman (Democrat, California) and Senator Frank Church (Democratic, Idaho) were blamed on the early projections. Citizens in western states claimed their votes didn't count. They had been disenfranchised, they said, because of the projection of Reagan's victory before the polls had closed in the western states. Exit polls became the focus of the attack.

California Secretary of State March Fong Eu commissioned a poll, which she claimed showed that more than 400,000 Californians did not vote because of the early projections. The House and Senate held a series of hearings starting in 1981. Through 1984, there was no legislation, but Congress passed resolutions before the 1982 and 1984 elections asking the networks to refrain from making projections until all polls in the continental United States had closed.

Public sentiment, at least in the western states, opposed projections and exit polls. Protectors of the voting franchise, such as the League of Women Voters, the Committee for the Study of the American Electorate, the quadrennial academic conclaves, and other do-gooders actively lobbied against the networks even though there was no reliable evidence showing any depressed effect on voter turnout or switching of candidate choice.

CBS News made an extensive search for two weeks immediately following the 1980 election for eyewitnesses to voters leaving the polls. None was found. The defeat of Ullman, Corman, and Church all could be easily explained by political circumstances. Furthermore, the margins of their losses were large enough that it would have required voter defections from the polling places even greater than those reported in the California secretary of state's study. As for that study, the pollster who conducted it, Mervin Field of the California Poll, publicly denied every conclusion of Ms. Eu's in an open letter he sent to the Los Angeles registrar of voters. It happens that the registrar was conducting his own study on Election Day, just as his office did for other general election years. It counted the number of voters going to the polls each hour of the day in a sample of Los Angeles voting precincts. The study showed no falloff in voter turnout (as a percentage of registered voters) in the later hours of Election Day in 1980. In fact, a slightly higher proportion of registered voters went to the Los Angeles polls after the NBC News projection in 1980 than voted during those same hours in 1976 when there was no early projection.

There also was a much-quoted study by John Jackson, based on re-interviews with participants in the National Election Study (the voting study conducted every two years by the Institute for Social Research at the University of Michigan, funded by the National Science Foundation). The House committee's report cited Jackson's study in its opening paragraphs, concluding from that report that voters were dissuaded from voting because of the early projections. On closer examination, however, the conclusion in Jackson's study found *only nine people* who said they did not vote because of the network projections. The voter validation study also presented information on actual voting records showing that one of the nine voters had actually voted and four more were not registered, which is hardly substantial enough evidence to justify the conclusions attributed to the study.

Wyoming, and later Washington State, passed legislation that made it illegal to conduct exit polls within 300 feet of a polling place, a distance that, for all practical purposes, made it impossible to conduct a valid exit poll. Similar anti-exit poll laws were passed in Florida, Georgia, Hawaii, Kentucky, Minnesota, Montana, Ohio, South Carolina, and South Dakota. A number of other states tried to impose the strictures of electioneering statutes on exit polls, most notably, California, Illinois, and Texas.

The networks resisted the pressure from Congress and from states' anti-exit poll legislation. They went about announcing election results as they always had. When a state closed its polls (or had closed the great majority of them, in states with multiple closing times), the networks reported what they knew about who had won. In the presidential contest, they added the electoral votes for the winning candidate from the states that were closed. When the electoral vote added to a majority vote, they announced the election of a president.

Many members of Congress, including Al Swift (Democrat, Washington State), cochair of the House Election Task Force, thought the networks' policy of calling races after polls closed was acceptable. What he and others did not like was the practice of hinting about election outcomes even if there was no outright declaration of the winner. Such characterizing crept into the analysis of the exit polls and was broadcast on all of the networks' early evening news broadcasts from 1976 through 1984, usually before the polls closed.

This practice usually occurred during the coverage of presidential primaries. It might also have happened during general election broadcasts, but it was not likely because there was too much other election news to report on states whose polls had closed.

The other implication of hints about the outcomes that were broadcast before poll closing that bothered Swift was that their continued use would defeat what he and the ranking Republican on the committee, Bill Thomas (Republican, California), saw as the one chance to end the projection controversy. Their proposal for uniform poll closing across the continental United States would fail if the networks continued to hint about election outcome before the polls closed or, worse, used exit polls to announce the winner before poll closing.

Following the 1984 election, Swift and Thomas urged the network news division presidents to give their assurances that they would stick to their policy of waiting until a state closed its polls before announcing the winner. They also wanted the networks to abandon characterization or any other analysis that hinted at the winner before a state's polls closed.

The networks' news chiefs agreed, even though there were strenuous objections from news producers and correspondents. The hard news view was, and still is, that news organizations should make no pacts with Congress or any other legislative body. Any agreement is a start down the slippery slope to surrendering the independence of news gathering to government control. But the agreement was made despite the objections. Swift and Thomas said of the networks' new commitments that the responsibility for ending the controversy now rested with Congress; the networks had done their part. They then saw to it that the House passed a uniform poll-closing law. After 20 years of controversy, an updated version of Frank Stanton's 1965 proposal cleared its first legislative hurdle.

Meanwhile, the networks decided to challenge the states' anti-exit poll laws. The first lawsuit was filed against the State of Washington and its zealous attacker of exit polls, Secretary of State Ralph Munro. Joining the networks in their challenge to the constitutionality of the law were *The New York Times* and *The Herald* of Everett, Washington. Leading the attack was the prominent First Amendment attorney, Floyd Abrams.

Washington State Federal Judge Jack Tanner said, during the trial, that the state would have to show that exit polls were disruptive to peace, order, and decorum at the polling place for him to uphold the state's law. He would not listen to arguments about the effects of projections on voter turnout or any other argument common to the controversy. His decision was for the plaintiffs, ruling the state law unconstitutional. The decision was upheld by the Ninth Circuit Court of Appeals and was not appealed to the Supreme Court.

Following the circuit court decision in early 1988, the media promptly went to the courts and successfully challenged the exit poll laws in Florida, Georgia, Kentucky, Minnesota, Montana, South Carolina, and Wyoming. None of these states appealed the decisions against them. This was probably due as much to the Ninth Circuit's decision as it was to the fact that the states, if they lost, would have to pay the challengers' court costs. With the weight of prior decisions against them, California, Hawaii, Illinois, Ohio, and Texas agreed not to interfere with the orderly conduct of exit polls.

The controversy was only slightly muted for the 1988 presidential elections as a result of the congressional action. The editorial writers, politicians, and other self-appointed protectors of the voting franchise were relatively silent. However, there was still a sense of public unrest, which may be stilled if uniform poll closing legislation is enacted.

How Exit Polls Are Conducted

An understanding of the technical details of an exit poll will demystify the process for the reader. It also will make it clear that this is an effort based on sound scientific methods and not a "gimmick" for collecting data such as 900-number telephone call-in polls.

In most respects, a high-quality exit poll is very much like any other scientific sample survey. It starts with a probability sample of voting precincts. Professional interviewers query a random selection of voters within these precincts. The instrument is a self-administered questionnaire. Respondent anonymity is maintained.

Exit polls have their own unique problems. The first and most serious for their use in an election night broadcast are logistical. Data are collected at precincts across a state, or across the nation, that are remote from the central computer in which they are processed. Each answer to each question must be transmitted by telephone to a processing center for the creation of a computer-compatible data file. A typical questionnaire has about 25 questions. In a national sample of 400 precincts, responses from 25 voters each would require the transmission from the precinct to the computer site of 250,000 pieces of information on election day. This has been done by identifying each question with a letter and each response with a number and reading the data over the telephone one question at a time. When the volume of data for state exit polls is added to this, the logistical problems can be staggering. Electronic means of transmitting the data are being investigated, but a practical and reliable method will not be available for some time.

Another problem special to election broadcasts concerns the almost simultaneous capture of data, then the analysis, and finally the presentation of the conclusions. In most survey research, a reasonable time elapses between the various stages of the process. There is time to discover and resolve problems in an orderly manner. That time frame is different on election night. The solution to avoiding chaos is the imposition of increased rigor. Quality control of the data is managed by an automatic mathematical solution rather than human judgment about the data. The weighting formula has contingent assumptions that depend on derived measures of association between elections and the resulting sampling errors associated with the estimates. Analysis of exit poll data is based on predetermined hypotheses about relationships among voting and other variables. It is only after the preplanned analyses are complete that there is time for further manipulation of the data.

With these considerations as background, various methodological steps can be investigated. The procedures described here are for a state sample, as all elections covered by the networks are state elections, including the presidential contest. National exit poll samples used by CBS News for an analytical overview are subsamples of the 51 state samples. Obviously, a national sample could be selected directly if individual state samples were not available. The procedures described here would need some slight modification for selecting a national sample, but they would still be applicable.

Sample selection. The selection of sample precincts to represent a state can be done more efficiently in a single stage from a complete list of precincts in the state. The alternative is to select a sample in two stages, by first selecting counties and then precincts within the sample counties. Although it is less work to obtain precinct lists and conduct research in selected counties, it is not worth the loss in efficiency. In this case, *efficiency* means that, for a fixed cost, the sample with the lower sampling error is preferred.

(A two-stage design would probably be more efficient for a national sample, but here we are discussing state samples.)

To select the state sample, it is best to compile a list of precincts as they existed for a recent past election for a statewide office. This complete list is called the "sampling frame." The more recent the past race, the fewer the changes local officials will have had time to make in precincts' boundaries, which will cause fewer problems in using the sample.

The sample is created so that each precinct has as many chances to be selected as it has voters. A precinct with 400 voters would have twice the probability of being included in the sample as a precinct with 200 voters. It represents Republicans and Democrats in proportion to their presence in the state, and it represents the different geographic parts of the state.

Changes in precincts' boundaries make it necessary to do research in each county's election office, where all precinct maps are available. This research can only be done by comparing maps including the current year's precinct boundaries with old maps that show the boundaries as they existed at the time the sample was selected. If a precinct's boundaries have changed, it is necessary to resolve the discrepancy between the old and new boundaries. It also is useful to get the past vote in the sample precincts for contests other than the one used for sample selection. These data are very useful for making reliable estimates.

Exit poll questionnaire. After experimenting with several different forms of questionnaires, we discovered that the one that works most reasonably well is a self-administered ballot that is approximately 5 1/2 by 8 1/2 inches. Questions should be printed in easily readable type, and questions can appear on both the front and the back of a single page. There should be no contingent questions, that is, ones that depend on the answer to a previous question; neither should there be any open-ended questions.

Experience has shown that, the longer the questionnaire, the poorer the response rate. An experiment on questionnaire length turned up some interesting data. The longest questionnaire was printed on an 8 1/2 by 11-inch page. The middle-sized version was half that, and the smallest was half again as large. The two larger versions asked about the respondent's vote, position on issues, some other opinions, and demographics. The middle-sized version had fewer questions. The smallest questionnaire asked only about the respondent's vote.

Response rates were in the mid-60% range for the longest questionnaire, about 80% for the intermediate version, and about 90% for the shortest questionnaire. However, the one with the best response rate also had the most serious bias on the vote question. The very short questionnaire, which only inquired about a person's vote, seemed to lose legitimacy with a select class of voters. The short version consistently overstated the Democratic vote, not just on this one occasion but in a series of trials. The most reliable questionnaire was the one of intermediate size. It can have up to 25 questions if both the back and the front of the page are used.

Interviewing. Interviewers should be experienced, that is, people who regularly conduct surveys. Their training starts by having them read through an instruction manual. They are then questioned on the material by a supervisor calling from election headquarters. If this is not adequate, a local supervisor will spend time on additional instruction.

Interviewers are stationed at the exits of the sample's precincts on election day. There is usually only one interviewer working at a time, except in some neighborhoods, where it seems more prudent to have two. They identify themselves to polling place officials and wear either a badge or a sash that shows the name of the news organization.

An interviewer approaches every k*th* voter as he or she leaves the polling place and asks him or her to complete a questionnaire. If the designated voter refuses, the interviewer marks the sex, race, and approximate age on a ballot. These data are used for a noninterview adjustment. The interval "k" should yield approximately 100 voters in the course of a 12-hour voting day. This is a rate that will keep the interviewer working at a reasonable pace and will provide a good estimate of the vote within the precinct.

Evaluation data[3]. It is reasonable to expect the overall sampling error of an exit poll to be larger than an estimate based on the actual vote returns in the same sample precincts. This is due to the additional component of sampling error from the sampling of voters. There is also a bias caused by the people who refuse to be interviewed.

Figure 4.1 contains a comparison of state estimates derived from exit polling and from actual vote returns in the same precincts. The figure contains a scatter plot of the two estimates. If there were no bias, the expected least-squares fit would be a 45-degree line through the origin. The actual fit, however, shows a Democratic bias in the exit polls of about two percentage points.

If one looks below the level of the state estimates to the individual precinct data, the same small, but persistent, bias in favor of the Democrats shows up. A comparison of the actual precinct vote with the exit poll results is shown in Figure 4.2, which resembles Figure 4.1. That is, the deviation of the expected line and the least-squares line indicate a similar bias.

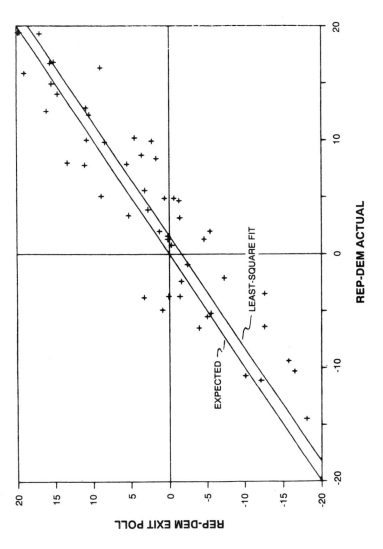

Figure 4.1. Estimates of Final Result: Exit Poll Results Versus Actual Vote

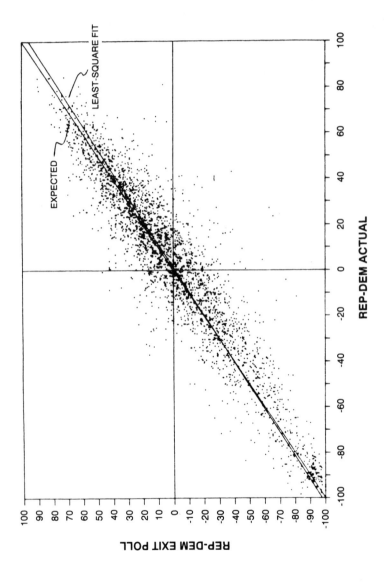

Figure 4.2. Precincts/Races: Exit Polls Results Versus Actual Vote

Notes

1. These polls were initially called "election day polls" at CBS News. NBC News called them "street polls," then "election day polls," and then "exit polls."

2. Editor's Note: There is a somewhat different version of the historical record presented in this chapter than in the previous chapter.

3. This section is adapted from a paper by Warren J. Mitofsky and Joseph Waksberg, "CBS Models for Election Night Estimation," delivered at the American Statistical Association Winter Conference, 1989, in San Diego.

5

Public Polls and
Election Participants

HARRISON HICKMAN

People concerned about the public release of poll results during election campaigns emphasize their potential impact on voters. Whether the fear is that knowledge of current election standings will dampen voter turnout or stimulate changes in candidate support, the focus is almost exclusively on how *average voters* might respond. This chapter proposes a broader view by including *political activists* as election participants likely to be influenced by this information, participants, in fact, more likely than average voters to be affected by the type of information conveyed in poll results. Most commentaries on the potential impact of public polls center on presidential elections; however, I argue that polls are more likely to influence voters and political activists in elections for lower offices. A final section reviews how campaigns respond to the release of poll results.

Given the controversy about the release and coverage of poll results during campaigns, it may be surprising that political science does not provide systematic answers to the issues central to the controversy: whether, to what extent, and how poll results affect voter turnout and preference decisions. This deficiency can be traced, in part, to the statistical models commonly used to explain elections. Most of these models address static and structural features of an election and ignore dynamic ones like candidate performance

AUTHOR'S NOTE: I acknowledge insightful critiques of an earlier draft by Doug Rose and Michael Traugott and the many helpful suggestions of Kirk Brown.

and campaign events. Some researchers have tried to remedy these deficiencies by supplementing the basic models with equations designed to capture dynamic elements of campaigns or with variables that summarize voter feelings toward the candidates, but the logic underlying the models remains untouched. As a general proposition, traditional models do not allow for the possibility that poll results can directly influence election outcomes, and, as a result, traditional sources provide few answers to the central questions.

The dominance of a needlessly narrow notion of the type of information conveyed by poll results also helps explain the absence of systematic answers. Most commentaries assume that poll results provide voters with a simple nominal ascription of current standings, conveying little more than who's ahead and who's behind, serving nothing more than a "scoreboard" function. In the conventional distinction between information concerning "game aspects" of a campaign and information concerning substantive aspects of a campaign, the presumption is that poll results belong exclusively in the former. Accepting this view means polls can affect election results only if we can prove "underdog" or "bandwagon" effects as well as an independent causal relationship between them and knowledge of poll results, a difficult chore at best. An alternative view is that information about poll standings communicates a broader range of information about the candidates' relative political skills, summary evaluations of candidates from voters who have had an opportunity to evaluate the candidates, and, perhaps, even cues about the types of social groups attracted to the candidates.

The usual presentation of poll results by print and electronic media is consistent with this broader alternative conceptualization. In presenting poll results, as in covering election outcomes, the media usually seek to explain rather than merely describe. Coverage of candidates and their campaigns differs qualitatively depending on their relative standing. Stories about candidates doing well in polls usually focus on what they are doing *correctly*—the policy positions, campaign strategies, and personal qualities that put them at the top of the preference rankings. Coverage of candidates doing badly in polls usually focuses on what they are doing *wrong*—various factors that put them behind front-runners.

My personal experience confirms this tendency. In hundreds of conversations with reporters, I have found that few if any reporters minimize the explanatory power of poll results. To the contrary, it is a rare reporter, indeed, who does not treat his or her poll story as a journalistic Holy Grail that explains the sum and substance of a campaign and its candidates. For example, the George Bush trailing by 15 points in May 1988 was the same

George Bush leading by 15 points four months later. Yet, at the time, reporters seemed to infer from the poll standings that the former was a spineless wimp running a totally inept campaign while the latter was a visionary leader at the helm of an electoral Rolls Royce. Neither, of course, was totally true.

The assumption that this wider scope of information is conveyed by poll results does not solve, per se, problems attendant to existing models of voter behavior. But it does provide an opportunity to consider *indirect* effects of polls, including those associated with the differing media coverage associated with candidate successes.

Critical Factors

Political science may not provide systematic answers to the central questions about the impact of *poll results* released during campaigns, but studies of the impact of *candidate performance in caucuses and primaries* during presidential nominating campaigns offer important insights. We expect that voters might respond to candidate performance in polls in much the way that they respond to actual events, such as primaries and caucuses—despite some important differences. No particular poll receives as much coverage as the outcomes of primaries and caucuses. Most people are decidedly more suspicious of poll results than of event outcomes, and competing information from other polls almost always mitigates the impact of any particular poll. But poll results and event outcomes both convey empirical information from a relatively impartial source about candidate performance, so responses to actual events are a useful starting point for understanding how election participants respond to poll results.

A study of media coverage in the 1976 presidential election finds that voters easily learn about candidates' chances of success and are "highly sensitive" to changes in them (Patterson, 1980; the quotes that follow are from pp. 119-132). This information is frequently and prominently communicated during a campaign and is strikingly simple compared with other information about candidates. The manner in which voters process information about a candidate's viability, which includes his or her performance and chances of winning the contest, varies according to their levels of commitment to a candidate. Voters more committed to a candidate are more selective in processing viability information, especially information unfavorable for their candidate. Voters less committed to a candidate are more likely to align their overall impressions of candidates with perceptions of the candidates' viability. But, as a general rule, "opinions about a candidate tended to align with their perceptions of his [sic] chances," and "most . . . reached a conclusion about a candidate's prospects before developing a firm opinion of him [sic]."

"Bandwagon" effects alone cannot explain election results. Take, for instance, Jimmy Carter's emergence in the 1976 primary season: "Carter's approval by other voters, his apparent command of the nominating race, and his lack of liabilities made him the natural choice of an electorate attuned to the race and devoid of strong preferences." Even this type of indirect bandwagon effect does not play a major role in general elections because of the tugs of party and policy issues, and leadership factors, and because "poll results seem to have less impact on [voters'] thinking than primary outcomes and delegate counts."

A recent analysis of "momentum" in presidential nominating campaigns addresses similar issues (Bartels, 1988; this discussion can be supplemented with Brady & Johnston, 1987). The evidence shows that perceptions of the candidates' likelihood of winning a nomination contest directly, indirectly, and interactively affect candidate's chances of gaining popularity and winning votes. Impressions of candidate success help voters overcome uncertainty about the candidates' true policy positions, suggesting that one function of information on election performance is to resolve uncertainty emanating from other factors.

On the other hand, not all polls affect all campaigns or all voters in the same manner. First, viability considerations have the greatest impact when at least one of the candidates is virtually unknown and diminish as voters learn more about candidates over the course of a campaign. Information mutes viability considerations. Second, viability considerations tend to be greatest when candidates cannot be distinguished clearly by their ideological orientations or their positions on major policy issues. Viability considerations help voters reach decisions when other decision criteria are inconclusive. Third, viability issues tend to work in tandem with preexisting, overarching evaluations of candidates rather than independent of them. Considerations of candidate and campaign performance tend to confirm and strengthen what voters already perceive in candidates. Finally, election poll standings are only one of the factors that might affect perceptions of a candidate's viability. In fact, these studies concentrate almost exclusively on candidate performance in actual election contests and mention polls only in passing.[1]

This can serve as the basis for assembling elements of a perspective that permits the possibility that poll results have an impact on the behavior of election participants. In the graphic summary of this formulation, factors are shown to vary along the ordinal x axis, ranging from a high to a low expected impact for the factors (Figure 5.1).

Orientation. The impact of poll results on election behavior depends on participants' orientations to election decisions. Participants with a strategic orientation—those inclined primarily to support candidates on their likelihood of winning—should be influenced more, and more directly, by poll results than participants whose orientation is on factors other than candidate viability. Election participants support candidates on the basis of various preferences. Partisanship, ideology, personality, likability, character, desire for change or continuity, and positions on policy issues are just some of the alternative decision criteria against which poll standings must compete if they are to have an effect on participant preference decisions. As a rule, poll results have the greatest impact on participants concerned primarily with candidate viability and the least impact on those primarily interested in other factors.

Participants' perceptions of the stakes of a contest play a role in shaping their ultimate orientation in a contest. This is obvious for those with a strategic orientation: The higher the stakes participants associate with finding the likely winning candidate, the more likely they are to make decisions based on evidence of a candidate's viability. In contrast, participants whose main interest lies in some other sphere of consideration—finding the most liberal or the most conservative candidate, for instance—should be more likely to set aside those considerations in favor of a strategic orientation if they believe the outcome of the contest involves especially high stakes. These voters are more likely to attach themselves to an ideologically acceptable but viable candidate rather than the candidate with the optimum ideological orientation when they believe the outcome of the contest is of great importance. In short, the higher the perceived stakes of the ultimate outcome of a contest, the more likely it is that candidate viability will play a role in participant choices— regardless of their basic orientation.

Salience. Second, poll results should have greater impact on participants' decision making when the data salient to their guiding orientation are not available or predictable from other sources. If a participant with a game orientation can reliably predict which candidate will win from other information, poll results will have little marginal impact on their preferences. Knowledge of poll results may confirm a prior inclination, but that knowledge will have minimal independent influence. It is also important to note that voters do not rely exclusively on poll results to estimate likely outcomes and that preferences can differ from expected outcomes. At a time when all national surveys showed Michael Dukakis leading George Bush (June 1988),

	Low ←	EXPECTED IMPACT OF POLLS	→ High
ORIENTATION	NONSTRATEGIC: Factors other than viability most important		STRATEGIC: Candidate viability most important factor
SALIENT DATA	KNOWN: Can be reliably predicted from other info		UNKNOWN: Cannot be reliably predicted from other info
URGENCY	LOW: No advantage to prompt action		HIGH: Prompt action beneficial
COMMITMENT	HIGH: Previous intention to support candidate		LOW: No previous intention to support candidate
PREDISPOSITION	INCONSISTENT: Results disagree with existing perceptions		CONSISTENT: Results agree with existing perceptions
TRUST IN POLLS	LOW		HIGH

Figure 5.1. Factors Contributing to Poll Impact

a Hickman-Maslin Research survey in New Jersey found Dukakis with a small lead in vote preference but Bush enjoying an even wider lead in perceptions of which candidate was more likely to win. The basis for this belief must have been independent of what voters knew about poll standings and their personal preferences. It also seems safe to assume that, even before publicly available polls, voters had perceptions of candidate viability and candidate performance and that impressions of viability and performance still can be formed without poll information through observation of the candidates and their campaigns.

Likewise, knowing that a candidate is performing well might be persuasive, even for participants with a nonstrategic orientation, if the participants are unable to predict reliably candidate comparisons on the dimensions that matter to them. At the very least, knowledge of a candidate's superior standing might shape participants' perceptions enough to stimulate support until the more salient data are available. Take, for example, a participant inclined to support the most liberal candidate but unable to uncover conclusive information about the candidates' ideologies or to resolve doubt left by the information that is available. The early days of the 1988 Democratic nomination process offered many illustrations; for example, Paul Simon supported both government funding of abortions for women who cannot afford them and a balanced budget amendment to the Constitution, while Dick Gephardt took contrasting views on both issues. Knowing only these positions, how could anyone searching for an ideological distinction between the candidates reconcile this? In cases like these, knowing that one candidate is performing substantially better than the other in the polls may be sufficient to stimulate a preference for one of the candidates until a satisfactory conclusion about ideology can be reached. In short, poll results provide information about candidates, and, in the absence of other information, knowledge of poll results should have an impact even for participants who do not have a strategic orientation. This is an especially important distinction for understanding the function of polls in elections characterized by low levels of candidate information.

Urgency. Third, the greater urgency participants associate with making a choice in a contest, the more likely poll results are to affect their decisions. Participants who feel a great urgency to make a choice are more likely to rely on information about candidate viability than those who have the luxury of waiting for more information. Urgency, of course, can flow from many sources. On the night before an election or any other decision deadline, urgency may flow from necessity. For others, urgency may attend more pragmatic considerations, considerations such as the

ones neatly summarized by former Louisiana Governor Earl Long's observation that "those who support me in the first primary get the jobs; those
who support me in the run-off get good government."

The utility of poll results for decision making in the face of urgency
reflects the type of information they convey. For one thing, poll results are
empirical and objective, handy features for people making decisions under
pressure. For another, they tend to be summary measures from which a wide
variety of considerations can be inferred. Poll results can summarize all the
elements or stereotypes of "likely winner" for participants with a game
orientation. They can capsulize indications of political skill for voters seeking
effective leaders ("he must be effective if he's doing this well"), candidate
ideology for participants with an ideological orientation ("candidates who
do best/worst with the electorate tend to be the most liberal/conservative"),
or even policy concerns ("people agree with me that crime is the biggest
issue, and people are supporting Candidate X"). "Doing well" is taken by
many participants as an indication of the general acceptability of a candidate—regardless of the particular definition they attach to "well."

Commitment. Fourth, poll results can be expected to have the greatest
impact for participants who have low commitment to any candidate in a
contest and the least impact with participants who have a high commitment
to a candidate. Voters with high levels of commitment to candidates tend to
filter evaluation-laden information about campaigns and candidates in a
manner advantageous for the candidate they prefer. Participants with less
commitment have fewer defenses against persuasive qualities of information
and thus are more likely to take on the perspective suggested by the information available to them.

A participant's level of commitment to a candidate also speaks to the
extent to which the participant has been able to reconcile available information about the candidates. A high level of commitment to a candidate usually
indicates that a participant has been able to reconcile most doubts involved
in selecting a candidate, at least for the time being, while lower levels of
commitment usually indicate that some doubts remain unresolved. In this
sense, knowledge of poll results interacts with the doubts implied by less than
total commitment to a candidate. Positive poll results should help resolve
those doubts to the candidate's advantage, while negative poll results may
add fuel to existing doubts.

Predisposition. Fifth, polls can be expected to have the greatest impact
when they are consistent with an established, even if ill-formed, disposition
toward the candidates. Positive poll results should have the greatest impact
on participants who have a preexisting favorable, or at least not unfavorable,

disposition toward the candidate most advantaged by positive poll results. Positive poll results may stimulate favorable feelings toward a generally unknown candidate, but the same results would be expected to have an even greater impact on participants with a preexisting favorable impression of the candidate. Conversely, poll results inconsistent with the participant's disposition toward a candidate should have comparatively little impact on the participant's decision making.

Trust. Finally, it also should be noted that the potential impact of a participant's knowledge of poll results varies directly according to the reliability he or she attaches to polls in general and to the particular poll under consideration. All things being equal, knowledge of poll results will have less impact on participants who "do not trust polls" and more impact on participants who tend to believe the accuracy of poll results. The level of trust that voters place in polls may be due to memories of polls that were "wrong" in the sense of showing candidates ahead who eventually lost, a general mistrust of such "newfangled notions," or even apparently conflicting information from multiple polls in one contest. Not even accounting for variations in the quality of polls in a race, statistical probability alone should ensure enough apparently discrepant information to raise questions of reliability among average voters—especially in relatively close contests.

Impact in Different Elections

The most recent frenzy of criticism about the proliferation of polls concerns the 1988 presidential election and the polls' potential impact on voters. We should note that few voters in presidential campaigns, especially during the general election period, have the characteristics associated with an expected high impact from knowledge of poll results.

There is little evidence of strategic voting in presidential general elections.[2] Alternative bases of voter preference—such as partisanship, policy issues and ideology, candidates' personality or likability, perceptions of leadership qualities, and performance by incumbents—dominate voter decision making in presidential elections. Given the abundance of readily available information about these factors, voters in a presidential election are able to learn what they want and need to know about candidates from available information other than poll results.

It is also rare for voters to feel special urgency to reach a decision in a presidential election. By experience if nothing else, voters understand that the election timetable progresses from nominating contests to conventions to campaigning and debates—and only then to voting. Until very close to Election Day, there is no reason for voters to feel urgency to reach more than a standing preference for one of the candidates. Voters can reassess their preferences as new information becomes available up to the point of actually voting, and there are no special rewards for making an early definitive commitment.

Although partisan dealignment and other factors may have reduced the overall level of voter commitment to candidates at any given point in recent presidential general elections, voters with no commitment to one of the candidates are indeed rare, as signified by the consistently low levels of "undecided" or "no preference" answers in surveys about presidential candidates from the time the nominating field is winnowed to two or three legitimate candidates to Election Day. Given the tendency of voters to interpret poll results in a manner consistent with their preferences, and given the variety of polls that are available, occasionally with discrepant results or at least conflicting emphases during the same period, voters are almost always able to find poll results consistent with their general inclinations. Even if they cannot find a poll that shows their candidate leading, they probably can find one showing him or her in an improving position. Even if they confront surveys and trends unanimously inconsistent with their preferences, voters can reconcile that apparent conflict with a nod to their doubt about the veracity of polls, an attitude confirmed in the preelection survey conducted in conjunction with this book.[3] (See Chapter 7.)

Looking to presidential general elections for a significant direct impact of polls on voters' candidate preference is a classic case of barking up the wrong tree. If polls are to have an impact on voters, it probably would be more productive to look at other types of elections. Taking just one step back and looking at presidential primaries offers several obvious illustrations. For one thing, there is almost always less demarcation between candidates in primaries on two traditionally important preference decision criteria: partisanship and policy positions. Primaries almost always include more candidates than most voters want or need to evaluate, and important distinguishing information is more difficult to come by during the primary season. This opens the door for summary information, such as data dealing with candidate viability, to play a role in pointing voters to candidates worth evaluating as serious potential choices and further shaping voter evaluations of them. In this manner, poll results during the nominating period *might* contribute to a winnowing role analogous to that of the outcome of early caucuses and primaries as well as to a role in feeding more substantive aspects of candidate evaluation.

This suggests that the nature of the impact of polls may vary at different points in voter decision making and at different points in an election contest. At least two features associated with high impact from poll results—the absence of data salient to a voter's orientation and low commitment to candidates in the contest—also characterize early stages of voter decision making, so we should expect polls to have more impact early rather than late in any contest. Even if early poll results stimulate a preference for a candidate, voters will be in receipt of dramatically more information when they make their ultimate voting decisions.

Another reason for examining primary campaigns instead of general elections concerns participant orientation. While the zero-sum structure of two-candidate general elections tends to discourage strategic considerations, the nonpartisan, multicandidate structure of primaries often encourages them. If voters are unable to decide which candidate they most prefer on nonstrategic grounds, the structure of multicandidate primaries allows them to vote on the basis of candidate viability. As Jesse Jackson and Paul Simon discovered in the 1988 Illinois primary, and Hart and Mondale found in the 1984 Democratic contest, these considerations can be manifest in votes *against* a candidate voters want to hurt as well as in votes *for* a candidate they want to help. As a general rule then, polls should be expected to have more impact in primaries than in general elections and more impact in multicandidate than in two-candidate contests (Figure 5.2).

If the expected impact of polls is greater in primaries than in general elections in presidential campaigns, the potential impact is even greater for other political contests. Presidential elections are the most different of American elections in several important ways. First, with the possible exception of elections for governor and mayor, information about the candidates is much more readily available to voters, and voters are more likely to seek information in presidential contests. The paucity of available information creates the possibility that poll information could have a more pronounced impact below the presidential level. In a nonpartisan, open seat race for county coroner, for instance, where voters are hard-pressed to learn any distinguishing information about the contestants, knowing something about candidate standing in the polls could provide enough information to establish a lasting, if not a final, preference for most voters.[4]

Presidential contests also offer voters many more opportunities than other races to assess candidate viability. One effect of the large number of primaries and caucuses during the nominating period is that poll results must compete with other, supposedly more reliable, information dealing with candidate performance. And, as noted above, numerous polls with differing emphases

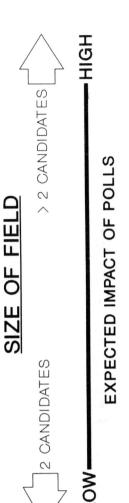

Figure 5.2. Expected Impact of Polls on Different Elections

are available at almost every step in presidential elections. So, even if we assume that the central feature of poll results is this type of nominal information, the impact is likely to be greatest when no alternative information is available. And this clearly applies more to elections below the presidential level.

It perhaps goes without saying that voters generally attach greater stakes to presidential elections than to lower-level races. When voters attach lower stakes to elections, they are more likely to engage in strategic voting, so they are more likely to find salient information in poll results in lower-level races.

For all these reasons, one should expect polls to have the greatest impact in races below the presidential level and to have greater impact in primary, nonpartisan, or multicandidate elections at every level.

Impact on Different Participants

From the discussion of critical factors, it follows that knowledge of poll standings is most likely to affect participants with strategic orientations who are (a) unable to reliably predict the outcome of the contest from other information, (b) feel great urgency to make a determination of candidate support, (c) have little if any commitment to a particular candidate, (d) have predispositions consistent with the direction of poll results, and (e) trust the accuracy of polls. Even when poll results directly influence voter preference, whether in the nominating phase or during the general election, the impact will be greater on political activists than on average voters. Political activists are much more likely than voters (a) to have a strategic orientation, (b) to feel urgency in making a commitment, (c) to have a lower or equal level of commitments to particular candidates, and (d) to trust polls. (See Figure 5.3.)

Political activists are motivated by different factors, but we can concentrate on financial contributors and potential endorsers to illustrate the relevant points.[5] The charge that poll information influences election participants assumes that everyone interprets poll results in the same manner with the same behavioral consequences—that is, that poll results help leading candidates and hinder trailing ones. While political activists, especially those with a strategic orientation, may place a premium on candidate viability and, ultimately, on winning, ordinary voters may look more favorably at an underdog who is trying to overcome long odds. The strategic orientation of activists and especially contributors means that they, more than voters, look like bettors at a horse race: They may talk more about long shots that win and pay big rewards, but they are more likely to be successful over the long

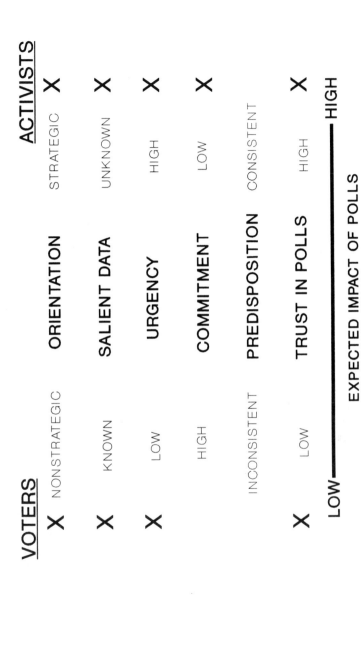

Figure 5.3. Distinctions Between Voters and Activists

113

term if they stick close to the established odds. In politics, poll results serve as a tote board for these strategic participants.

Although the most frequent types of donations are no doubt friends giving to friends on the basis of personal solicitation and allies giving to allies on the basis of ideological and partisan factors, contributors are more likely to give money in close races, and candidates must convince contributors that their candidacies are viable (see Jacobson, 1980, pp. 71-75; Jacobson & Kernell, pp. 35-39). Presidential candidates enjoy a surge of financial assistance when they are successful in early contests and see the pace of contributions slow dramatically as their candidacies become endangered. To assume that candidate viability is not a central factor, one must conclude that the candidates and their fund-raisers lose friends over the course of the campaign or that they change their ideologies, party affiliations, and policy positions enough to discourage contributions.

Urgency also affects political activists much more than voters at large, and candidate activities take into account the tendency of activists to monitor early events more closely than voters and to make earlier commitment decisions. In much the way that John Kennedy used primary contests to prove to party bosses his (a Catholic's) electoral viability, candidates today use the pre-primary period to convince potential contributors and other activists of the viability of their efforts. Even when a candidate is speaking to public audiences, the purpose is as much to impress opinion makers, potential contributors, and other political elites as to win the support of average voters who might be persuaded by it. In this respect, candidates' suspicions are not unfounded, for, unlike average voters, political activists anticipate that their commitment, if not their contribution, will bring special benefits, and they have learned through experience that the most important money and support to any politician comes early. Earl Long's aforementioned comment contains wisdom gleaned from experience as well as humor. Finally, political activists tend to be much more sophisticated than other voters in using polling information for decision making.

Political activists find special value in polls and easily connect polling information with their commitment decisions for several reasons. Because their decision making traditionally occurs early in the process, and because their orientation to a race tends to be strategic, these participants crave information bearing on the likely outcome of the race. Unfortunately, little reliable empirical information is available. Fund-raising is one alternative empirical measure, but every potential contributor knows that, if fund-raising rather than vote-getting were the best measure of viability, John Connally would have been the Republican presidential nominee in 1980. Likewise, the fascination with early straw polls demonstrates that activists are willing to place significant value in viability measures—even those much less reliable than poll results. Polls are important to political activists because they bear directly on their orientation to the race and provide the data most useful for addressing their fundamental decision criteria.

As is the case for average voters, however, poll results are more likely to affect the decision making and behavior of political activists in races below the presidential level. Media coverage and analysis of candidate viability usually are available later and are less sophisticated in lower-level races. As a result, poll results are less likely to compete with other estimations of viability and, therefore, to play a bigger role in activists' decision making.

By the same token, polling information is most difficult to obtain, certainly from public sources, in races below the level of president, mayor, governor, and U.S. senator. One is tempted to say that this reflects a proper technical judgment, because races for state senate, single-member city council or county commission districts, and even Congress often involve complicated and expensive sampling problems because of the vagaries of district geography and turnout. Even so, newspapers and other media outlets seldom include questions about races below the level of U.S. senator even when they occur in areas easy to replicate in a telephone sample. Down-ballot statewide offices, like superintendent of public instruction or state auditor, are no more difficult to sample than a race for governor or U.S. senator, but statewide media polls often do not include them. But whether the concern is survey cost, itself an unspoken commentary on the importance of the race to the media organization and the voters, or a quiet understanding that it is in these races that poll results could be most influential in shaping voter attitudes and behaviors, the result is the same: Campaign insiders must rely on estimates of candidate viability other than polls or on polls commissioned by the candidates themselves.

Candidates and their campaign managers recognize the importance of candidate viability for persuading political activists, and they recognize the special value of polls in this process. Nothing demonstrates this recognition more clearly than the distinctive way campaigns communicate with potential contributors and other activists. Even when public polls are not available, campaigns almost always include their own private survey results, complete with a "confidential" memorandum from the pollster, in information distributed to potential contributors and other activists. Conversations and meetings with potential contributors and other activists emphasize poll standings. When candidates are not present, political insiders' conversations concentrate on candidate viability. "Who's ahead?" is asked thousands of times more frequently than "what's his (or her) position on the Midgetman?" or any other question about candidates' positions on policy issues.

In contrast, poll standings are seldom part of candidates' paid communications with voters at large—the expenditure with which candidates wager on their political futures. This is not due to a dominating preference for policy concerns among candidates and their advisers or because this type of information cannot be communicated in snappy advertising formulations. As campaign slogans, "John Smith: First in the Polls, First in Our Hearts" or "Jane Johnson: You know what's she's done in the horse race; just think what she'll do in the Senate" works just as well as "Marvin Marcos: Manila in the Senate" or "Don J. Ceour: New Ideas for Colorado's Future."

Communications with average voters usually only mention polls or other messages about candidate viability under three circumstances. When candidates are under attack, they occasionally use references to poll standings to ascribe motivations to the candidate responsible for the attacks: "Trailing in the polls and election day just two weeks away, my opponent has launched a vicious and misleading attack on my sterling record of accomplishment for the people." When candidates find themselves losing, they occasionally refer to their standings in an attempt to establish themselves as underdogs with honorable motivations who deserves voter sympathies: "When the history of this campaign is written, let it be said that what was important to us was not whether we won or lost but the fact that we told the truth about the problems we face." Finally, trailing primary candidates occasionally argue that they would be stronger general election candidates than the other primary contestants. This tactic rarely appears in paid advertisement, and a saying common among campaign professional neatly summarizes estimations of its value: "Electability is the last gasp of a dying campaign."

These exceptions notwithstanding, the most common tendency is for candidates to emphasize viability concerns when addressing activists and nonviability concerns when addressing voters. The reason for this pattern of campaign communication is simple. Campaigns and candidates address questions central to election participants' decision making, things that matter to them. Voters make their decisions on the basis of factors such as partisanship, ideology, personality, likability, character, desire for change or continuity, and positions on policy issues, and that is what candidates and campaigns address when they communicate with voters at large. If poll results would persuade voters to support a candidate, it is a safe bet that poll results would be a focal point in candidates' paid communications. Campaign communications with political insiders, especially current and potential contributors, emphasize poll results because candidates and campaigns know that these considerations are key to activists'—not voters'—decision making.[6]

The Reactions of Campaigns

Campaigns react to the public release of poll results according to predictable patterns, patterns congruent with the general tendencies discussed above. The basic alternatives are obvious; campaigns can have a positive reaction or they can have a negative one. These reactions tend to vary according to candidates' position in the poll standings and according to the congruence between poll results and campaign perceptions of audience expectations.

Interactions between standings and expectations are more revealing than either one of them individually. As a general rule, when poll results exceed what campaigns believe key groups expected the polls to show, campaigns take a positive, confirming approach and use the results in a proactive manner to strengthen those perceptions. When poll results show a candidate doing worse than the campaign's perceptions of existing expectations by key groups, they usually take a negative, disconfirming approach and use various tactics to undermine the credibility or significance of the poll and to argue that the poll results do not show a true picture of the race and/or its likely outcome.

Candidate standings are critical, however, regardless of the relationship between poll results and expectations. Results from three 1987 Des Moines *Register* surveys of likely 1988 Democratic caucus attendees illustrate the point (see Table 5.1).

In this case, campaigns for several candidates can find good news for themselves and bad news for their opponents. Paul Simon can argue that the December results confirm his continuing lead over all challengers and that the closest challenger has not made a statistically significant gain. Dukakis can argue that October reports exaggerated his demise and that he remains in second place. Gephardt can argue that he is essentially tied with Dukakis, and both Babbitt and Jackson can argue that their positions are statistically indistinguishable from Gephardt's.

An understanding of prepoll expectations, however, is necessary for an understanding of the impact of these results and the probability that a candidate will be successful in convincing the poll audience of his or her interpretations of the results. For example, if the poll audience expected Simon to be further ahead than he is, even results showing a good standing

TABLE 5.1   Iowa Caucus Poll Results (1987)

Candidate	August	October	December
Paul Simon	13	24	35
Mike Dukakis	14	18	14
Dick Gephardt	18	14	11
Jesse Jackson	10	11	9
Bruce Babbitt	9	8	8
Al Gore	2	3	3
Joe Biden	10	—	—
Pat Schroeder	6	—	—
No preference	18	22	20

will not necessarily have a positive impact. If expectations were that Gephardt or Dukakis were even with or ahead of Simon, the results might not be good for them despite their relatively good positions. Likewise, if expectations were that Babbitt and Jackson would be trailing the field, the poll might simply solidify that impression.

The expectations and standings dimensions can be combined, as shown in Figure 5.4, as a vehicle for stipulating a general scheme of campaign response scenarios. It is best to think of the reactions of campaigns as attempts to confound or confirm the general tenor of the results, in terms of the interactive effects of expectations and absolute standings. In both cases, however, "spin," the interpretation campaigns want attached to the information, is the essence of a campaign's response.[7]

Regardless of the campaign's analysis of the likely impact of the release of survey results, there is a commonality in the style of their responses. In an earlier time, campaign responses tended to be comparatively passive and reactive. They handled inquiries with straightforward responses and little more. Today, the approach is more aggressive and proactive, much in the manner that campaigns attempt to spin the results of debate performances. Rather than waiting for inquiries to come to them, campaigns work to sell their versions of polls from the instant they are aware of the results. The candidate, campaign manager, and spokesperson disseminate carefully crafted interpretations through print and electronic interviews, press releases, and radio actualities. Mailings that include the poll results and the campaign's spin are out within days, and there is increasing use of fax machines for dispensing the information within hours.

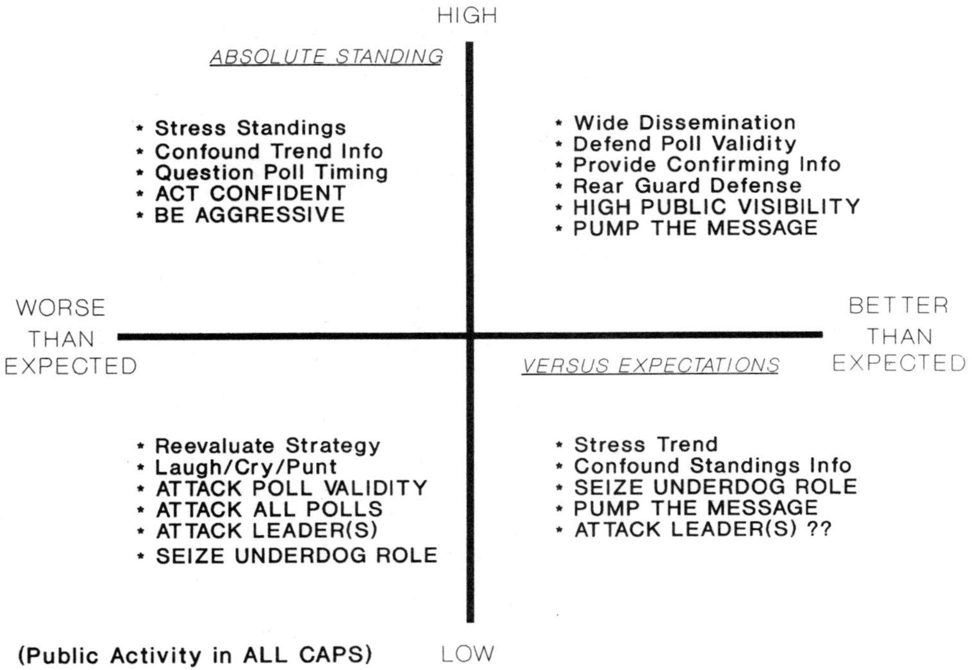

ABSOLUTE STANDING

HIGH

WORSE THAN EXPECTED

Stress Standings
* Stress Standings
* Confound Trend Info
* Question Poll Timing
* ACT CONFIDENT
* BE AGGRESSIVE

* Wide Dissemination
* Defend Poll Validity
* Provide Confirming Info
* Rear Guard Defense
* HIGH PUBLIC VISIBILITY
* PUMP THE MESSAGE

BETTER THAN EXPECTED

VERSUS EXPECTATIONS

* Reevaluate Strategy
* Laugh/Cry/Punt
* ATTACK POLL VALIDITY
* ATTACK ALL POLLS
* ATTACK LEADER(S)
* SEIZE UNDERDOG ROLE

* Stress Trend
* Confound Standings Info
* SEIZE UNDERDOG ROLE
* PUMP THE MESSAGE
* ATTACK LEADER(S) ??

LOW

(Public Activity in ALL CAPS)

Figure 5.4. Likely Campaign Responses to Various Poll Results

119

Campaigns marshall evidence from other public polls or even private polls commissioned by the campaign, reports of organization and financial activities, and endorsements by key groups or individuals to buttress their spins. The nature of the collateral information depends on how a campaign wishes to spin the results.

Selecting the proper audience to receive the results and the campaign's explanation of them are equally important; if the campaigns are the spinners, who are the "spinees"? The major targets are political activists—the election participants that poll results are most likely to affect—including three basic subgroups: current supporters, potential supporters, and opinion leaders. Current supporters need encouragement in the face of bad and disappointing results, while good results can be used to motivate them to work harder or contribute more. Campaigns use positive results to persuade potential supporters and attempt to minimize the damage from negative ones.

As Figure 5.4 indicates, campaigns confronting polls showing good standings that exceed expectations always take confirming actions. They want this news widely reported, and they work to ensure that it falls into the proper hands and minds as quickly and as forcefully as possible. If there is ever a situation in which a campaign wants to communicate poll results to the public, this is it. But the key target remains the activists. They try to create a "bandwagon" effect, to pull in contributions and endorsements from individuals who might be stimulated to act by the news. The appearance of good news in political campaigns is not predictable, so, when it comes, campaigns must make the most of the opportunity it presents.

Campaigns shown to be doing better than expected take two common responsive actions, regardless of their absolute standings. They always take an "I-told-you-so" attitude, stressing the fact that they are doing better than expected, usually marked by a positive trend compared with previous polls, thus justifying the strategies they have been following. Second, these campaigns normally take advantage of the increased attention that accompanies exceeding expectations and stress the campaign messages that supposedly have led to their surprising showings.

Campaigns in leading positions also must fight rearguard actions as well, as their opponents will be working to undermine the impact of the poll results. Confounding tactics are numerous, but they fall into a predictable pattern. Campaigns confronted with poor standings attempt to put the results in the best light. They might argue that the interviews were conducted at an especially beneficial time for the front-runner. The leader's campaign might recently have finished a run of television ads (as was true in the case of Paul Simon prior to the December survey reported in Table 5.1) or may have been the beneficiary of a prominent media story.[8] Trailing candidates may focus on the fact that they have more resources available for the remainder of the campaign, and they may bring forward key endorsements sooner than originally planned.

Trailing candidates may be tempted to ignore poll results and hope the story will not be as prominent if they are not part of it. This option carries risks because media outlets, especially at the state and local levels, give prominent play to their own polls: Polls cost media outlets too much money for them to give the story short shrift. This holds even when the polls are of dubious quality (such as mail surveys) or are totally contrary to other polls conducted at similar points in time. Likewise, suggestions that "Candidate Jones had no comment on the survey that shows him trailing the field" can be taken as an indication that the candidate accepts the general accuracy of the poll results.

Another ploy in the face of unfavorable poll results is for trailing candidates to limit their comments to the poll and avoid making other significant pronouncements during that news cycle. The reasoning is that they do not want potentially good stories played in the context of their "desperation" or to be overwhelmed by the poll story. If they are going to attempt to make nonpoll news, it usually will be in a media market where the poll results are *not* a big story. This often means they can go to a media market not covered by the outlet that commissioned the poll, because media outlets seldom give prominent coverage to others' polls.

The most common response, however, is for trailing candidates, especially those shown to be doing less well than expected, to raise questions about the technical quality of the poll. They raise questions about the size of the sample and the screening procedures used to define eligible respondents. They argue that the proportions of various subgroups are over- or underrepresented in the sample or that their position relative to the leaders is distorted in some other way. In his presidential campaigns, George Wallace was famous for arguing that his supporters were less likely than others to respond to surveys, a tactic ironically used more recently by Jesse Jackson. Trailing candidates also challenge the political motivations of the organizations conducting or commissioning the poll, and they cite examples when similar polls have been "wrong" in past elections.

Except for candidates in the weakest electoral positions, attacks on polls tend to be made out of the view of the general public. Rather, they direct commentaries at campaign insiders and reporters covering the campaign. Professional pollsters retained by the campaign often draft the commentaries in the form of a document that can be distributed to key supporters and opinion leaders or suggest "talking points" for use in detailing problems in the offending survey.

The arguments campaigns make against polls often take on ironic qualities. For example, campaigns do not hesitate to ignore the strictures of sampling error when claiming they are ahead. Campaigns that find themselves trailing another candidate by less than the margin of error, however, are suddenly blessed with great statistical insight and claim that the polls show the two candidates to be "even." In the same manner, campaigns occasionally criticize specific aspects of public polls, such as weekend interviewing, unrepresentative proportions of key electoral groups, and a small sample of likely voters, even though the professional pollsters retained by the campaigns might rely on identical if faulty procedures. In fact, one frequently finds campaigns criticizing a poll at one point in the campaign but defending it at another point. The commissioning agency is the same, the polling organization is the same, and the polling techniques are the same. What changes are the relative positions of the candidates in the results.

Illustrations from 1988

The 1988 presidential general election offered several useful illustrations of how campaigns respond to poll results. Each business day between the Democratic convention and Election Day, the Dukakis campaign sent a summary of *Talking Points* by fax to Democratic campaign professionals and opinion leaders around the country. (The quotations that follow in this section are from copies of the fax material.) The campaign hoped the distribution of these talking points would contribute to an understanding of the strategy and tactics—a formidable goal in itself—and create consistency in what Democrats across the country were saying about the campaign.

An early theme was to suggest that Robert Teeter, the Republican presidential campaign pollster, controlled George Bush. On August 3, the talking points attributed President Reagan's veto of the defense bill and decision to allow plant-closing legislation to become law with Teeter's reported belief that "a veto of the defense bill would be helpful to the Bush campaign" and an 80% approval rating for the plant-closing legislation. Bush's support for day-care funding was cited as a third example. In sum, the Dukakis campaign argued, "If there is one consistent theme to the Bush campaign it is: when polls conflict with principles, the polls win every time." Readers were left to presume that Dukakis would never do this.

On August 5, poll results were portrayed in a substantially more positive light in the "spinning" of a Gallup survey. And why shouldn't they be—the survey showed Dukakis to be ahead:

> Galluping Along - A new survey released by the *Gallup Organization* yesterday gives Dukakis a wide lead over Bush across the country. Dukakis holds a lead of roughly ten points over Bush, besting him in nearly every region of the country. Most encouraging is the news from voters in the Rocky Mountain states. Pollster [Andrew] Kohut claims that "politically transformed" voters in the West may be the key to Democratic victory in November. "They are most strongly in favor of free health care for the needy, national health insurance and help for the homeless," said the survey.

Over the next week, talking points suffered serious cases of whiplash as the spin was alternatively set in opposite directions. The points of August 10 offered excellent examples of a campaign lowering expectations and mixing and matching polls:

> POLLS: We've always said that this is going to be a tight race. The media is [sic] reporting that Dukakis' lead in post-[Democratic] convention polls has narrowed this week. Gallup polls released yesterday afternoon report Dukakis leading Bush 49% to 42%. Polls are historically volatile at this stage of the campaign as the numbers from the 1984 campaign illustrate: a Gallup poll showed Mondale 19 points behind Reagan the week before the Democratic convention and a News-week poll taken directly after the convention had him 2 points ahead — a 21 point swing. After the Republican convention the polls should be around where they were before the conventions.

The interest of the Dukakis campaign in lowering expectations was evident in the fact that they ignored a CBS News/*New York Times* survey released on the evening of August 6 showing Dukakis ahead by 17 points, 50% to 33%.

On August 12, the full circle from optimism to realism to optimism seems complete:

> NEW NBC POLL:—A new NBC poll shows: (1) Duke leads Bush by 14 points; (2) 53% of voters believe Bush was "very involved" with Iran/Contra; (3) 44% believe he's behind the high deficit; (4) 38% associate him with Administration scandals like Ed Meese. MSD is rated better than Bush on handling the deficit, drugs and crime. A final note: 73% of those who heard the MSD medical story believe that Dukakis was the victim of "dirty tricks" by his political opponents.

But realism reared its ugly head again on August 18:

> POLLS: A poll today in the Washington Post showed Dukakis' lead narrowing to
> 49%-46%. This is exactly what we expected: it's going to be a very close, tough
> race. The Republicans are getting a bounce from their convention coverage, and
> we could very well trail in some polls after tonight.

The talking points of August 23 suggested that the expectations of the
Dukakis campaign were correct, but there was an increasing sense that polls
were unreliable after all:

> POLLS: Yesterday, Newsweek published a poll that showed Bush leading
> Dukakis by 51% to 42%. CBS released a poll that showed Bush leading by 46%
> to 40%. Both polls were taken either during or just after the Republican Conven-
> tion. Kevin Phillips, a Republican pollster [sic], dismisses these post-convention
> polls as "statistical gibberish." We expected Bush to get a big bounce out of the
> Convention (Mondale-Ferraro gained 21 points).

In the same release, the same two surveys seemed more believable when they
showed voters much more supportive of Democratic vice presidential nominee Lloyd Bentsen than of Dan Quayle, his Republican counterpart. If it
occurred to the Dukakis campaign that the coverage that supposedly helped
Bush also hurt Quayle, it was not evident in their talking points. In a similar
fashion, they did not seem to consider the possibility that the same type of
"bounce" might have accounted for Dukakis's showing in the surveys during
May and immediately after the *Democratic* convention.

Only two significant mentions of polls appear in the talking points during
the month of September: The September 15 fax mentions an ABC
News/*Washington Post* poll showing Dukakis "up by 3%" and postdebate
talking points mentioned surveys showing Dukakis as the "winner" of the
first meeting with Bush. Other than that, the consistent pattern of surveys
showing Bush sustaining a six- to ten-point lead went unmentioned.

The talking-point releases for October were a different matter, as the
Dukakis campaign struggled to undermine the impression that the trend was
moving strongly in Bush's direction. The release of October 5, the day of the
Bentsen-Quayle debate, illustrated how campaigns attempt to link an unexpectedly high standing with the campaign message:

> SAY HEY: "Dukakis is closing the Gap with Bush" says today's *New York Times*.
> The message is getting through, and it's working. To recap: Bush stands for the

status quo; Dukakis stands for change; Bush stands for complacency; Dukakis stands for change; Bush stands for running in place; Dukakis wants to move forward. Bush would settle for the bronze; Dukakis wants the gold for America; Bush is looking for an intentional walk; Dukakis wants a home run. Dukakis wants America to be number one.

And it's working. According to today's CBS/NYT poll, the race is tightening up. It's: Bush 48%, Duke 46%. Ten days ago, just after the Prez debate, it was Bush 46%, Duke 40%.

The following day, poll data connected the vice presidential debate to what the Dukakis campaign argued was the trend of the campaign. The main source was an ABC survey conducted just after the debate, which showed Bentsen ahead by 51% to 27% as the perceived winner of the debate ("a nearly two to one margin"). Furthermore, "the ABC poll also showed that Bentsen's win helped Dukakis. Before the debate, Bush led Dukakis 50%-45%. After the debate, Dukakis picked up 3%. Now the race is a statistical dead heat: 50% - 48%." The concentration on trend when the standings were unfavorable and even the selective use of statistical significance to spin the surveys paled in comparison with their use of a small group experiment for their own advantage:

> USA TODAY: *USA TODAY*'s "debate meter" showed that Bentsen was a big hit with American voters. "Quayle's performance raised doubts about his ability to serve as President," among the 100 registered voters gathered in Omaha to score the debate. Before the debate, 29 people said Quayle would be a "bad" President. After the debate, that figure jumped to 50. Before the debate, Bush/Quayle led Dukakis/Bentsen 46-39. After the debate, Dukakis/Bentsen were *ahead* 45-34— an [sic] remarkable 18 point swing. The President of the American Association of Public Opinion Research, Bob [sic] Meyer, added: "There was a dramatic switch away from Bush. Either their doubts about Quayle increased to the point where it tipped their voting decision or seeing Quayle made those existing doubts an important ingredient in their vote."[9]

Selective adherence to statistical rules was a consistent pattern in the talking points throughout the period from the vice presidential debate through coverage of the second presidential debate, as the Dukakis campaigns picked and chose through numbers in search of a positive trend. On October 11, the focus given to an ABC/*Washington Post* survey was as follows:

QUAYLE FACTOR: The polls show that Quayle is becoming a big factor in the election. ABC/Wash Post poll: GB-50% MSD:47% with a margin of error of +/– 4.5%. (Last week numbers: GB-51% MSD-44%). Sam Donaldson: "the race is a virtual dead heat." More important: "the overall impact of Quayle's performance was to shift about 2% of the electorate to Dukakis." (W. Post).

Of course, the same reasoning that showed the race "a virtual dead heat" showed that the debate had no statistically significant impact in voter preference (but never mind). The Dukakis campaign even found good news in the second presidential debate, a debate widely perceived to have been won by Bush as soon as Dukakis metaphorically stepped over his wife's body in response to the first question. First came a memo purportedly distributed to campaign staff members arguing that Dukakis "won [the debate] last night according to a *USA Today* California poll." Additional evidence of Dukakis's "winning" performance came from NBC and *USA Today* focus groups with "swing voters":

> It's swing voters who will decide this election, not voters previously committed to one candidate. . . . The polls that show a Bush win fail to note the obvious - Bush led the trial heat by a few points going into the debate [10 points according to The Hotline/KRC survey], and committed Bush voters are skewing the score for Bush.

Later the same day, additional information showed that the *USA Today* study of "likely but weakly committed voters" consisted of a sample of 100. The predebate matchup showed Bush ahead 50 to 42, while the postdebate score was 46 participants for each candidate. The Dukakis talking points characterized this as "a decisive 8-point swing." Neither the margin of sampling error for a sample of 100 nor an ABC News survey showing Bush the debate winner by a 16-point margin were mentioned in either fax.

The last references to polls during the campaign revealed a measure of the campaign's desperation. On October 17, the Dukakis staff argued that "the election is still up for grabs" through reference to a most unlikely source: "GB's pollster, Bob Teeter, says that 12-14% of the voters have not made up their minds — the winning majority is still undecided." In the second reference, we find an illustration of how evaluations about a candidate's absolute standings depend on one's perspective and the standings' relationship to expectations:

COMEBACK TRAIL: A new ABC/Washington Post poll last night reveals a closer and more competitive race than "conventional wisdom" would have you believe: Bush 52% to MSD's 45%, with a 3.5% margin of error. The poll was taken between Oct. 12-18. A Harris poll put the margin at 9%.

They did not mention that an NBC/*Wall Street Journal* survey released October 16 found Bush with a 17-point advantage, more than enough cushion to offset the unlikely possibility that Dukakis would win the votes of all undecided voters.

The Dukakis campaign did mention the NBC/*Wall Street Journal* survey on October 28 when it was useful for showing a positive trend: "GOOD NUMBERS: A new *NBC/Wall Street Journal* polls [sic] shows an 8 point movement toward MSD over the last week: the poll indicates only a 9 point difference between Dukakis and Bush-down from 17 in the previous NBC/WSJ poll."

On November 2, less than a week before Election Day, the Dukakis campaign made a final gasp of competitiveness. They reported that "according to the national tracking poll conducted by KRC Research Associates, Bush's lead has dropped 5 points from Saturday to Monday." What they did not say was that the poll's total sample found Bush with an 8-point lead and the "drop" was between nightly waves of 333 interviews. They also referred to an ABC News/*Washington Post* survey that "shows 20% more people think Bush waged a 'dirty' campaign compared to MSD" and to a CBS News/*New York Times* poll that "shows that 1 out of 5 voters say they [are] still open to changing their minds in the final week." It is not surprising that they neglected to mention that the two surveys had Bush ahead by 12 and 13 points, respectively.

The Role of the Press

The press plays a central role in the responses of the campaigns to the release of poll results. It is through the press that word of the poll standings reaches most election participants; campaigns can reach only a limited number on their own, even if the participants are limited to activists. Press reports also are more likely to be believed. As shown in the Dukakis example, even campaigns understand that press reports of poll results are more credible than those of the campaign. Most important, the extent to which information communicated by poll results extends beyond simple information about candidate standings depends in large part on the way the press plays the results. When campaigns are trying to spin poll results, journalists are the most likely spinees. If audience expectations are important in the impact of poll results, the expectations of the press are even more important.

"Played by the press" should not be taken to imply that the press only extends the meaning of poll results when they provide extensive analytical commentary. Simple descriptions of poll data hold potentially significant meaning for election participants. Deciding, for instance, whether to emphasize the absolute standings or the trend since the most recent survey may totally alter the implications of a press report. Likewise, concentrating on the spread between a well-known incumbent and an unknown challenger may show the challenger in a much worse light than, say, concentrating on the vote among voters who know both candidates or the relationship between the incumbent's vote and the 50% majority mark.

As suggested in several of the examples quoted from the Dukakis talking points, the press almost always errs on the conservative side when reporting poll results. For example, imagine a race in which one candidate is shown to be four points ahead of a challenger in a survey with a margin of sampling error of plus or minus four points. Statistically, the probability that the leading candidate is eight points ahead is just as great as the probability that the candidates are "even." Yet, the possibility of the wider margin seldom receives equal play in poll coverage. This can be shown in a simple graph overlaying the actual probability distribution of the spread between two candidates in a survey showing a four-point gap (plus or minus four at a 95% confidence level) and an estimated probability distribution based on the usual portrayal of press accounts. (See Figure 5.5.)

On the other hand, the press almost always seems to give inordinate attention to marginal gains by trailing candidates. The press played the shift in the Bush-Dukakis margin from 51%-44% to 50%-47% in surveys with sampling margins of 4.5 points *each* as a meaningful gain for Dukakis—at least in the short term. Strictly speaking, there was an almost identical probability that the race did not change between the two polls. But the fact that Quayle did not perform well in his debate with Bentsen led many in the press to believe Dukakis would gain in its aftermath, and that is how the story played. Likewise, a challenger who moves from 12 points behind to 9 points behind, from 46%-34% to 45%-36%, for example, often will be portrayed as "gaining ground," even if the gain is not statistically significant. The tendency to stress trends rather than absolute

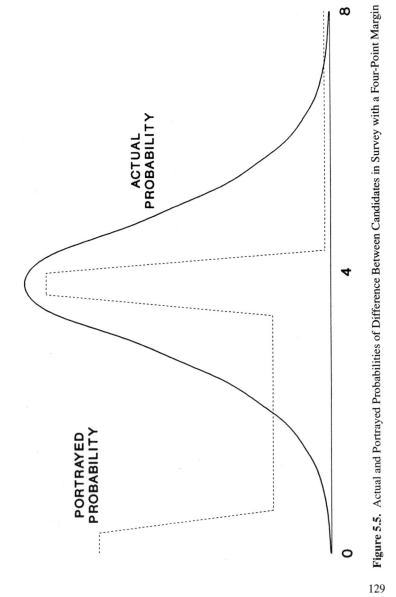

Figure 5.5. Actual and Portrayed Probabilities of Difference Between Candidates in Survey with a Four-Point Margin

129

standings seems to be exaggerated when the shift in the margin is from double to single digits.

These and other tendencies in press coverage can be traced to features that distinguish journalists from other election participants. All the above characteristics associated with political activists apply even more to journalists. Journalists clearly take a strategic view of election outcomes: Who wins and who loses is the centerpiece of the news of elections. Information relevant to this orientation is almost uniquely communicated in poll results. Every journalist can cite at least one example of when reporting from the field gave an erroneous impression of the likely outcome of a contest; the most famous example may be the *Washington Post*'s coverage of the 1976 Wisconsin Democratic primary, when their field reporting suggested Morris Udall would decisively defeat Jimmy Carter. The next time someone longingly wonders what ever happened to the good old days when reporters covered campaigns by knocking on doors, it seems fair to remind them of this episode. Polls allow journalists to address the likely outcome of a contest from behind a veil of objectivity, and polls offer journalists a scapegoat when there is an unanticipated outcome. Better that "the polls were wrong" than "I was wrong."

Urgency also influences the press, although in a somewhat different manner than it affects political activists. Journalists are under pressure from editors, from career considerations, and from competitiveness to get to a story first; and, in elections, the story is who will win. Even if the pressure is not to predict who will win, there is a natural inclination to cover a campaign in terms of a certain structure. Identification of the front-runner and the strength of his or her lead, the top challengers, and others who might have a legitimate chance of winning offers a context from which events can be explained throughout the race. Poll results provide this context, if only to confirm evidence from other information, and they offer an antidote to the myopic perspective attendant to being "on the bus."

The journalists' code of objectivity also means they are not likely to have a high level of commitment to any candidate, a tendency also associated, above, with political activists. Unlike activists, however, journalists are not bound to sustain their preferences after they determine which candidate is most likely to win. Journalists' perspectives can shift in the face of new information and changing poll results, while activists tend to be locked into their commitments.

Others have examined the extent to which news coverage tends to emphasize game aspects of campaigns. Mentioned less frequently is the extent to which journalists stretch, if not distort, poll results into more substantive commentaries on the candidates involved in a campaign. Although voters' greater concern with factors other than candidate viability provides them a natural defense against the direct influence of poll results, most voters are less cognizant of the indirect ways poll results influence coverage of the types of things that do concern them when making election decisions. Information reaching voters about a candidate's political skills, personal popularity, skillful handling of policy matters, or performance in office that flows from a journalist's analysis of poll results is somewhat like a fighter or a cruise missile coming in under enemy radar. Voters have defenses against the influence of polls on their decision making, but the defenses are not impenetrable.

Commentators concerned about the potential for poll results to influence voters need only to look around their newsrooms to find the perpetrators of that influence. If journalists truly wish to minimize the influence of polls on voters, they should be more careful in distinguishing between the types of information they communicate under the guise of reporting about poll results.

The analogy of sports coverage may be a useful one to keep in mind. Play-by-play announcers inform viewers of the score of the game and provide simple descriptions of action on the field. The role of color commentators is entirely different. They attach deeper meanings to the score and the behavior of the players, focusing viewer attention on examples of good and bad traits in teams, players, and coaches. Pat Summerall's role may have a more linear quality and may seem dull by comparison, but viewers are free to extend or not to extend the meaning of the information he provides—as they find it useful to their own purposes. In contrast, John Madden's role has a much greater influence in shaping viewer impressions of the players, teams, and coaches participating in the game. He does this by looking behind the scoreboard and action on the field to the motivations and fundamental qualities of the game participants, including physical skills, mental agility, and character traits.

Through experience, if nothing else, viewers of professional football games understand that play-by-play and color commentary have different functions and provide different types of information. Journalists concerned about the influence of poll results on voters are well advised to understand and honor this fundamental distinction also.

Notes

1. Steven J. Brams (1978, pp. 216-221) is one of the few political scientists I have found who explicitly examines the potential impact of the public release of poll results on an election outcome. In this passage, the focus is on the impact of preelection polls on elections under approval voting. The understanding of poll data, however, clearly falls into the "game" category.

2. The fact that the field is usually limited to two major opposing candidates is another reason for the absence of strategic voting in presidential general elections. One supposes that strategic voting was more common in 1968 and 1980 when George Wallace and John Anderson, respectively, ran significant third party campaigns. That also might help account for the fact that both Wallace and Anderson lost support as Election Day approached. The potential for strategic voting in multiparty elections is also the best justification for banning the release of polling data in the final weeks of campaigns in countries like France.

3. So many polls are available in contemporary presidential elections that one suspects voters process the results through the lens of their current candidate preference and use polls much as a sports fan uses a scoreboard. Observers of presidential contests, like regular viewers of professional basketball, know that almost no lead is insurmountable. In this respect, Michael Dukakis was no different than the Miami Heat, a team that frequently loses after holding large leads, and George Bush was no different than the Los Angeles Lakers, who won despite an early 29-point deficit during the 1988 NBA playoffs.

4. There are, of course, exceptions to the degree to which the critical factors affect each type of election. For example, some congressional elections stimulate wide interest and some gubernatorial elections do not. This discussion and the ordinal relationships suggested in Figure 5.2 speak to general tendencies.

5. Paid campaign staff probably belong in a separate category because their contractual obligations to a campaign and the informal mores of professional campaign workers discourage switching preference among candidates until the initial candidate one supported is elected or eliminated.

6. Yet another reason poll results do not play a critical role in presidential general elections is the fact that strategic contributors are legally excluded from direct participation. Although the recent emphasis on "soft" money provides opportunities for their participation in *party* spending, the over $50 million from the Federal Treasury given to major party candidates greatly reduces the *necessity* for candidates to tap into the financial-viability nexus in presidential general elections.

7. The discussion of "scenarios, standards, and benchmarks" in F. Christopher Arterton (1984, pp. 143-192) explores the way campaigns work to set and achieve expectations.

8. Benefits also come from unexpected sources: While former North Carolina Governor and Duke President Terry Sanford was running for the U.S. Senate in 1986, the Duke basketball team reached the NCAA Final Four. In the aftermath, Sanford's personal popularity ratings with voters in the state improved significantly.

9. For reference, even if one presumes the 100 participants were randomly selected and, therefore, "representative" of voters in Omaha, it should be noted that the range of possible sampling error for a sample of 100 is plus or minus 10 points.

References

Arterton, F. C. (1984). *Media politics: The news strategies of presidential campaigns*. Lexington, MA: Lexington.

Bartels, L. M. (1988). *Presidential primaries and the dynamics of public choice*. Princeton, NJ: Princeton University Press.

Brady, H. E., & Johnston, R. (1987). What's the primary message: Horse race or issue journalism? In G. R. Orren & N. W. Polsby (Eds.), *Media and momentum: The New Hampshire primary and nomination politics* (pp. 127-186). Chatham, NJ: Chatham House.

Brams, S. J. (1978). *The presidential election*. New Haven, CT: Yale University Press.

Jacobson, G. C. (1980). *Money in congressional elections*. New Haven, CT: Yale University Press.

Jacobson, G. C., & Kernell, S. (1983). *Strategy and choice in congressional elections* (2nd ed.). New Haven, CT: Yale University Press.

Patterson, T. E. (1980). *The mass media election: How Americans choose their president*. New York: Praeger.

6

Public Attitudes About
News Organizations,
Campaign Coverage, and Polls

MICHAEL W. TRAUGOTT

Editors and reporters look forward to presidential campaigns because they provide some of the best content for news coverage. Although the inherent newsworthiness of campaigns and elections has always been present, the patterns and style of coverage have changed dramatically over time. And one of the most visible and significant of those changes has been the incorporation of the results from polls and surveys as a routine part of the coverage (Crespi, 1980; Gollin, 1980, 1987).

This trend has been viewed as both a blessing and a curse, depending upon whether one is a producer or consumer of the news (Kovach, 1980; Ladd, 1980; Von Hoffman, 1980). These perceptions depend in some degree upon the phase of the presidential election campaign during which the polling results are being reported (Traugott, 1985). Both the quality of the data and their possible impact on the electorate vary in terms of the number and visibility of the candidates—in the primaries versus the general election—and the voters' interest in the campaign. And an important factor in how poll results are evaluated and what kind of impact they have depends on whether they are used as part of routine reporting of the campaign up through election

AUTHOR'S NOTE: The views presented in this chapter are solely those of the author.

day or whether they are used to project the winner on election night (Sudman, 1986; Tuchman & Coffin, 1971).

The 1988 presidential campaign represented just the latest in a string of campaigns since the 1960s in which the use of polls increased and the quality of coverage was affected by the availability of more survey data. As part of a significant effort to study and report upon press coverage of the campaign and voters' response to it, the Times Mirror Company commissioned the Gallup organization to conduct a series of surveys during calendar year 1988 as part of a project titled "The People, the Press, & Politics."[1] In conjunction with results of earlier studies dating back to 1985, these surveys provide an important perspective on how the public evaluated the media's performance during the 1988 campaign, including the work of pollsters.

This chapter reviews the findings from the recent Times Mirror surveys in terms of some of the concerns the public has been expressing about the influence of news organizations on the presidential nomination and election process. Particular attention is devoted to the role of polls and pollsters, distinguishing between preelection polls that track the relative standing of the candidates and those polls used by networks on election night to project the winner of the race. It concludes with a call for more empirical research on the ways polls may affect candidate preference as well as voter turnout.

Politics, Polls, and Press Coverage

Presidential campaigns are inherently newsworthy because they involve a contest for the highest office in the land, decided on a schedule that is relatively well known in advance. The campaign encompasses all of the standard criteria of newsworthiness (Graber, 1988) in that it involves a conflict with high impact and with well-known figures. Events take place both on an organized daily schedule and in an established chronology of important dates along the way. The caucuses and primaries, conventions, debates, and Election Day itself permit editors and producers to allocate resources to coverage in a rational and cost-effective way. The participants in the process—or their principal staff members—are willing sources for reporters, even if they won't always speak on the record.

There are characteristic patterns in coverage of presidential campaigns that have been observed through systematic empirical studies since the 1970s (Marshall, 1983; Patterson, 1980; Robinson & Sheehan, 1984). These studies show that coverage tends to emphasize the conflictual elements of the contest, focusing upon who is ahead or behind ("horse race" coverage) and the strategies each candidate will have to employ for the remainder of the contest (Arterton, 1984). At various points in the campaign, but especially during the primaries, the amount of coverage that candidates get varies with their success in securing votes and delegates and affects public assessment of their viability and electability (Brady & Johnston, 1987). And the tone of the coverage also varies with how well the candidates do, frequently in relation to how well they are expected to do.

Because of the disproportionate emphasis on these types of news, a common complaint is that coverage of the issues suffers. Despite the fact that it is difficult to describe how much of each type of coverage is "enough" to ensure a well-informed citizenry by Election Day, there is an underlying assumption that more attention should be devoted to coverage of the candidates' issue and policy positions. Reporters (and their editors) frequently complain that the new styles of campaigning, in which the candidates emphasize broad themes and their personal qualifications, preclude more issue coverage because such discussion and debate does not take place among the candidates themselves.

Given these tendencies in press coverage and their relation to contemporary campaign styles, polling provides an important reportorial tool to supplement "horse race" journalism. Here a useful distinction can be drawn between those who conduct polls for major media organizations and editors and reporters from other media organizations who are responsible for incorporating poll results into their political coverage. Those who conduct their own surveys argue that independent control over the content of their questionnaires—deciding for themselves what is newsworthy—is an important justification for what they do. Editors and producers in these news organizations argue that this control over content distinguishes them from those who report survey results released by major independent polling firms or by the candidates. This would be a more compelling argument if it had been clearly demonstrated that the content of the press coverage emanating from these two groups of media organizations was considerably different in qualitative terms. But, in both cases, there is a tendency for the poll-based stories to lead with the "trial heat" numbers that indicate who is ahead or behind.

The use of polling is even more compelling given the tendency toward "precision journalism" that is currently extant in the profession (Meyer, 1973). The use of polling data lends a semblance of objectivity to the reporting, based upon the statistical terminology used to describe the data collection methods and the implied precision of the numerical representation of percentages computed from the data. But this belies the fact that, leaving the details of sampling and respondent selection methodology aside, reporters are writing about concepts like "Reagan Democrats" or "committed supporters" that may be either conceptually flawed or based upon the flimsiest of operationalizations from survey questions.

The "average reader" has neither the methodological training nor the inclination to conduct a serious or sustained evaluation of polling results in any given election campaign. Recent research suggests that both the general public and media elites believe that preelection polls are usually accurate in their estimates of the outcome (Kohut, 1986; Roper, 1986). Although polls in general are viewed as a good thing, there has been a concern among media elites that the reporting of poll results interferes with the political process (Kohut, 1986).

The most serious question raised by the use of polls in campaign reporting is their impact on the electorate. Given the proliferation of polls in current campaign coverage, at least in the number of references to polls if not the actual number of polls conducted by national organizations, in conjunction with a growing political science literature that shows the effects of voters' perceptions of candidate viability and electability on their eventual vote choice (Bartels, 1988), it seems clear that a review of purported "underdog" and "bandwagon" effects is in order.

To the extent there is a crisis of confidence in the public's evaluations of press coverage of campaigns and the use of polls, it is now centered on assessments of the appropriateness and utility of "exit polls" conducted by TV networks on Election Day for the purpose of projecting the winner. There is a clear uneasiness among voters that these media projections violate their individual right to make a private decision that will have an impact on the electoral process. This gets aggregated to a normative concern about the integrity of the political process itself or the intrusion of television networks on it when they use exit polls in this fashion.

All of these questions were addressed anew in "The People, the Press, & Politics" survey project. In the discussion that follows, the broad outlines of the study are described, followed by a presentation of some of the main findings that relate to public attitudes toward press coverage of the campaign and the role of polls and pollsters. In the concluding section, the significance of these findings and their meaning for the 1992 campaign are discussed.

The Times Mirror Survey Project

Dating back to 1985, Times Mirror has had an interest in exploring and understanding several of the observed inconsistencies in public opinion regarding the American media and their performance in reporting various kinds of news stories. Beginning with a general survey of attitudes toward the press and eventually focusing upon special topics such as the press's coverage of terrorism and what became known as the Iran-Contra affair, the Gallup Organization was engaged to measure and analyze the public's views on these issues.

One of the central findings of the earliest study (Times Mirror, 1986) involved an explication of "the riddle of two-mindedness" by which the public affords high ratings to the press as an institution but at the same time has substantial reservations about many areas of its performance, including coverage of specific stories. A natural extension of this work was to focus upon press coverage of the 1988 presidential campaign—in a general way, as a venue for the special coverage that the presidential selection process engenders by nature of its newsworthiness, and, on occasion, by looking in detail at public reaction to stories that involved particular conflicts or generated unusual debate and criticism. There were notable examples of the latter during the 1988 campaign, including the press's reporting of Senator Gary Hart's liaison with Donna Rice, then Vice President George Bush's confrontational appearance on the *CBS Evening News* with Dan Rather, and the selection of Senator Dan Quayle to form the Republican ticket.

The broad outlines of the Times Mirror survey project provided several opportunities to pursue repeated public assessments of press performance during the campaign as well as to measure reaction to breaking news stories. A substantial element of the project involved the use of a new typology of the American electorate, developed by the Gallup Organization, to explain the dynamics of candidate preference and eventual voting behavior during the campaign (Ornstein, Kohut, & McCarthy, 1988). The generation of the typology was based upon a lengthy series of questions, usually administered in hour-long face-to-face personal interviews with probability samples of the adult population in the United States. In all, the Times Mirror survey program conducted under the heading "The People, the Press, & Politics" involved surveys with six independent samples as well as two reinterview surveys conducted on the telephone. More than 14,000 Americans were asked their opinions about politics in general and about the 1988 presidential candidates and their campaigns.

A substantial amount of information was gathered on the public's evaluation of press performance during the campaign, including assessments of the influence of news organizations on the candidates' success in securing their parties' nominations and eventually winning the election; the amount of coverage of campaign events; the influence of advertisers and pollsters during the campaign, including both campaign consultants and media polls; and election night projections of winners based upon "exit polls" of people leaving their voting places. These data are discussed and analyzed in the following sections.

There are a number of general points that should be kept in mind in what follows. Although the American public may have relatively strongly held views about what appropriate press behavior is—or at least what they are willing to tolerate in the behavior of the media—the Times Mirror surveys, as others, consistently show that the public does not understand very well or very clearly how reporters go about their work. And this is the genesis, as well as the explanation, of the riddle of two-mindedness.

For example, the media as an institution generally receive high marks for the "watchdog" function they serve at the same time that individual reporters are excoriated for invading the privacy of public figures, including politicians. This derives from a lack of public understanding of what "enterprise" in reporting means and of how hard reporters have to work at times to extract information from reluctant politicians. In the same vein, the media are evaluated positively for their "surveillance" function in keeping the public abreast of how the presidential campaign is progressing but criticized for projecting winners on election night before all citizens have had a chance to cast their votes in privacy, uncontaminated on the West Coast by information about how their eastern counterparts have already voted.

Negative public reaction will not automatically translate into government action, regulation, or policy changes. Nor should it, because of the very safeguards of freedom of the press that are built into the American political system by the U.S. Constitution. A certain amount of dynamic tension between the press and the public must be taken as a given, understanding that it will inevitably have an effect upon the credibility of the media and, ultimately, their public support.

Public Evaluations of 1988 Campaign
Coverage, the Polls, and Pollsters

The Times Mirror surveys measured public attitudes toward general and specific elements of press coverage of the 1988 presidential campaign in five areas: (a) the influence of news organizations on who was nominated and who was elected president, (b) the amount of coverage of the campaign, (c) the influence of advertisers and pollsters as well as evaluations of pollsters, (d) evaluations of reporting who was ahead and behind in the polls, and (e) the projection of winners on election night.

With a great deal of consistency across the various stages of the campaign, the American public was concerned about the influence of news organizations on which candidates became the presidential nominees or became president. With five measurements taken between November 1987 and October 1988, most Americans (more than half in four of the surveys) indicated that news organizations have "too much" influence. There was a decline in the proportion offering this response through the end of the primary process, from 59% to 49%, but a majority expressed equivalent concern about news organizations' influence on which candidate would be elected president at the end of the general election campaign (see Table 6.1).

Concern about the influence of news organizations was most likely to be expressed by the best educated and most politically sophisticated members of the public, including those who were most likely to follow public affairs and were most knowledgeable about politics. Self-described Republicans and Independents were more concerned about the role of news organizations than were Democrats.

Public concern about the influence of the media did not arise from the amount of campaign coverage they generated. About six in ten of those surveyed indicated they thought that news organizations were giving "about the right amount" of coverage to the campaign, while only one in five found it excessive (see Table 6.2). Assessments of the job that news organizations were doing in covering the presidential campaign were generally positive, but these job ratings declined across the campaign. By the time of the postelection interview, one in three voters (30%) gave news organizations a rating of "only fair" for the job they had done in covering news about the presidential campaign in 1988 (see Table 6.3).

TABLE 6.1 Concern About the Influence of News Organizations on Candidate Success

Date of Survey	Too Much (percentage)	Right Amount (percentage)	Too Little (percentage)	N
November 1987	59	31	5	(1,501)
January 1988	51	37	4	(2,109)
May 1988	49	41	4	(3,021)
August 1988	54	41	1	(1,000)
October 1988	58	36	3	(2,006)

NOTE: Exact question wordings are given in the Appendix. Percentages do not add to 100% because "don't know" responses are excluded.

TABLE 6.2 Perceptions of Quality: Amount of 1988 Campaign Coverage

Survey Date	Too Much (percentage)	Right Amount (percentage)	Too Little (percentage)	N
November 1987	21	58	16	(1,501)
May 1988	24	62	7	(3,021)

NOTE: Exact question wordings are given in the Appendix. Percentages do not add to 100% because "don't know" responses are excluded.

At the end of the campaign, voters were asked if they were the editor of their local newspaper would they increase or decrease the coverage of the 1992 presidential campaign or state and local campaigns. In both cases, slightly more than half said they would leave it "about the same"; but respondents were twice as likely (35% to 18%) to indicate a preference for increasing coverage of state and local campaigns (see Table 6.4).

The issue of pollsters and their influence on the presidential nomination and election process was confounded in the 1988 campaign by separate public debates about the role and influence of private pollsters who serve as campaign consultants and provide strategic advice, as opposed to "media pollsters" who collect and disseminate data for public consumption as part of the news-making process. Americans were equally divided as to whether

TABLE 6.3 Perceptions of Quality: Ratings of News Organizations' Campaign Coverage—1988

Survey Date	Excellent (percentage)	Good (percentage)	Only Fair (percentage)	Poor (percentage)	N
May	14	57	19	3	(3,021)
August	20	43	23	12	(1,000)
October	14	46	30	9	(2,006)

NOTE: Exact question wordings are given in the Appendix. Percentages do not add to 100% because "don't know" responses are excluded.

TABLE 6.4 Recommended Level of Coverage for the 1992 Campaign

Recommendations	Presidential Campaign (percentage)	State and Local Campaigns (percentage)
Increase	18	35
Decrease	22	8
Leave about the same	57	56
N	(2,325)	(2,325)

NOTE: Exact question wordings are given in the Appendix. Percentages do not add to 100% because "don't know" responses are excluded.

or not private pollsters and advertising consultants had "too much influence" or exerted "about the right amount of influence" on who got the nomination or was elected president. But members of the most politically sophisticated groups in the electorate—those best educated and most politically active and involved—were the most likely to be concerned about their influence (see Table 6.5).

After the election was over, however, voters were asked to "grade" various participants in the campaign process for the role they played. They assigned the highest grades to themselves and to George Bush, closely followed by the Republican party. At the next level, they assigned approximately the same grades to Michael Dukakis and "the pollsters." Lower grades were assigned to "the campaign consultants"; the voters were divided into two groups in assigning grades to "the press." One in eight of the voters (13%) gave the pollsters an "A" for their conduct during the campaign, and another three in

TABLE 6.5 Perceptions of the Influence of Advertisers and Pollsters on Which Candidate Becomes President

Date of Survey	Too Much Influence (percentage)	Too Little Influence (percentage)	About the Right Amount (percentage)	N
January 1988	38	5	45	(2,109)
October 1988	43	8	44	(2,006)

NOTE: Exact question wordings are given in the Appendix. Percentages do not add to 100% because "don't know" responses are excluded.

ten (29%) gave them a "B." The low grades assigned to the press for their performance during the campaign seemed to reflect long-standing negative attitudes toward certain forms of press behavior among various groups in the electorate. Republicans and Bush voters gave the press lower grades than did Democrats and Dukakis supporters, and those with high levels of education were less likely to assign high grades as well (see Table 6.6).

Late in the 1988 campaign, respondents were asked to assess the value of reporting who was ahead in the polls. Nearly one-half of those surveyed (47%) held the opinion that such reporting did not improve the coverage of the election, compared with less than four in ten (38%) who felt it did. Only 7% volunteered that they thought it had no effect. By a similar plurality, respondents were also likely to believe that such reporting is "a bad thing for the country" as opposed to a "good thing" (45% compared with 38%). In conjunction with earlier findings reported above, it was not so much a question of the accuracy of the results that was being called into question but the intrusiveness of the continual presentation of the "trial heat" results—the reporting of who is ahead and behind—that was the source of concern (see Table 6.7).

Although popular assessments of pollsters and polling through the course of the campaign were relatively positive, and the public was ambivalent about the publication of poll results before the election, public sentiment took on a distinctly more negative tone when questioning turned to election night projections of the outcome of the presidential race by television networks. The increasing use of "exit polls" has been one consequence of rapid technological change in the areas of vote tabulation, data collection and processing technologies, and the application of the latest survey methods to the design of studies of voters as they leave the polls. As a matter of evolving

TABLE 6.6 The Voters' Grading of the Conduct of Campaign Participants

Campaign Participant	A	B	Assigned Grade (in percentages) C	D	F	MEAN G.P.A.
The voters	19	30	28	10	7	2.47
George Bush	15	34	26	13	11	2.29
The Republican party	11	34	31	12	10	2.24
The pollsters	13	29	29	12	11	2.22
Michael Dukakis	9	29	40	13	7	2.20
The Democratic party	7	26	45	13	7	2.13
The campaign consultants	5	20	37	14	8	2.00
The press	8	22	33	19	16	1.87

NOTE: Exact question wordings are given in the Appendix. Percentages do not add to 100% because "don't know" responses are excluded.

TABLE 6.7 Attitudes Toward Reporting Who's Ahead in the Polls

Question	Percentage
Does reporting who's ahead improve coverage or not?	
improves coverage	38
does not improve coverage	47
has no effects	7
	(N = 2,325)
Is reporting who's ahead a good or bad thing for the country?	
good thing	38
bad thing	45
neither	12
	(N = 2,325)

NOTE: Exact question wordings are given in the Appendix. Percentages do not add to 100% because "don't know" responses are excluded.

network policy, the use of this information on election night has changed over time as well (as noted in Chapter 4 by Mitofsky). This issue has been a recent source of contention since the early call by NBC News of the 1980 presidential election and the move by all three networks to use exit poll results for projections in 1988.

In the Times Mirror postelection survey, one-quarter (24%) of the nonvoters indicated they had heard the results of Election Day polls, and 7% of the self-described voters said they had heard such results *before* they voted. Because of the constitutional issues involved, Congress and representatives of major media polling organizations have been unable to reach an agreement about how to deal with the reporting of such results on election night. However, federal legislation to bring about uniform poll-closing hours in the 48 contiguous states is again under consideration (Bonafede, 1989).

In the first Times Mirror survey in 1985, one of the coverage situations that respondents were asked to evaluate involved election night projections of presidential election winners. Slightly more than half of the respondents said this was an issue that concerned them. Using "split half sample" procedures to ask the question in two different forms, generally similar results were obtained by asking about actions the government might take or about self-imposed censorship by the networks (see Table 6.8.) A substantial majority of respondents (72%) indicated that it was more important that networks should not report such results if they discourage voting, while only one in five (18%) indicated they thought it was more important that networks have a right to tell their viewers who has won the election as soon as they think they know. About half (51%) felt the government should *not* allow early projections, while 42% said the position of no government involvement "in deciding when and how to report about elections" was closer to their own. In each case, half the respondents (54% and 51%, respectively) indicated that the reporting of election night projections was an issue that concerned them. Although measurement of the extent of public concern about this issue is subject to variation due to the form in which the question is posed, the magnitude and valence of the public's concern is clear (as noted in Chapter 7; see also Table 6.8.).

Conclusions

The Times Mirror surveys demonstrate the public's ambivalence toward the role and influence of news organizations in the presidential selection process, with a healthy dose of skepticism about the appropriate role for polls as an element of campaign coverage. These data should serve as a red flag for journalists and pollsters alike because they raise the prospect of a loss of public support for the use of polls as an integral part of reporting on political campaigns. This is only a cautionary note, because reporting policies in news

TABLE 6.8 Attitudes Toward Media Projections of Election Winners

Question	Percentage
The role of the government	
Government should not allow	
early election projections	51
Government should not get	
involved	42
	(N = 1,049)
The role of the networks	
Networks should not report	
because it discourages voting	72
Networks have a right to report	
the projected winner	18
	(N = 1,055)

NOTE : Exact question wordings are given in the Appendix. Percentages do not add to 100% because "don't know" responses are excluded.

organizations should not be driven by public opinion any more than they should be by advertisers, for example. Nevertheless, the maintenance of public credibility and approval in news organizations is an important goal because it ultimately will ensure independence and freedom from excessive regulation.

One potential problem for news organizations and journalists is that those who are most likely to be concerned about the nature of contemporary political reporting, the role of polls in general, and the potential effects of network projections are the best educated, most politically sophisticated, and most active citizens. This means that they are also the most likely to make their views known to both media and political elites and to demand change. Although there may be no scientific or legal basis for responding to demands for change from these activists, news organizations are likely to be subjected to extended pressure from these readers and viewers.

Given the current state of methodological advancement, the debate centers not on such factual matters as whether the polls are right or wrong, that is, whether they are providing accurate or misleading information. Rather, the issue involves a contest of normative positions that pits news organizations' rights to collect and disseminate information without any prior restraint or control against the public's concern about the intrusiveness of data about who is ahead and behind on their decision-making process through the course of the campaign. Part of the problem arises from the proliferation of polls, or at least the public's perception that there has been an increase in the number conducted or in the frequency with which they are being cited in news reports. Some of this concern could almost certainly be alleviated if the reporting of poll results were less preoccupied with "horse race" treatment of who is ahead or behind and more devoted to explaining the dynamics of the campaign and the relationship between citizens' policy and issue concerns and the candidates' responses to them.

Many voters differentiate between the use of data by the networks and print journalists as Election Day nears, although this distinction may not necessarily exist clearly and independently in the minds of the vast majority of the public. At the very conclusion of the campaign, the greatest levels of concern focus on the use of exit polls by the networks to project winners on election night, before everyone has voted.

It remains an empirical question as to what difference the reporting of poll results makes, how this may vary at important stages of the campaign, and how it is related to the size of the lead the polls are showing. But the prospect of such effects, particularly as they may affect levels of voter participation, can create public doubt about the integrity of the electoral process.

This suggests that a two-pronged approach is needed. On the one hand, more research is needed to explicate the relationship between public knowledge of and attitudes toward polls during the campaign and the voters' preference for candidates. And, on the other, some form of self-restraint by news organizations is indicated in the frequency of their polling efforts and the way in which they report the results. In combination, this will preserve confidence in the process and maintain levels of participation in it.

Appendix: Selected Questions from the Times Mirror Surveys

In general, how would you rate the job news organizations have done in covering news about the presidential campaign in 1988: excellent, good, only fair, or poor?

GO88334   October 1988   Q. 602

How much influence do you feel news organizations have on which candidates becomes presidential nominees ["candidate becomes president" after the nominees are known]: too much influence, too little influence, or about the right amount?

GO88002	January 1988	Q. 56
GO88174	May 1988	Q. 502
GO88334	October 1988	Q. 603

And how about advertising consultants and pollsters? (IF NECESSARY, PROMPT: How much influence do you feel advertising consultants and pollsters have on which candidates become their parties' presidential nominees? ["candidate becomes president" after the nominees are known] Would you say they have too much influence, too little influence, or about the right amount?)

| GO88002 | January 1988 | Q. 57 |
| GO88334 | October 1988 | Q. 604 |

So far, do you think news organizations are giving too much coverage to the 1988 presidential campaign, too little coverage to the campaign, or the right amount?

| GO88174 | May 1988 | Q. 503 |

Some people feel that the government should require that the TV networks make no projections on the outcome of elections on election night until the polls have closed and everyone has voted. Others feel that the government should not be involved in deciding when and how to report about elections. Which position is closer to your opinion?

| GO85108 | June 1985 | Q. 57 |

What's more important—the right to report or not to discourage voting?

| GO85108 | June 1985 | Q. 57 (Form II) |

In your opinion, does the reporting of who is ahead in the polls improve the press coverage of the election, or not?

| GO88334 | October 1988 | Q. 607 |

In your opinion, is the reporting of who is ahead in the polls a good thing or a bad thing for the country?

GO88334   October 1988   Q. 608

During this campaign, did you feel you learned enough about the candidates and the issues to make an informed choice between Bush and Dukakis, or did you find it difficult to choose because you felt you did not learn enough from the campaign?

GO88177   November 1988   Q. 12

Students are often given the grades A, B, C, D, or Fail to describe the quality of their work. Looking back over the campaign, what grade would you give to each of the following groups for the way they conducted themselves in the campaign?

First . . .

The press	The Republican Party	Michael Dukakis
The pollsters	The Democratic Party	The voters
The campaign consultants	George Bush	

GO88177   November 1988   Q. 14

If you were the editor of your local newspaper four years from now, would you increase, decrease, or devote the same amount of space to coverage of the *presidential* campaign?

GO88177   November 1988   Q. 15

How about the amount of space devoted to *state and local campaigns*? Would you increase it, decrease it, or leave it about the same?

GO88177   November 1988   Q. 16

Note

1. The Times Mirror Company, a highly integrated information company with interests in broadcast and cable television, publishes books, magazines, and several newspapers, including the *Los Angeles Times, Newsday,* and *New York Newsday* and the *Baltimore Sun* newspapers. Its specialized periodicals include the *National Journal.* Through its vice president for public affairs, Donald S. Kellermann, it has long been active in producing information to stimulate

public discussion of important issues concerning the role of the media in contemporary life. Times Mirror has recently opened a Center for Press & Public Policy in Washington, D.C. Additional information about their surveys can be obtained by contacting Mr. Kellermann, Director of the Center, at 1875 Eye Street, N.W., Washington, D.C. 20006.

References

Arterton, F. C. (1984). *Media politics: The news strategies of presidential campaigns.* Lexington, MA: Lexington.

Bartels, L. M. (1988). *Presidential primaries and the dynamics of public choice.* Princeton, NJ: Princeton University Press.

Bonafede, D. (1989, May 20). The networks' call. *National Journal,* pp. 1242-1244.

Brady, H. E., & Johnston, R. (1987). What's the primary message: Horse race or issue journalism. In G. R. Orren & N. W. Polsby (Eds.), *Media and Momentum.* Chatham, NJ: Chatham House.

Crespi, I. (1980) Polls as journalism. *Public Opinion Quarterly, 44,* 462-476.

Gollin, A. E. (1980). Exploring the liaison between polling and the press. *Public Opinion Quarterly, 44,* 445-461.

Gollin, A. E. (1987). Polling and the news media. *Public Opinion Quarterly, 51*(Suppl.), 86-94.

Graber, D. A. (1988). *Mass media and American politics* (2nd ed.). Washington, DC: CQ Press.

Kohut, A. (1986). Rating the polls: The views of media elites and the general public. *Public Opinion Quarterly, 50,* 1-10.

Kovach, B. (1980). A user's view of the polls. *Public Opinion Quarterly, 44,* 567-571.

Ladd, E. C. (1980). Polling and the press: The clash of institutional imperatives. *Public Opinion Quarterly, 44,* 574-584.

Marshall, T. (1983). The news verdict and public opinion during the primaries. In W. C. Adams (Ed.), *Television coverage of the 1980 presidential campaign.* Norwood, NJ: Ablex.

Meyer, P. (1973). *Precision journalism.* Bloomington: Indiana University Press.

Ornstein, N., Kohut, A., & McCarthy, L. (1988). *The people, the press, & politics.* Reading, MA: Addison-Wesley.

Patterson, T. E. (1980). *The mass media election: How Americans choose their president.* New York: Praeger.

Robinson, M. J., & Kohut, A. (1988). Believability and the press. *Public Opinion Quarterly, 52,* 174-189.

Robinson, M. J., & Sheehan, M. (1984). *Over the wire and on TV.* New York: Russell Sage.

Roper, B. W. (1986). Evaluating polls with poll data. *Public Opinion Quarterly, 50,* 10-16.

Sudman, S. (1986). Do exit polls influence voting behavior? *Public Opinion Quarterly, 50,* 331-339.

Times Mirror. (1986). *The people & the press.* Los Angeles.

Traugott, M. W. (1985). The media and the nominating process. In G. Grassmuck (Ed.), *Before nomination: Our primary problems.* Washington, DC: American Enterprise Institute for Public Policy Research.

Tuchman, S. & Coffin, T. E. (1971). The influence of election night television broadcasts in a close election. *Public Opinion Quarterly, 40,* 315-326.

Von Hoffman, N. (1980). Public opinion polls: Newspapers making their own news? *Public Opinion Quarterly, 44,* 572-573.

7

Public Reactions to Polling News During the 1988 Presidental Election Campaign

PAUL J. LAVRAKAS
JACK K. HOLLEY
PETER V. MILLER

The use of sample surveys to conduct preelection and exit polls has become a major part of the coverage given by the news media to presidential elections. Some even claim that the "horse race" aspect of these polls (i.e., which candidate is leading) has become *the* major focus of the media's campaign coverage. Regardless of whether one agrees with this extreme view, it is obvious that findings from preelection and exit polls have been given considerable attention by the American media in their coverage of recent national elections. This is especially true of the national dailies and the television networks, which currently do most, if not all, of their own election polling.

A concern, of course, is whether a catch-22-like principle is operating. By first measuring and then reporting on public opinion about which candidate is leading, are the media affecting the subsequent opinions and behaviors on which they are reporting? And evidence from scientific research would

AUTHOR'S NOTE: In addition to our own work on the questionnaires used in the study reported here, we would like to acknowledge the suggestions from several of the other contributors to this book, especially Dr. Michael W. Traugott.

suggest that this *is* likely to occur. In both the physical sciences and the social sciences, it is an accepted principle that, in measuring something, the measurer, by the very measuring process itself, may affect what is being measured—both at the time the measurements are made and thereafter. In most cases in science, though, considerable effort is taken to minimize the likelihood of this measurement "bias," and/or the effect is reasoned to be "so small" that it is not considered important.

But just the opposite process takes place in the realm of election polls, the news media, and elections. The media's reporting of election poll results does exactly the reverse of suppressing their possible effects on subsequent public opinion and behavior. Instead, if knowing how others say they are going to vote changes how some people vote (or, at least, how they "say" they will vote), then, by publicizing poll results, the media are enhancing the chance that whatever effect *might* occur *will* occur.

With this concern in mind, the use of polls in presidential election news coverage over the past few decades (compared with the first half of the twentieth century) has emerged as a "story" in and of itself. A number of journalists as well as media critics and other scholars have addressed the scope and nature of the role of poll findings in election news coverage. But this discussion has often clouded the distinction between the election surveys themselves and the media's reporting or misreporting of the findings.

Many media observers appear not to question the claim made by some that the use of polls played a larger role in the 1988 national election coverage than in earlier presidential elections. Yet, a content analysis we conducted of the front pages of four major newspapers (the *Chicago Tribune*, the *Los Angeles Times*, *The New York Times* and the *Washington Post*) for the four months prior to the elections in 1984 and 1988 indicated that there was an 11% *decrease* in the proportion of page-one presidential campaign stories that focused on the results of preelection polls. The actual number of preelection poll stories also was *down*—20%.

Although major newspapers may not have increased the number or proportion of prominent news stories they ran about the 1988 election that focused on poll results, we suspect that a "big change" may have taken place at smaller newspapers and television stations throughout the nation. Were we to conduct a content analysis of the use of polling news by smaller media organizations, we would expect to find a sizable increase across the last two decades as the effects of the computer revolution and the use of social science research methods by journalists ("precision journalism") have become more widespread. Indirect evidence for this hypothesis comes from a national survey of daily newspapers conducted in 1989 (reported in Chapter 10), which found that 40% of the nation's daily newspapers are now directly involved in political polling, either conducting election surveys themselves and/or contracting for them. Thus it is not at all surprising that many people felt they were being bombarded by poll results in 1988.

Anticipating this as an issue that merited scientific study, we began planning a research project in April 1988 to measure the public's exposure and reactions to the media's use of polling in their coverage of the developing 1988 presidential campaign. Our purpose was to gather reliable information about a subject on which there has been a lot of talk and speculation but little hard data. The research we planned, and are reporting in this chapter, was part of our larger commitment to study this topic, which included our 1989 symposium (see Chapter 1) and this book.

We wanted to learn what the public thought about the media's use of polls in covering the 1988 presidential election, and we wanted to do it in a way that would allow us to study it *as it was occurring*. Thus, we decided to conduct a survey of adults whom we would interview both before and after the November 1988 election. Prior to the election, we would ask them about their exposure to preelection polls in the media and what they thought of this type of news. After the election, we wanted to see whether their attitudes toward the media's use of preelection polls had changed and what they thought about the television networks' use of exit polls to project a winner on election night. We also wanted to gather information that would help us make some estimates about the possible influence of these polls on voter turnout and voting in the 1988 presidential election.

As will be explained in detail in this chapter, our findings include the following:

- The public had a fairly high interest in campaign news, and most people thought they were adequately informed.
- The vast majority of those we surveyed thought the media had treated George Bush and Michael Dukakis fairly, although perceptions changed somewhat after the election.
- The preelection polls that the media used to report horse race stories provided information to which the majority of the public attended. Nearly everyone knew Bush was ahead in the polls. Two out of three adults reported they were interested in news stories that contained preelection poll results, and a similar proportion said they found the news informative, although few said it was useful in helping them decide which candidate would get their vote.
- Although the majority of adults had some faith in the accuracy of preelection polls, there was also evidence of some skepticism.

- A large proportion of the population regarded the polls as harmful to the political process. This was especially true of the exit poll projections used by the television networks to project a winner on election night. In fact, a majority of Americans felt so negative about this that they favored legal restrictions against the media conducting this type of research.
- Perhaps most important, we found evidence to suggest that preelection polls have an effect on how some people vote and on whether some citizens even turn out to vote.

For those readers without a lot of interest in social science methods, we recommend that the following section should at least be skimmed. For others who want to learn the details of our research methods before proceeding to our findings (page 156), we have tried to include enough information to satisfy this interest.

Survey Methodology

The telephone survey conducted for this project was funded by Northwestern University's Medill School of Journalism, Northwestern's Institute for Modern Communications, and the Northwestern University Survey Laboratory. All the data collection was carried out by the Survey Laboratory's professional interviewing staff at its centralized telephone facility using standardized telephone interviewing procedures.

Panel Design

A two-wave panel survey was conducted with a national probability sample of 1,103 adults who were interviewed during the five weeks prior to the 1988 election: October 2, 1988, through November 6, 1988. Each of these persons was "randomly" selected from the adult members of her or his household using a standard version of the "last birthday" respondent-selection technique. Of the 1,103 respondents interviewed prior to the election, 940 (i.e., 85%) were successfully reinterviewed during a three-week period after the election: November 10, 1988, through December 2, 1988. The survey's overall degree of precision (i.e., margin of error) was plus/minus three percentage points.

Sampling was done via random-digit dialing (RDD), a standard technique that allows telephone interviews to be conducted with households throughout the nation regardless of whether a household's telephone numbers is listed or unlisted. Given that approximately 95% of the nation's households have a telephone, RDD affords the most cost-effective manner of reaching a highly representative cross-section of the American public.

In the case of our survey, a two-stage sampling procedure was employed, with stage 1 sampling used to identify approximately 250 telephone area code/prefix/suffix combinations (i.e., the first eight digits of a ten-digit long-distance telephone number) that reached residential households throughout the nation (*including* Alaska and Hawaii). These numbers were then used in stage 2 to generate the actual pool of telephone numbers that were dialed to reach the 1,103 respondents.

A total of 2,585 RDD numbers were processed in stage 2. A number was called as many as ten times if it rang but was never answered, or if an eligible household was identified and the designated respondent was unavailable but did not refuse to cooperate. Overall, about one-third of the telephone numbers (31%) were found to be "nonworking" or "nonresidential" at the time they were first dialed and thus were dropped from the sampling process.

Of the other 1,777 telephone numbers, 239 (or 13%) reached households that refused to participate in the survey. In another 308 cases (or 17%), the telephone rang but was not answered during the 10 separate calls on different days and at different times (experience with RDD surveys indicates that many of these numbers are actually nonworking numbers but have no message that informs a caller of that fact). In another 127 cases (or 7%), an eligible respondent was not, or could not be, interviewed because he or she was never available at the time of the call, was not English speaking, was ill, or was on vacation.

From the standpoint of representing the opinions of the American public, the quality of this sample is quite good. In conservative terms, the 1,103 respondents represent 62% of the telephone numbers that "may" have reached a household. Eliminating the 308 numbers that were never answered (none of which had answering machines connected), the 1,103 completions represent a response rate of 75%. Comparing the sample of 1,103 with the total number of completions plus the total number of refusals (239) yields a response rate of 82%. All of these rates are reflective of what credible surveys should achieve.

For the postelection wave, only 163 of the 1,103 preelection respondents were not reinterviewed. Thus, of the original respondents, 11% simply could not be contacted during the postelection survey field period (e.g., not home, out of town, sick, or number changed), and only 4% refused to participate. Overall, compared with the 940 (85%) who were reinterviewed, these 163 adults were slightly more likely to be Blacks and those with less formal education. Neither of these differences was of a magnitude to suggest any meaningful misrepresentation of public opinion as measured by our postelection sample.

Questionnaire Content

The questionnaires that were used in both the preelection and the postelection surveys were developed carefully and thoroughly pilot-tested. Given the financial resources that were available for this survey project, we were limited to developing preelection and postelection questionnaires that would take approximately 10 minutes to administer. The content of the questionnaires included a robust set of standard items on voting intentions and background and demographic factors. In addition, items were developed to measure a wide range of aspects of the public's exposure and reactions to the 1988 preelection and exit polls and other presidential campaign news reported by the media. These included items measuring awareness of these polls, recall of poll results, interest/attention to polling news, value of polling news, credibility of polling news, influence of poll results, and a test sequence to assess the public's understanding of the margin-of-error concept.

Furthermore, to test for the effects of preelection polling news on voting intentions, an experimental variation of the voting-intention item was employed during our preelection interviewing. For a random half of those interviewed each week, interviewers first told the respondent which presidential candidate was leading in the most recent polls that were being reported by the news media *and then* asked the respondent for whom he or she would vote. During each of the five weeks prior to the election, the actual wording of this "experimental" version was changed to reflect the most recent poll results. For the other random half, interviewers simply asked about voting intentions *without* mentioning recent poll results.[1]

For the test sequence used to assess a respondent's understanding of "margin of error," all respondents were first asked how well they understood the concept. Then, with the exception of those who responded that they did not understand it at all, each respondent was given an actual test to determine whether he or she could correctly apply the margin of error concept in a hypothetical poll situation.

Analytic Approach

The data were weighted to adjust for variations in the preelection sample due to several factors. These included the number of telephone lines per household, the number of adults per household, gender, age, race, education, income, and region of residence. This weighting procedure is a standard statistical technique that makes a survey's findings a more accurate estimation of the entire adult population than would be the case without weighting.

As presented in the following sections, a variety of multivariate statistical procedures were used to analyze the data. In addition to reporting simple percentages, multiple regression analyses were used to identify a statistically significant "profile" of individual differences in the way different items were answered. For the technically sophisticated reader, these results are reported only for those independent variables (i.e., the demographic and background factors) that had significant beta weights ($p < .05$), while controlling for (a) the importance of the election outcome to the respondent, (b) whether or not the respondent was registered to vote, and (c) which version of the preelection questionnaire had been administered.

As reported below with additional detail, the experimental variation we employed with the voting-intention item allowed us to use several statistical procedures to test for possible "bandwagon" and/or "underdog" effects. In particular, one approach used was to develop a statistical model of the kinds of people who intended to vote for each candidate, using *only* the registered voters who were *not* first told of the recent poll results before being asked about their voting intentions. This model was then applied to the group of registered voters who *were* told about recent poll results; this was done to predict which candidate they would have voted for had they not been "exposed" to our experimental item manipulation. Their "predicted" voting intention (from this statistical model) was then compared with their actual voting intention as reported during the interview, as part of our approach to testing for bandwagon and/or underdog effects. We urge readers to view these results as suggestive and not as a definitive test of whether a bandwagon effect and/or underdog effect occurred in the 1988 presidential election.

Findings

Attitudes Toward General Election Coverage

With the presidential campaign being the major news event of 1988, Americans were exposed to a tremendous amount of information in newspapers and magazines and on television and the radio. Some media observers argued that this level of coverage was "overkill" and that it lowered the public's attention to the election and its related issues.

Overall, though, our survey found a fairly high level of interest in news about the ongoing presidential election campaign. Only 13% of adults reported they were not at all interested, whereas half (51%) reported considerable interest (i.e., persons who said they were either "quite" or "very" interested). Those with the greatest interest in news about the presidential campaign were women, older adults, those with more education, those with more income, those more conservative on political issues, and people who identified themselves with a political party.

Not all Americans thought the election outcome would make a difference to the future of the nation, with about one in six (17%) saying it really wasn't very important whether Bush or Dukakis won. On the other hand, two-thirds of the public felt it was very important to the nation's future which of these men was the next president. Non-Whites, political conservatives, those from lower-income households, Republicans and Independents, and those with the greatest daily exposure to the news media were most concerned about who would win the 1988 election.

Overall, the vast majority of Americans (85%), said they were "informed" about the presidential campaign. Even allowing for some "social desirability" in this response, this is a further indication of the salience of the news coverage of the 1988 campaign. Those who were most likely to feel "uninformed" were adults with the least daily exposure to the news media, with less education, with less income, not employed, older, with no party affiliation, White, and female.

Prior to the election, most Americans thought the media were being fair in their treatment of both Dukakis and Bush, with about three in four Americans feeling that way. After the election, a slightly *smaller* percentage thought Bush had been treated unfairly (21% versus 26% feeling that way before the election), whereas a slightly *greater* percentage thought Dukakis had been treated unfairly (33% versus 27% feeling that way before the election).[2] These pre-post election differences were most likely due to some people adjusting their opinions in lieu of the election outcome. It is not surprising that party affiliation was highly correlated with the individual's assessment of the fairness of the media's coverage of the two candidates, as clearly shown in Table 7.1.

In addition to news coverage of the campaign, we all were exposed to a good deal of political advertising in the mass media. As part of our post-election interviews, respondents were asked about their exposure to and assessment of the presidential candidates' ads. Seven in ten (71%) said they had seen about the same number of Bush ads as Dukakis ads, 21% reported seeing more Bush ads, and 8% said they saw more Dukakis ads. (Those with

TABLE 7.1 Fairness of Media Coverage and Party Affiliation
and Timing of Assessment

| | Percentage Saying Media Coverage Was "Unfair" | | | |
| | Coverage of Bush | | Coverage of Dukakis | |
Party Affiliation	Preelection	Postelection	Preelection	Postelection
Democrat	17	16	32	42
Republican	40	30	22	26
Independent	24	24	23	31
Nonpolitical	19	14	26	24
All respondents	26	21	27	33

greater exposure to the Bush ads were more likely to say they saw "many more" Bush ads than were those with greater exposure to Dukakis ads likely to say they saw "many more" Dukakis ads.) More than four times as many Americans thought the Bush ads were more effective (47%) than thought Dukakis's ads were more effective (11%), with four in ten not regarding either candidate's ads as more or less effective. It is not surprising that upper-income Republicans were most likely to rate Bush's ads as more effective.

Summary. Our survey found that most Americans reported that they paid attention to and valued the information provided by the news media in covering the 1988 presidential campaign, in particular, those in the higher socioeconomic strata. But, as would be expected, these opinions typically were mediated by political affiliation.

Awareness of and Interest in Preelection Polls

A prominent proportion of the news coverage prior to the 1988 election was related to the results of surveys; some conducted *by* media organizations, some conducted *for* media organizations, and other independent surveys merely reported *in* the news media.

In the month before the election, seven of ten Americans (71%) reported that they were aware of "opinion polls" that were predicting who would win the presidential election. Furthermore, 95% of those who said they knew of such polls also were able to name George Bush as the candidate who was leading according to the polls.[3] Those Americans most likely to be aware of these opinion polls were more educated, older adults with the greatest daily exposure to the news media, those who were employed, people who defined themselves as politically conservative, and people who identified with a political party.

The public reported varying levels of interest in and attention to the news stories that covered opinion poll results on the Bush-Dukakis race. Whereas only about one-third (31%) said they were not interested in this type of news, 39% reported being "somewhat" interested and the remaining 30% indicated greater interest. An almost identical split was found by a follow-up item that asked about the amount of "attention" paid to such news stories: 29% said they basically did not pay any attention, 43% said they paid some attention, and 28% reported paying a fair amount of attention. Overall, those people most likely to closely follow poll stories were Republicans and those with the greatest daily exposure to the news media.

After the election, when asked to look back at the amount of preelection polling stories about the presidential campaign reported by the media, most Americans (66%) said the media had given too much play to these types of stories. Of others with differing opinions, 25% thought the amount of coverage had been "right," 4% thought it had been "too little," and 5% were undecided. Older adults, those with more education, and those with the greatest daily exposure to the news media were the ones most critical of the news media on this count.

Summary. Our survey indicated that most Americans were aware of the polling results reported in the news media before the 1988 election, and almost everyone knew that the polls were predicting that Bush was in the lead. Overall, citizens expressed somewhat varied sentiment about the extent to which they were interested in this type of news about the election. But there was a much clearer consensus of opinion that the media had used too many polling stories in their 1988 preelection coverage of the presidential campaign.

Credibility and Value of Preelection Polls

Given that most Americans were aware of the preelection poll results reported by the media and were at least somewhat interested in this type of news, what did the public think about the accuracy of the polls?

About half of the public (52%) reported that they generally believed the opinion poll results reporting who was leading in the presidential race, 38% said they generally did *not* believe them, and the remaining 10% did not feel strongly one way or the other. Providing further insight on the perceived credibility of the 1988 opinion polls, when asked how accurate they thought most of these polls were, only 13% of the public said they believed them to be "not at all accurate." The vast majority of the public attributed at least some accuracy to the polls; 60% said most of the 1988 presidential polls were "somewhat accurate," 20% thought most were "quite accurate," and 7% said "very accurate."

The level of credibility that Americans assigned to the 1988 opinion polls on the Bush-Dukakis race varied across demographic groups. Those *least* likely to believe the poll results during the month before the election were older adults, Blacks, Democrats, Independents, those without any political party identity, and self-defined liberals.

Compared with other types of news stories on the presidential campaign, a majority of the public (63%) thought polling stories were, in fact, "informative" as opposed to being "uninformative." Younger adults, people with less education, non-Whites, Republicans, Democrats, and Independents found news about polling results most informative.

With most adults saying that they found polling results credible and at least somewhat informative, what value, if any, did Americans place on this type of information in helping them decide which presidential candidate would get their vote?

Among registered voters, two-thirds (68%) stated that the preelection polling news was of no use whatsoever to them in making the decision. Even more striking is how highly correlated this assessment was with educational attainment. As shown in Table 7.2, as the educational level of respondents increased, the self-ascribed value of polling information in helping one make a voting decision consistently and markedly decreased.

An additional perspective on the "value" of preelection polls is provided by the finding that more Americans felt poll stories that reported "which candidate was leading in the race for president" *harmed* our political process in 1988 than felt this type of news *helped* the process. (This closely parallels results reported by Traugott in Chapter 6). Specifically, 44% thought preelection polls were at least somewhat harmful, whereas 36% found them useful; the remaining 20% did not view them as either harmful or useful.

Given the results of the 1988 preelection polls (i.e., George Bush *was* leading throughout the entire preelection field period of our survey), it is not surprising to find that Democrats were most likely to view the media's use of poll results as "very harmful," with 18% of Democrats feeling this way compared with only 5% of Republicans. Nevertheless, this assessment was not completely explained by party affiliation: There also were strong educational differences within the population, with college graduates most likely to view preelection polling news stories as harmful.

TABLE 7.2 The Value of Polling Information in Deciding Own Vote and
Level of Educational Attainment: For Registered Voters

Educational Attainment	Percentage		
	Not at All Useful	Somewhat Useful	Quite or Very Useful
Eighth grade or less (100)[a]	53	22	25
Ninth through eleventh grade (95)	57	22	21
High school graduate only(331)	66	23	11
At least one year of college (169)	74	20	6
College graduate only (116)	77	18	5
At least one year of graduate school (84)	82	16	2
All registered voters (897)	68	21	11

a. Number of registered voters in each educational subgroup appears in parenthesis.

Summary. Overall, Americans attributed at least some degree of credibility to the 1988 preelection polls on the Bush-Dukakis race. The public appeared to sense that the poll results reported by the media prior to the election were not always accurate but most often were. (By this, we do not mean to suggest that the public formed this judgment because of a true understanding of the technical—that is, "stochastic" or probabilistic—nature of sample surveys. Rather, the public seemed to have some "gut-level" feeling about the accuracy of most presidential preelection polls reported by the news media).

Public opinion about the effect of news about preelection polls on our political processes also varied, but a plurality of Americans believed that the media's reporting of the horse race aspect of these polls did more harm than good to the presidential election process.

Understanding the Precision of Preelection Polls

As noted above, the public appeared to have some sense that preelection polls were not always accurate in identifying which candidate was actually leading at the time a survey was conducted but, nonetheless, that the polls reported by the media on the Bush-Dukakis contest generally were accurate.

In an attempt to measure the public's understanding of the precision/imprecision of sample surveys, such as preelection polls, we included a *test* within our preelection questionnaire. First, respondents were told, "Sometimes when the media report the results of an opinion poll, they say that the poll has a 'margin of error' of so many percentage points." Respondents then were asked, "How well do you understand what this means?"

Now, one can rightly argue that any question that asks survey respondents to admit they might not know something may suffer from the effects of the common desire of people to present themselves in a positive light (i.e., the well-documented "social desirability" bias). Although this may have happened to some extent in our questioning, only one-third of the public (33%) responded that they understood the concept of margin of error "completely." In contrast, 36% said they understood it "only somewhat," 12% said "not really very much," and 18% admitted they did not understand it at all. (Young, White, upper-income, male college graduates with some political party identity were the persons most likely to say they understood "completely" what was meant by margin of error.)

With the exception of those persons who said they did not understand the concept at all, respondents were then asked the following test question, in which the actual percentages were varied (see Table 7.3):

> If an opinion poll, with a margin of error of plus or minus ___ percentage points, found that George Bush had ___ percent of the vote and Michael Dukakis had ___ percent, what conclusion would you draw about the election? Would you think Bush was actually leading, . . . that Dukakis was actually leading, . . . or that the race was so close that this poll could not accurately predict who was leading?

As shown in Table 7.3, there was considerable variation in the public's "accuracy" across the six versions of hypothetical item wording, which varied the Bush percentage, the Dukakis percentage, and the size of the margin of error. About eight in ten of those asked the first, second, and fourth versions of the question gave a correct response, whereas far less than half answered correctly to the other three versions.

On closer inspection of the actual responses given to each version (i.e., not whether the answer was right or wrong but which response choice was made), respondents were most likely to say that "this poll could not accurately predict who was leading," *regardless* of the actual percentages contained in the item wording. For those versions (1, 2, and 4) in which this response *was* the correct answer, the majority were correct. Yet, when this response was not the correct answer (versions 3, 5, and 6), the majority were incorrect. To us, it appears that in each of the versions of the item many people simply "guessed" that the hypothetical poll was not accurate enough to predict the leader regardless of which version they were asked rather than

TABLE 7.3 "Accuracy" on Margin-of-Error Test Question

Version	Item Wording	Percentage Correct[a]	Incorrect
1	Bush = 51%, Dukakis = 49%, M.O.E. = 2%	84	16
2	Bush = 52%, Dukakis = 48%, M.O.E. = 3%	81	19
3	Bush = 53%, Dukakis = 47%, M.O.E. = 2%	38	62
4	Bush = 53%, Dukakis = 47%, M.O.E. = 5%	81	19
5	Bush = 54%, Dukakis = 46%, M.O.E. = 4%	20	80
6	Bush = 46%, Dukakis = 54%, M.O.E. = 4%	19	81

a. Correct answers were as follows: version 1, too close to tell; version 2, too close to tell; version 3, Bush leading; version 4, too close to tell; version 5, Bush leading; version 6, Dukakis leading. In versions 5 and 6, the confidence intervals for Bush and Dukakis touch. We subscribe to the view that this situation should be interpreted as a lead for whichever candidate has the greater support.

reaching this conclusion due to an actual understanding of the margin of error concept.

Although this approach to investigating the public's understanding of survey precision may not be definitive, our findings suggest that most Americans probably do not have a good understanding of what margin of error means. Even respondents' self-assessment of their understanding (as measured by the previous item) was *uncorrelated* with test accuracy, as was educational attainment. (Of interest, women were significantly more likely than men to give a correct answer to the test item, despite men believing themselves to be more knowledgeable.)

Summary. As measured by this test sequence on margin of error, Americans did not demonstrate much of an understanding of the concept. These findings provide food for thought to those in the news media and academe who debate how much explanation should be presented about survey methods in news stories that report survey results. The results also reinforce the view that Americans have a long way to go before they adequately understand the limitations of information generated via sample surveys.

Effect of Preelection Polls on Voting Intentions and Election Expectations

Past research has found differing results on the long-standing question of whether preelection polls can influence voting behavior and thus the outcome of elections. Here it is not our intent to review that body of literature. Suffice

TABLE 7.4 Voting Intention and Experimental Condition
for Registered Voters

| | Experimental Condition | |
| | Control (N = 459) (percentage) | Treatment (N = 455) (percentage) |
Candidate Preference		
Support Bush	51.8	45.4
Support Dukakis	34.9	40.0
Undecided	13.3	14.7

it to say that some studies have suggested there may be a "bandwagon" effect, in which some persons appear to be influenced to vote for whoever is leading in the polls, whereas some other studies have found evidence for an "underdog" effect, in which some persons appear to be influenced to vote for whoever is behind in the polls. Still other studies have not found evidence for either type of effect.

To further test this issue, we incorporated an experimental design variation into the Bush/Dukakis voting-intention questions used in our preelection survey questionnaire. As mentioned earlier, a random half of those interviewed before the election were asked a standard voting-intention question, whereas the other half were first told which candidate was leading in the recent national polls reported by the news media and *then* were asked about their voting intentions.

At first glance at the results of this manipulation, there appeared to be no statistically significant effect on voting intentions when recent poll results were made salient immediately *before* asking persons how they would vote. This is shown by the percentages in Table 7.4; the differences shown in this table are within the size of the survey's sampling error and thus are *not* statistically significant. Therefore, they should not be interpreted as reliable evidence for one type of effect or another.

As we reported earlier, though, less educated Americans were most likely to say that news stories about preelection polls were "very useful" in helping them make their voting decisions (see Table 7.2). This suggested that educational differences might have "interacted" with our item wording manipulation. And, in fact, when the effect of the experimental manipulation was tested separately for persons of different educational levels, significant differences between the two versions *were* found.

Specifically, when persons who did not graduate from high school were told that Bush was leading in the polls—as he was during the entire field period in which our preelection survey was conducted—there was a significant *increase* in respondents' uncertainty about which candidate they would vote for, compared with those with similar levels of educational attainment but who were not told that Bush was leading (see Figure 7.1). This increase in uncertainty among those without a high school degree who were given poll information resulted in losses of fairly equal size for both Bush and Dukakis.

Unlike their less educated counterparts, high school graduates' uncertainty level did not change when recent poll results were made salient, as shown in Figure 7.2. Rather, when high school graduates (with no college experience) were told that Bush was leading in the recent opinion polls, a significant *decrease* occurred in support for Bush, with a comparable *increase* in support for Dukakis. This is an example of the classic underdog effect of supporting the apparent/expected loser.

Finally, for persons who had pursued their education beyond high school (regardless of whether or not they had earned a college degree), being told that Bush was leading in the recent polls had *no effect* on their reported voting intentions compared with their similarly educated counterparts for whom recent poll information was not made salient. As illustrated in Figure 7.3, the nearly identical proportions of Bush supporters, Dukakis supporters, and undecided voters under both versions of the voting-intention item is a testament to the oft-found pattern of better educated persons being more resistant to external sources of influence—in this case, being told (or reminded) about public opinion poll results showing Bush to be leading.

A statistical modeling of possible bandwagon and underdog effects. The following section presents the results of a statistical approach we used to further investigate the possibility of bandwagon and underdog effects. In reviewing these findings, the reader is reminded that, in addition to sampling error, there are many other potential sources of imprecision in survey data (e.g., respondents not always providing reliable responses) and that these sources could contribute in some unknown way to our specific findings. We say this to urge readers to use caution so that our findings will not be taken for anything more than what they are—informative, within the context of our experimental manipulation, but possibly not reflective of what happened in the actual election.

As we will report elsewhere in much greater detail, our methodological and statistical approach to measuring the possible impact of the "horse race" aspect of preelection polling news on the public's voting intentions provides

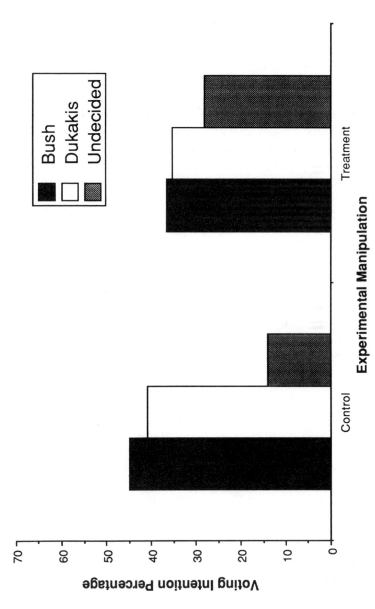

Figure 7.1. Effect of Media Polling Results on Voting Intentions for People Who Are Not High School Graduates

167

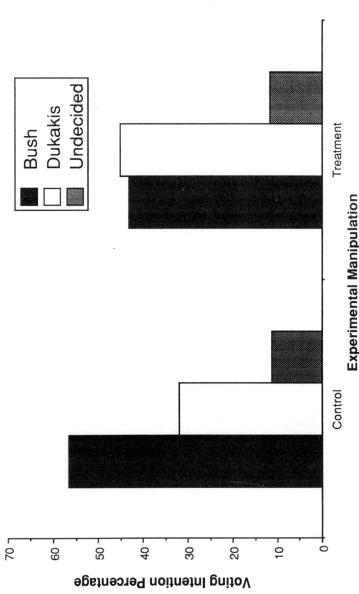

Figure 7.2. Effect of Media Polling Results on Voting Intentions for People Who Are High School Graduates with no College

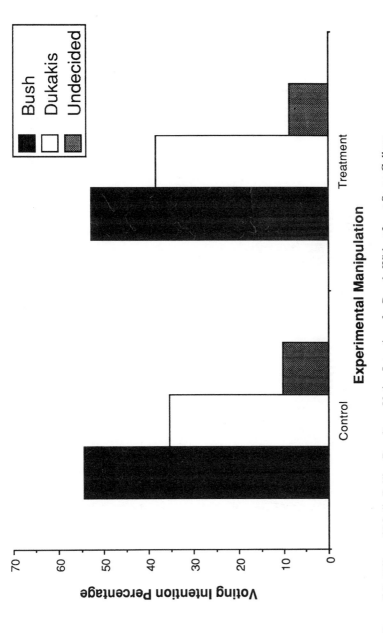

Figure 7.3. Effect of Media Polling Results on Voting Intentions for People With at Least Some College

169

a way to *disentangle* possible bandwagon and underdog effects. That is, in other studies, researchers have looked at the possibility that the effect of exposure to preelection polling news stories created *either* one type of effect *or* the other. Instead, we have reasoned that these two possible effects should be viewed *and tested* as separate phenomena—both of which could occur within an electorate during the same preelection period.

As such, past research that found evidence for an overall bandwagon effect may actually have measured a situation in which the bandwagon effect was of larger absolute magnitude than a companion underdog effect. Similarly, past research that found evidence for an overall underdog effect actually may have measured a situation in which the underdog effect was larger than a companion bandwagon effect. Finally, past studies that found no evidence for either effect (overall) may have obscured a situation in which both effects were of similar magnitude, thereby canceling each other out with a superficial appearance of "no effect."

With this reasoning, we began by employing a statistical procedure (discriminant analysis) that can be used to determine the best set of factors to accurately "predict" an outcome. In this case, the predicting factors used were personal demographics and background measures (e.g., gender, age, political party affiliation) gathered in the preelection survey from the registered voters in our sample, and the outcome measure was voters' intention to vote for either George Bush or Michael Dukakis.

This statistical procedure was first applied to all registered voters in our sample who were asked the control version of the voting-intention question sequence ($n = 459$), that is, persons who were *not* told about recent polling results. This analysis identified a set of demographic and background factors that significantly predicted whether the voter was a Bush supporter,[4] a Dukakis supporter, or undecided at the time of the preelection interview. This predictor equation was highly significant from a statistical standpoint, with an overall level of accuracy of 76% ($p < .0001$).

Next, the results of this first step were used to predict how the registered voters in our experimental condition ($n = 454$) *would have* expressed their preferences had they not been told first that George Bush was leading. That is, each of these persons was categorized as to whether he or she "should" have been a Bush supporter, a Dukakis supporter, or an undecided voter had he or she merely been asked his or her voting intentions without being also told of the recent poll results.

At the third step in this procedure, we compared how the registered voters in our experimental condition were *predicted to vote* (using the results from the previous step)—had they not been first told about the

TABLE 7.5 Predicted Versus Actual Voting Intention for Registered Voters in Experimental Condition

| | Actual Voting Intention | | |
Predicted Preference	Support Bush (percentage)	Support Dukakis (percentage)	Undecided (percentage)
Bush Supporter	67.7	18.5[a]	13.7
Dukakis Supporter	11.0[b]	76.5	12.5

a. The "underdog" effect.
b. The "bandwagon" effect.

recent opinion polls—with what they *actually said* in the preelection interview after they were told about the polls. This comparison is shown in Table 7.5.

Of those registered voters in the experimental condition who were predicted supporters of George Bush ($n = 250$), about one in five ($n = 46$) demonstrated the underdog effect by expressing a preference for Michael Dukakis after they were told that Bush was leading in the polls. (Of the 46 persons who showed the underdog effect, 93% reported in our post-election survey that they had voted for Dukakis on Election Day, compared with 99% of the predicted supporters of Bush who did *not* exhibit the underdog effect, who reported voting for Bush on Election Day.)

In turn, of those registered voters who were predicted supporters of Michael Dukakis ($n = 136$), about one in ten ($n = 15$) demonstrated the bandwagon effect by expressing a preference for Bush after being told he was leading in recent polls. (When interviewed after the election, 87% of these 15 persons said they had voted for Bush on Election Day, compared with 98% of those predicted supporters of Dukakis who did *not* exhibit the bandwagon effect, who said they had voted for Dukakis on Election Day.)

In terms of the absolute numbers of voters in our survey data base, the underdog effect, as measured by this methodological/statistical approach, represented three times as many persons as the bandwagon effect.[5] Looking back at the more superficial analyses of these data presented in Table 7.4 and Figures 7.1-7.3, one can see indications of an "overall" underdog effect for Dukakis. In Table 7.4, this trend was not statistically significant. When broken down by educational levels, it showed up only in the group whose highest level of educational attainment was a high school diploma, as shown in Figure 7.2.

With the use of a more sophisticated analytic approach, our findings suggest the possible occurrence of *both types* of effects but, in this case, of different magnitudes. If these "experimental" findings accurately portrayed what happened in the real election, one sees that, even with an underdog effect three times as large as a bandwagon effect, Bush's lead over Dukakis still was sufficient to win the election.

Our approach can also be used to form a profile of types of people most likely to exhibit the bandwagon or the underdog effect. Using another statistical procedure—multiple regression—we found that younger adults, those who did not identify with the Democratic party, and employed persons were most likely to demonstrate the bandwagon effect.

In contrast, "Reagan Democrats" and those without a political party affiliation, women, liberals, and unemployed and lower-income persons were most likely to demonstrate the underdog effect.

In addition to these demographic profiles, our data showed that voters who did not make their presidential choice until the later stages of the campaign (i.e., after September 1988), as reported in our *postelection* interviews, were the ones most likely to exhibit either the bandwagon or the underdog effect.

The public's expectations of the election outcome. Apart from the possible influence of preelection polling results on voter choice, it is almost indisputable that news stories about the horse race aspect of preelection polls are related to the expectations the public forms about the outcome of the presidential election.

When asked who they thought would win the election, the majority of Americans, throughout the six weeks prior to the election, said they expected it would be George Bush. As shown in Table 7.6, this proportion was not a steadily increasing trend as Election Day neared, but, in general, more people did expect Bush would win toward the end of the campaign than earlier in October; fewer thought Dukakis would win; and the proportion of "uncertains" remained fairly constant throughout this period.

From a demographic standpoint, those most likely to expect a Bush victory were males, non-Blacks, and Republicans. Furthermore, among the group not told recent poll results, those persons most likely to expect a Bush victory reported (a) having high awareness of preelection polls, (b) having knowledge that Bush *was* leading in the preelection polls, (c) being interested in news stories that reported poll results, and (d) believing these news stories.

Further evidence for the *direct* influence of preelection polls on the public's expectations was the finding that, prior to the election, those persons who expected Dukakis would win but who were administered our question-

TABLE 7.6 Preelection Expectations of the Election Outcome by Week of
Interview and Questionnaire Version[a]

Expectation	Percentage Week of					
	Oct. 2	Oct. 9	Oct. 16	Oct. 23*	Oct.30*	Nov 6.*
Control condition:						
Bush will win	57.6	59.9	75.5	79.6	62.4	77.9
Dukakis will win	21.6	20.6	10.9	2.7	15.9	0.0
Uncertain	20.8	19.5	13.6	17.7	21.7	22.1
Experimental condition:						
Bush will win	50.9	62.2	70.1	65.8	78.6	55.4
Dukakis will win	24.8	15.0	9.1	7.4	10.3	11.4
Uncertain	24.3	22.8	20.8	26.8	11.1	33.1

a. "Questionnaire Version" refers to which condition the respondent was in in the experimental manipulation of the voting intention question.
* Identifies a significant difference in expectations under the control versus the experimental conditions.

naire version in which they were told the recent polls results (thus they were told Bush was leading in the polls) were significantly *less* confident about a Dukakis victory than their counterparts who were not first "reminded" what the polls were saying. (The opposite effect was not observed—that is, persons who expected Bush to win, and who were reminded of recent polling results that he was in fact ahead, were *not* more confident of a Bush victory than those who were not reminded of the polls.)

Registered nonvoters and expectations of the election outcome. As is well known, a large percentage of eligible Americans do not vote in elections. Of this group, many are registered to vote but fail to do so for a variety of reasons. For the 1988 presidential election, approximately 89 million citizens voted (48 million for Bush and 41 million for Dukakis), approximately 25 million were registered to vote but did not, and approximately 48 million adults never registered.

Those persons in our survey interviewed after the election who said they were registered to vote but reported they did *not* vote (*n* = 86) were queried as to *why* they had not voted.[6] One in ten of these registered non-voters (11%) stated that their expectation of a George Bush victory influenced their decision not to vote. Furthermore, another one in ten (9%) said they thought this expectation "may" have contributed to them not voting. Together, this represents about one in five registered nonvoters who said they were, or may have been, influenced by the preelection polls' prediction of a Bush victory. Furthermore, we believe that this is quite likely to be an *underestimate* of the proportion of nonvoters who were so influenced, as it would be "socially desirable" for some respondents to deny that these expectations were instrumental in leading them not to vote.

With our findings about registered nonvoters in mind, it is interesting to project them to the general population and speculate about their possible effects on the outcome of the 1988 presidential election. In reviewing the following section, please note that we are *not* suggesting that this is what *did* happened in 1988; rather, these findings and the associated projections are illustrative of what *could* have happened.

Considering the precision of population projections from this size of subsample (plus or minus eight percentage points), these registered nonvoters who acknowledged they may have been influenced by their expectations of a Bush victory represented approximately 3 million to 7 million Americans. This, of course, is a very large number of potential voters; certainly large enough to change the outcome of a close race were these persons to exhibit different candidate preferences from those citizens who *did* cast their vote.

Overall, though, these persons in our survey who reported that they did not vote, at least in part because they expected a Bush victory, were evenly split in saying for which of the two candidates they would have voted. Thus these findings, albeit based on a very small subsample within our survey, suggest that the results of this election would *not* have changed had these 3 to 7 million Americans voted.

Who were these persons who apparently did not vote because they expected "the election was going to be a certain victory for George Bush and so it didn't matter much if you voted or not"?

Taking into consideration a host of demographic/background factors and information about these persons' exposure to and attitudes toward preelection polling news stories, it is especially interesting to find that these individuals were persons with high daily exposure to the news media and who had reported in our preelection survey that they found news stories with polling results on the Bush-Dukakis race to be "very informative."

Of further interest is the finding that, as a group, *all* of those in our sample who reported they were registered but did not vote (i.e., not just those who said their expectation of a Bush victory may have kept them from voting) gave the following candidate preferences: 47% for Dukakis and 34% for Bush, with 19% remaining undecided/uncertain. Taking these results (i.e., the 47% versus 34%, Dukakis/Bush split) and projecting them to what could have happened had all these persons (representing approximately 25 million Americans) who were registered but failed to vote actually voted this way, one can estimate that Dukakis may have received as many as 14 million more votes and Bush as few as 6 million more votes. Had this "extreme case scenario" occurred, and we acknowledge that the probability that this would have happened is extremely low, the popular vote could have yielded a Dukakis "victory" (a reminder that these are popular vote projections, not electoral college projections) with 55 million votes to Bush's 54 million.

Again, we want to remind readers that these population projects are speculative, given the many potential sources of imprecision inherent in all survey data, including ours. Nevertheless, they represent estimates taken from what we believe is a highly credible survey data base and are not numbers we merely "pulled out of a hat."

Summary. At a minimum, it seems safe (and logical) to conclude from our findings that news stories about preelection polling were a major determinant of the public's expectations of the 1988 presidential election outcome, that is, a Bush victory.

It remains for future extensive research to provide a more definitive analysis of whether or not news about preelection polls influences voting, turnout, and election outcomes. In the case of our survey, it was demonstrated that *both* an underdog effect and a bandwagon effect appeared to have occurred, at least within the controlled context of our experimental manipulation. Whether this also happened in the actual election is only speculation, but we believe the issue merits considerable and serious consideration by pollsters, journalists, and other media executives.

Of greater importance, our findings—that approximately 20% of registered nonvoters may not have voted because their awareness of preelection polling news stories made them think a Bush victory was a foregone conclusion—further reinforce the view that the media's reporting of the "horse race" aspect of preelection polls influences persons within the electorate and affects their behavior. Whether the effect of this influence is of a size or nature to change the outcome of an election remains debatable. If it does, it seems reasonable to assume that its size and nature may vary from election to election. This too will need to await further investigation, but, again, we believe it merits serious consideration by the media and the polling community.

Awareness of and Reactions to
Election Day Exit Poll Projections

Apart from the public's reactions to *preelection* polls, there has been a lot of attention given to the public's reaction to the way the television networks use Election Day exit polls to project a winner, oftentimes early in the evening—in fact, even before voting has ended in the western states. But before presenting our findings about these exit poll projections, it is important to make certain of the distinction between the exit polls themselves and the projections that are made with the aid of exit poll results by the television networks.

National Election Day exit polls for the presidential election have come to be the most comprehensive and reliable source of information about *who* voted for whom. This follows from the fact that no other reliable set of data has such large sample sizes, and thus no other set of data can be used to reliably break down the vote along many varied demographic and attitudinal factors. *The New York Times*, for example, printed a "Supertable" (see Chapter 2) within a few days after the 1988 election showing the detailed demographic makeup of the Bush and Dukakis vote.

For the most part, the public appears unaware of this aspect of exit polls. Instead, the public seems to equate exit polls with election night television projections of the winner. Thus it was this "projection" aspect of exit polls about which we gathered information in our postelection survey.

The findings of our postelection interviews indicated about four out of five adults (78%) watched at least some of the presidential election coverage on television the night of November 8, 1988. More of the people who watched reported viewing ABC (49%) than either NBC (43%), CBS (41%), or CNN (12%), with nearly a third (29%) watching more than one of the networks. Four-fifths of the persons who watched the election night coverage recalled that they had heard by 10 p.m. eastern time that George Bush was the projected winner—a time at which voting was still going on in the western parts of the nation.

What was the viewing public's reaction to the networks' projections when they first heard that a projected winner was being announced? Nearly half (46%) of the public reported it "displeased them that a projection was being made by the networks before all the voting was finished." Most of the others (42%) said it "didn't really matter to them," whereas 12% reported it had "pleased them." It is not surprising that Dukakis supporters were significantly more likely to report being displeased by the fact the networks had made an "early" projection, but even one-third of Bush voters said they were dis-

TABLE 7.7 Reaction to the Networks Making Projection by Reported
Presidential Vote

	Percentage	
Reaction to Projections	*Supported Bush*	*Supported Dukakis*
Pleased with networks	18.6	2.8
Neither pleased nor displeased	47.6	35.2
Displeased with networks	33.8	61.9

pleased (see Table 7.7). Apart from this difference between Bush and Dukakis supporters, better educated viewers were most likely to be displeased with the networks.

When asked *what* displeased them about the networks making projections, most "displeased" viewers felt it was unfair, especially to people on the West Coast, and that it may actually keep some West Coast residents from voting. In the words of a male high school graduate from Minnesota, "At 9 p.m. in the Midwest, people on the West Coast still have [time] to vote; they could be influenced that their vote would have no impact on the outcome." A female college graduate from Kansas explained she was displeased with the networks because she believed, "People don't vote on the West Coast and other (non-presidential) candidates don't get a fair shot." Even a middle-aged woman from Florida, where voting had ended before the projections were made, said, "We felt *our* vote didn't count."

Along these lines, when specifically asked what effect, if any, network projections had on "people in the West who hadn't voted," the majority of Americans (51%) felt they made residents of western states less likely to vote, compared with 27% who believed the "early" projections of a Bush victory had no effect and 11% who thought they made people more likely to vote. (In addition, 5% thought the effect was a mixed one, and 6% were uncertain of the effect.) Those most likely to think network projections dampened voting on the West Coast were older, employed, upper-income adults, those who identified themselves as Democrats or Independents, and those who *lived in the West.* (See Chapter 4 for a discussion of the effects of projections on voter turnout.)

Value of election day exit polls. With the finding that few Americans viewed the 1988 network exit poll projections positively, it is not surprising that we found that a majority of the public, 52%, felt the network projections were "harmful" to our political process. This compared with only 25% who regard these projections as "useful" and 23% who did not believe the projections had an effect on our political process. Better educated, older adults, those with the greatest daily exposure to the news media, and Democrats were most likely to view election night projections as "very harmful."

In addition to expressing displeasure with network projections, the 1980s have seen heated political debates on legislating against exit polling. In our postelection survey, the majority of Americans (52%) said they would favor a law "to restrict the media from projecting a winner in the presidential race on Election Day until all voting has stopped across the nation." In contrast, 42% said they would oppose such a law, at least in part because they believed "this would be a violation of freedom of speech that is guaranteed by the First Amendment." (The remaining 6% of the public was undecided.) Those most likely to favor a law restricting early projections were lower-income, older adults, Blacks and Whites, Democrats, and persons with the greatest daily exposure to the news media.

Summary Overall, our findings on the public's reaction to exit poll projections reinforce the view that, at a minimum, the networks have created a public relations problem for themselves. Whether or not exit poll projections affect voter turnout and thus election outcomes will await further study, although, as Mitofsky notes in Chapter 4, there is no compelling evidence at this time. But, for now, there *is* considerable evidence that a sizable percentage of Americans do not view them favorably.

Summary and Implications: What Was Learned?

When we began planning for this study in early 1988, we anticipated that there would be considerable debate about the manner in which polls would be used by the media to cover the presidential election campaign. Our expectation was based on what had taken place over the last few decades, as polling and the media's usage of it became entrenched in presidential campaign coverage. And a heated (negative) discussion *did* take place toward the end of the 1988 campaign, and it has continued. This includes the controversies surrounding "problems" with the preelection polls and exit polls used by the media to cover the New York City mayoral and the Virginia gubernatorial elections in November 1989.

Within this context, it has been our intent to gather empirical evidence to provide reliable information to add to the discussion. We believe our 1988 preelection-postelection panel survey has done this, in particular, because it gathered data on these issues *as they were occurring*. Rather than merely speculating about how the public reacted in 1988 to this type of news coverage, as was done by some "informed" media observers, the results we have presented can clarify much of the debate and allow it to be concentrated on what, if anything, the media should do in planning for the use of polling in future coverage of election campaigns.

As we have shown, during the 1988 presidential election campaign, the American public had a fairly high level of interest in campaign news, and most people felt they were adequately informed about the candidates—at least to their own satisfaction. The vast majority judged the media's treatment of Bush and Dukakis as fair. All in all, these are quite good marks for what journalists did in 1988.

News about preelection polls that the media used to report the "horse race" aspect of the presidential campaign *was* noticed by the vast majority of Americans. In fact, nearly everyone who was aware of preelection polls knew that George Bush was "leading."

Two-thirds of the public said they were interested in news stories that reported preelection poll results about the Bush-Dukakis race. A similar proportion said they found this type of news informative, but very few went as far as saying that this information was useful in helping them make a decision about whether to vote for George Bush or Michael Dukakis. Those most likely to acknowledge that the preelection polls helped them make their voting decision were the less educated among the population.

Although most of the public appeared to place at least some faith in the accuracy of the 1988 preelection polls, there was other evidence that the poll results and related news stories also were viewed with a fair amount of skepticism. If our test of the public's comprehension of margin of error is reflective of Americans' basic understanding of surveys, then we would assign most Americans a failing grade. This lack of understanding of survey research indubitably contributed to the public's mixed (and somewhat inconsistent) view of 1988 preelection poll credibility. To many Americans, if not most, the "mystique" of sampling a few hundred or even a few thousand persons to accurately represent the opinions of tens of millions just doesn't seem possible, despite experience from the outcome of many previous elections that preelection polls often are extremely accurate.

It is not surprising that it was the better educated segment of the population who were most discriminating about election polling news. Also, among those persons with strong political party ties, there appeared to be some tendency to like the bearer of "good news" and dislike the bearer of "bad news." In 1988, with the media reporting that the polls were showing Bush in the lead, it was traditional Democrats who often reported the most negative views toward this type of news.

The concern the public has about election polls is highlighted by the large proportion that regarded them as *harmful* to the political process that elected the president. This was especially true for the public's assessment of, and personal reactions to, the television networks' exit poll projections on election night: Here, a majority of Americans reported feeling so negative that they said they would favor legislation to restrict the media's right to conduct this type of survey research. Although much remains to be debated about whether or not the media's use of election polls is good or bad for our democracy, our results clearly show where the majority of Americans currently stand on this issue.

We also have presented considerable evidence that addressed the issue of whether or not the media's reporting of preelection polls directly or indirectly influences voter turnout, actual voting, and thus, possibly, the outcome of elections. At least within the controlled context of our experimental test of the bandwagon effect and the underdog effect, we found evidence for both in the 1988 presidential election, and, as logic would suggest, it was those voters who made up their minds late in the actual 1988 campaign who were most likely to demonstrate either effect.

Although we readily acknowledge that our findings may not reflect the actual behavior of those who voted in the 1988 election, it seems reasonable to suggest that, if our "minor" manipulation was able to demonstrate effects, then so should the real world—with all the "power" of preelection poll news bearing full weight upon voters.

Yet, with even greater implications than that of possible bandwagon or underdog effects, there are the not-unexpected findings that public expectations of a George Bush victory were closely linked to Americans' exposure to preelection poll news and that *these expectations* contributed directly to the decision of many registered voters *not to* vote. To the extent that this actually happened in 1988, we firmly believe that this potential influence of polling news on the electorate does *not* aid our democracy. Our findings suggest several issues that merit further consideration regarding changing the way the media view their use of election polls and survey research in general, for that matter.

We have presented considerable evidence that the media's use of poll findings in their 1988 presidential election coverage received a good deal of attention from the public. Simultaneously, there is considerable evidence to suggest that Americans do not understand the strengths and limits of election polls and thus are not "well-informed consumers" when it comes to processing this type of news/information. As such, the media need to seriously rethink their responsibility to educate the public about news that is generated via surveys. For the public to make full and proper use of the type of news the media present about election polls, and, thereby, to become a better informed electorate, the public needs to be exposed to more critical reporting about "good" and "bad" surveys and about the intelligent use of news that is generated via survey research. (See Chapter 9 for further discussion of this issue.)

Of course, for this to occur, we will need to see an improvement in the media's own understanding of valid survey methods and the valid use (i.e., reporting) of information that is generated via valid surveys. Too often, inadequately trained reporters, editors, and producers are expected to run news that comes from "sources" (in this case, sample surveys) about which they can't or don't think critically. This must change, with more than mere lipservice given to the need for change.

It also follows from this reasoning that the media must set higher standards for the survey research methods they use on both the editorial/news *and* the business/advertising sides of the industry (and many in the polling community should set higher standards for the research services offered). This is especially needed at the media outlets through which the majority of Americans directly receive their news. It simply is not enough for the *Washington Post* and ABC News, for example, to do it right; we need greater discretionary use of survey research shown by less prominent and smaller dailies, weeklies, consumer and trade magazines, and radio and television stations. Until journalists and the polling community get their own houses in order, the public's ability to make intelligent use of the information generated via surveys, such as election polls, is not likely to improve.

Furthermore, and if only from the standpoint of self-interest, media executives, other journalists, and pollsters should realize that in an age of declining survey response rates coupled with the looming threats new telephone technologies pose for telephone survey validity, the quality (i.e., accuracy) of the information that can be gathered via sample surveys for the media's own needs will deteriorate *unless* something is done to stem the tide of nonresponse.

Until the public better appreciates the value of valid survey research methods and the information these methods are capable of generating, we are likely to see a continued erosion of the public's participation in survey research, thereby diminishing the likely accuracy of surveys, such as election polls. We suggest media executives put into practice the maxim, "An educated consumer is our best customer."

In addition to these broad implications—but not unrelated to them—media executives, other journalists, public policy makers, pollsters, and other scholars must continue to monitor, study, and discuss the manner by which elections poll findings are used by the media to cover political campaigns and elections. Although one might argue that neither the bandwagon nor the underdog phenomenon can or should be "countered" in a democracy built upon freedom of speech, the media should not look the other way in acknowledging their responsibility to improve and increase the participation of the American electorate in our presidential and nonpresidential elections.

To the extent that preelection poll news and exit poll projections decrease this participation, the media should mount a serious, cooperative, and aggressive campaign to counter this trend. If the media want to continue the unrestricted freedom to use and report election polls as newsworthy information, they also *must* take responsibility to work to counter the negative fallout that may result from this type of news.

Notes

1. The wording of the standard or "control condition" item is as follows: "If the presidential election were being held today, would you vote for the Republican ticket of George Bush and Dan Quayle or for the Democratic ticket of Michael Dukakis and Lloyd Bentsen?"

The wording of the "experimental condition" item during the first week of October 1988, which we modified each week to reflect the most recent opinion polls, is as follows: "*Most recent opinion polls are showing that Bush has a slight lead over Dukakis.* If the presidential election were being held today, would you vote for the Republican ticket of George Bush and Dan Quayle or for the Democratic ticket of Michael Dukakis and Lloyd Bentsen?"

The wording of the experimental version of the voting-intention question was changed for each of the weeks of the field period. In week 1, the wording referred to Bush's "slight lead"; in week 2, it was Bush's "very small lead"; in week 3, it was Bush's "consistent, small lead"; in week 4, it was Bush's "consistent, clear lead"; in week 5, it was Bush's "consistent, sizable lead"; and, during the final weekend before the election, it was Bush's "consistent, but narrowing lead."

2. About 10% of those interviewed before the election did not have an opinion of the fairness of the media's coverage of Bush and Dukakis; about 5% expressed no opinion in the postelection interview. The percentages presented in the text are for those respondents who offered an opinion.

3. This was measured by the following item: "Do you recall if Bush or Dukakis is currently leading in those polls?" Throughout the field period of our preelection survey, Bush was in fact leading in most, if not all, of the major polls.

4. Supporters of Bush or Dukakis also included those persons who were "leaning" toward either candidate.

5. For the statistically oriented reader, we want to readily acknowledge that the "predicted" scores contain an "error" component. That is, the respondents in the off-diagonal groups in Table 7.5 (i.e., those representing the bandwagon and underdog effects) are not exact (i.e., error-free) measures of each group's actual size. Of note, though, their off-diagonal counterparts in a table

including *only* those in the *control* version of our questionnaire (i.e., those for whom polls results were not made salient) showed proportionately fewer persons in the "bandwagon cell" and the "underdog cell"; that is, the distribution of "prediction errors" in the original model differed from the pattern observed in Table 7.5.

6. The respondents used in these analyses were all persons who reported in the *postelection* survey that they were registered to vote but did not. Elections studies have consistently found that some people do not give accurate answers when they are asked whether they are registered, and whether they voted, and, if so, for whom they voted. We acknowledge that this is a likely source of some error in our data.

With this in mind, though, it is worth noting that in the *preelection* survey, 78 of these 86 respondents reported that they were registered to vote, 7 others reported that they planned to register before the deadline for the election, and only 1 of these 86 persons giving information in the preelection survey possibly inconsistent with his postelection response regarding his registration status. Yet, even in this one case, the respondent may have registered to vote even though he reported in the preelection survey that he did not intend to do so.

Although this does not prove that these people all gave accurate post-election responses, it is worth noting that the information gathered during the two waves of the study had an extremely high level of internal consistency.

8

Media Use of Preelection Polls

FRANK W. McBRIDE

The 1988 presidential campaign confirmed two realities about preference polls and their use in the media. The first reality is that there is no shortage of preelection polling in a presidential election year. A compilation of Bush-Dukakis trial heats, put together by *Public Opinion* magazine, included over 100 measures that were taken during the last six months of the campaign. Because *Public Opinion* might not have learned of all presidential preference polls, the actual number could have been higher. The 1988 campaign also provided daily tracking of the presidential race from Labor Day through November—an added bonus for the most voracious consumers of public opinion data.

The second reality is that use of preference poll results by the various media is a controversial practice. One concern is that the widespread interest in public opinion data, a manifestation of "horse race" coverage of elections, detracts from the central issues of campaigns. Another concern, the concern that will be the focus of this chapter, is that publicly released polls, as used by the media, have a significant and inappropriate influence on the behavior of political actors—the candidates, the campaign organizations, voters, and nonvoters.

Although there is just cause for concern, this concern is often directed away from the true problems that can be caused. First, "fear of polls" is often manifested in the assumption that the voting public mindlessly uses poll data to choose a candidate—that a bandwagon effect improves the public standing of the candidate that leads in the polls. In truth, experience refutes such an effect among the voting public. The real impact is more serious. Instead of scaring away voters, poll results tend to scare away campaign contributors who might otherwise back the trailing candidate.

Another reason that concern is misdirected is that the controversy over polling hits an apex during the years of presidential contests and is aimed at the presidential contest. Media polls have minor effects on the presidential race after the nomination process, but considerable impact on subpresidential races. For this reason, the potential for public polls to influence the political system is a danger in 1990 and 1994 as well as in the next presidential year of 1992.

A primary goal of this chapter will be to show why a bandwagon effect among the mass electorate is not a major cause for alarm. At the same time, another goal will be to show how preelection polling can have a pernicious influence on the democratic process. A final goal will be to provide some suggested defenses against the future misuse and abuse of public polls so that they can inform the interested public within the confines of responsible journalism.

An Attempt at Reconstructing Reality

Before examining the pitfalls that the media frequently encounter when using preelection polls, it would be worthwhile to reconstruct the "true" standings of Bush and Dukakis during the final six months of the 1988 campaign period. Needless to say, the only true measure of ballot strength was taken on November 8 when over 90 million people turned up at the polls. However, a rough idea of where Bush and Dukakis stood, at any given point in time, can be estimated by averaging a number of polls that were taken during a short period of time.

During the last six months of the 1988 campaign, dozens of national preference polls were conducted—perhaps as many as one per day on the average. Because of this proliferation, many polls conducted in short periods of time could be averaged to find a more stable estimate of who was leading and by how much at different points in the campaign. These averages, when "trended," provide a relatively stable and plausible pattern of change in presidential vote preference rather than the abrupt and unexplained shifts shown by unique polls taken a week or two apart.

The first 18 points on the trend chart in Figure 8.1 are each based on a minimum of six polls. The poll results were compiled and reported in the November/December 1988 issue of *Public Opinion* magazine. To be

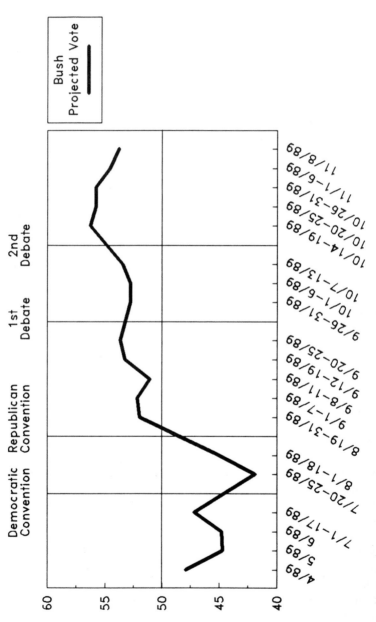

Figure 8.1. Bush Projected Vote (based on aggregate public poll results)

included in this analysis, polls had to be conducted by reputable and non-partisan organizations. They also had to include a minimum of 800 respondents and had to be based on representative national samples. As a result, each point on the chart is based on thousands of cases and a variety of polls rather than any one unique study. The last point of the chart is based on the actual November 8 results.

While this methodology is designed to account for the margin of error inherent in a single poll, it certainly cannot eliminate error. However, it should offer a more precise estimate of the presidential vote percentages that Bush and Dukakis would have received had the election been held during any of the time periods prior to the election.

The figures on the trend chart are plausible in light of actual campaign developments. It is a fair assumption that Bush would trail between April and the first half of July. The Republican nomination process essentially ended on Super Tuesday when Bush buried his GOP rivals in all primary states. Media attention was shifted to the still unresolved Democratic nomination process—a process in which Michael Dukakis began to emerge as the likely standard-bearer for his party.

Bush dropped to the low 40% range immediately after the Democratic National Convention (July 18-21, 1988) but quickly rebounded and passed Dukakis after the Republican convention (August 15-18, 1988)—an indication of the value of having the media spotlight to oneself. The analysis of aggregated poll results shows that, from Labor Day on, Bush always retained the lead.

A slowdown occurred after the first debate on September 25. Dukakis, in his first appearance with Vice President Bush, not only held his own but also, by the accounts of experts and the public alike, "won" the debate. Thus, during the following days, Bush slipped. After this short period of slippage, the Bush campaign got back on track.

Another period of slippage occurred during the final two weeks of the campaign when Bush came under fire for the negative tone of his campaign. The slippage continued through Election Day and ended at just under 54%. This final projected figure proved to be nearly identical to Bush's actual vote share.

Given that presidential campaigns traditionally start on Labor Day, there was much for the media to report during the two months leading up to Election Day—appearances, debates, tactics, gaffes, and so on. However, as the trend chart suggests, there was little true news regarding the possible outcome. Nonetheless, the misuse of poll results sometimes led to the creation of "news" when there was nothing new to report. Some of the reasons that this happened in 1988, as well as in the past, were poorly timed polls, misinterpretation of margin of error, and small sample size.

Timing

In politics, timing is supposed to count for a great deal. The same is often true of public opinion polls. An interesting example of how the timing of a poll can significantly influence (and distort) results occurred during the presidential election in 1984. During that year, it was generally acknowledged that Ronald Reagan would comfortably win reelection. Because speculation was never based on who would win, the major guesswork for students of politics concerned the number of states that Reagan would take on Election Day.

Despite the fact that polls were pointing to a Reagan victory, a midsummer poll actually placed Walter Mondale ahead of Reagan by two points (in effect, a statistical tie). The poll in question was taken immediately after Mondale's well-publicized and historic decision to place Geraldine Ferraro on the Democratic ticket. Given the enormous coverage of and widespread interest in this unprecedented choice of a running mate, Mondale might indeed have "moved the numbers." The problem is that his "lead" was a mere blip lasting perhaps 48 to 72 hours. Subsequent polls pointed to the inevitable Reagan victory.

The polling organization that conducted this study was probably pleased with its coup, but, aside from quickly fielding a poll and disseminating the results, there was little to boast about because the poll's validity was short-lived. Despite the questionable value of strategically timed polls, the media and their polling operations still show considerable zeal for fielding flash polls and reporting their potentially dubious results.

The enthusiasm for this practice was widespread during 1988. Although dozens of polls were conducted during the entire year, a large proportion were started soon after (within three days) of four prominent events—the Democratic convention, the Republican convention, and the two presidential debates. Although over 100 public polls were conducted during the last six months of the campaign, at least a quarter of them were fielded in only a 12-day period.

In all fairness, polls that follow major campaign events often capture genuine change but change that may be short-lived. For example, Bush's political recovery began with the Republican National Convention and the postconvention polls reliably indicated that he was back on track. On the other hand, poll measures taken immediately after prominent events may merely measure voting intentions through a prism of unbalanced media coverage or hype and hoopla that the electorate soon forgets or deems irrelevant.

In effect, it is often the case that polls become part of a self-fulfilling prophecy. The polls are conducted to monitor an expected change, actually show the expected change, and then are used to explain what has happened. However, it is often the case that "what happened" only happened for a short period of time—perhaps no longer than the few days during which the poll was conducted. For this reason, when dealing with such results, journalists' interests in the nature of the possible development must be tempered with a sensitivity to the potential longevity of the development. Again, measured change can always be genuine because a campaign is a dynamic process. But, taking a measure of public opinion can be like taking an individual's pulse. In both cases, readings can be incorrect after a flurry of activity. The safest bet for avoiding illusory poll results is to eschew data collected so soon after an event. It might be argued that such a practice slows down the process of reporting news. However, there is no crime in failing to report data that are not newsworthy.

Margin of Error

Newspaper stories that use poll results are often followed by little boxes that remind readers of the poll's margin of error and explain what it means. The electronic media often mention the "plus or minus" aspect of a result in passing. However, this acknowledgment of the inherent imprecision of poll data is often little more than a footnote—a footnote overshadowed by a story that treats the results as if they were chiseled in granite.

Information about sample sizes, margin of error, and so on is often treated like a statistical coda with little bearing on the news story. In truth, such information has to be taken into consideration when reporting poll results. The failure to do so has led to poor, misleading, and erroneous interpretations of results.

A common journalistic mistake is to use poll results to interpret randomness. For example, the margin of error for a simple random sample of 1,000 people would be plus or minus three percentage points. This would mean that, if a poll showed a candidate with 47% of the vote, the only conclusion that could be drawn with reasonable confidence would be that the candidate's true vote share ranged from 44% to 50%. Thus a subsequent poll showing the candidate with 44% of the vote might or might not indicate slippage of his or her support. While most journalists understand this, many are unwilling to acknowledge the possibility that voting preferences have not changed between the two polls. Often, the most fantastic explanations for these possibly meaningless shifts are offered for public consumption.

Another common, related misuse is to conclude that a candidate is winning (or losing) when, accounting for margin of error, there is no difference between the candidate and his or her rival(s). Perhaps the emphasis on "horse race" coverage demands that someone must be winning. However, a 47% to 45% poll lead must be declared a "statistical tie" unless the poll is based on a very large number of interviews (e.g., 10,000).

Sample Sizes

Lack of sensitivity to the margin of error issue often is manifested in the use of small overnight polls or figures that are based on one night's returns from a partially completed poll. While a poll based on a small sample size can certainly be accurate, there is greater reliability in larger studies. However, the desire to report figures often leads to the use of studies with small samples—as small as 300 interviews—that have twice the margin of error of a standard national poll.

A notable example of this occurred during the summer in 1988. ABC News reported two polls, conducted only days apart, which painted two completely different pictures of the presidential contest. One showed Bush and Dukakis tied, and the other showed Dukakis with a double-digit lead over Bush. Peter Jennings was at a loss to explain this discrepancy. The problem was that each poll had sample sizes of less than 400. After taking each poll's high margin of error into account, there might have been no discrepancy.

Effect of Media Polls on the Electorate: The Primaries

If publicly released polls truly affect voters, the most likely opening for such influence would seem to occur during the primary period. Given a number of little-known candidates who share one party label, voters can face considerable uncertainty. A poll would provide some information for reducing this uncertainty—a means of separating the "serious candidates" from the "also rans"—if voters actually felt that this "horse race" data were pertinent.

If poll results were truly influential during primaries, John Glenn, and not Gary Hart, might have served as the thorn in Walter Mondale's side in 1984's

Democratic nominating process. Polls taken during late 1983 and early 1984 showed Glenn and Mondale as having comparable potential for winning the Democratic nomination and doing battle with Ronald Reagan. The Iowa caucus results, where Glenn failed to distinguish himself from Rueben Askew, George McGovern, Ernest Hollings, and others, put the Ohio senator's campaign to a quick end. The Iowa results also put previous polling results into proper perspective.

A more likely hypothesis is that actual vote tallies taken during the primary process are more important than poll results as part of the voters' decision-making process. Perhaps the impact of actual results even eclipses that of poll results. One reason is that the candidates with the best finishes demonstrate genuine vote-getting ability as opposed to the soft support of preference polls. A second reason is that primary winners are rewarded with a disproportionate amount of media attention while the remaining candidates receive relatively little coverage.

Effect of Media Polls on the Electorate: General Election

The idea that the media might aid a bandwagon effect for a presidential candidate who leads in publicly released polls is persistent despite a lack of compelling evidence. In fact, if any effect truly exists, there might be an underdog effect for the candidate who is believed to be trailing.

Those who would subscribe to either hypothesis first have to assume that the electorate has a general sense of who is leading in the polls. There is no question that plenty of data were available for the voting public to make a judgement in 1988. Scores of national surveys were conducted between the close of the Republican convention in July and the eve of the election. And, as in the past, polls figured prominently in the coverage of the presidential contest.

While the number of polls was staggering, the more important question was the extent to which voters were aware of the findings. In general, voters were fully aware that Bush was leading as the campaign came to a close. A study conducted by Market Opinion Research for the Bush campaign on November 6 and 7 revealed that 86% of registered voters believed that Bush was leading Michael Dukakis in preference polls. Only 5% believed that Dukakis was ahead, 3% felt that the race was a tie, and 6% were unsure. (These findings are consistent with those reported in Chapter 7.)

The public's general assessment of the horse race accurately reflected the near unanimity of reputable, publicly disseminated studies. Therefore, because most voters knew how the horse race was going, the 1988 presidential campaign serves as an excellent laboratory for testing bandwagon and underdog effects.

Figure 8.1 shows that Bush's projected vote share, based on the aggregate poll results, generally climbed from the close of the Republican convention until it peaked in mid-October at 56%. This figure began to decline in late October to the Election Day figure of just under 54%. These findings certainly preclude any overall (surface) bandwagon effect as Bush, the apparent leader throughout the final two months of the campaign, actually lost some ground during the final two weeks.

These findings could point to an underdog effect. During the final days of the campaign, Dukakis was portrayed as making a spirited effort despite unfavorable odds. Market Opinion Research polls conducted during the final days of the campaign showed that many voters were impressed with the intensity of Dukakis's final push for support. However, although many voters were indeed attracted to Governor Dukakis's bid for a Harry Truman-style finish, there is mixed evidence that Bush's drop during the final two weeks might have been due to an underdog effect for Dukakis.

First, the Bush campaign was under fire for the tone of its advertising—advertising that many felt flew in the face of the "kinder and gentler" messages of the candidate. Second, during the final days of the campaign, Bush was being treated more like a president-elect than a candidate. The seeming inevitability of a Bush victory, and the proximity to the election, might have subjected him to more intensive voter scrutiny. Perhaps a small portion of his earlier supporters could not make the final commitment to a President Bush.

Instead, I would argue that, if there is a likelihood of a bandwagon or underdog effect, it would be with subpresidential-level races. In most cases, voters are less informed about these races than they are about presidential contests. Therefore, there is a possibility that voters would look for some means of cutting their information costs in order to make their ballot choice.

In reality, it is unlikely that any sizable proportion of voters use polls as a guide to choosing the probable winner. If they did, candidates who trailed in preference polls would be buried by a bandwagon effect. What often happens is that the trailing candidates exceed any expectations that polls might create—perhaps because of an underdog effect, but, more likely, because dormant partisans "come home" on Election Day.

The most relevant effect of media use of polling data is that, to many, it is disturbing at a normative level. A significant portion of voters believe that the political process is somehow subverted by a "democracy" of randomly selected individuals. There is a widespread belief that these polls are inaccurate. Another possible problem is that many voters are concerned that poll results influence others.

As reported in Chapter 7, the preelection survey conducted by Northwestern University in the fall of 1988 showed that 12% felt polls were not accurate and 59% rated polls as only somewhat accurate. This low level of confidence is very unflattering in light of the fact that the most widely publicized November polls estimated Bush's popular vote in the 52% to 56% range—all acceptable figures when allowing for margin of error.

Voters give little evidence that they use polling results as part of their own voting decision. Market Opinion Research, which polled for the campaign of George Bush, routinely asked voters why they were supporting Bush or Dukakis. It was an extremely rare occurrence to find a voter who would acknowledge he or she was voting for the candidate currently ahead in the polls. Also, the Northwestern preelection survey showed that only 10% of voters viewed polling data as "quite useful" or "very useful" in deciding how to vote.

Although voters do not appear to be influenced by polls, a 43% plurality view them as harmful to the political process. Only one-third (33%) see them as useful and 23% regard them as neither harmful nor useful. The Northwestern study did not query voters as to why polling information was harmful to the political process, but I believe a possible reason is that voters feel that others are heavily influenced by polls.

This fear that polls influence others certainly applies to exit polls. Slightly more than one-half (53%) of voters surveyed by Northwestern after the election believed that the projections of Bush's win made West Coast voters less likely to go to the polls. Another 10% felt that the projections encouraged voting and 5% felt that the projections had a mixed effect. In total, over two-thirds (69%) of those surveyed believed that there was an effect.

If voters perceive exit polls to be influential, they might also believe that preelection polls are influential. And, if they do, they might believe that preelection polls not only affect the likelihood of voting but also affect the actual vote choice of others.

Such a projection onto one's fellow citizens, coupled with a general sense that polls are not very accurate, would lead voters to believe that polls, and their use in the media, truly play an insidious role in the democratic process. Therefore, even if mountains of evidence show that preelection polls have no impact on voting behavior whatsoever, a new strategy for handling poll results might be warranted for the simple purpose of reminding voters that it is they, and not polls, who drive the electoral process.

Effect of Media Polls on the Campaigns: The Presidential Level

Public polls released just prior to the 1988 New Hampshire primary played an important role in the tactical decisions of the Bush campaign. Polls taken before the Iowa caucus showed Vice President Bush with a comfortable lead in this first primary. However, Bush's poor showing in Iowa turned Senator Robert Dole into the Republican front-runner. Dole's polling, public polls, and pundits agreed that Bush, the previous front-runner, might be knocked out of contention. The Bush campaign, without its own New Hampshire polls, was compelled to rely on the grim projections of public data and decided to attack Dole for "straddling" the issue of tax increases.

Bush's nine-point win in New Hampshire—38% to 29%—over Dole was by no means overwhelming. However, these results, when juxtaposed against the previous expectations of a Dole victory, proved disastrous for Dole. Though considered the front-runner for a few days, Dole found himself reeling. The senator's campaign never recovered from the turn of events in New Hampshire. And George Bush never had to look back over his shoulder.

While it was interesting that the Bush campaign based a major decision on public polls, the more important lesson of New Hampshire was how the combination of expected outcomes and voting booth realities can quickly turn the primary process upside down. During the prenomination period, the mixture of media poll results, the actual primary and caucus outcomes, and the "spin" that the campaigns put on both could be likened to rocket fuel. The mixture can ignite and quickly launch a successful campaign or it can explode and immediately end a campaign. This danger often declines over the course of the primary period and certainly diminishes during the general election period.

This volatile mix of poll results, actual results, and "spin" created an explosion for Senator Dole. For Dole, the problem was not losing to Bush but losing after many political pundits had deemed the senator to be the front-runner.

In contrast, the 1984 Democratic caucus in Iowa is an example of how the volatile mix ignited for a successful launch. Walter Mondale was expected to win in Iowa and did so with almost one-half of the vote. What was unexpected was that his closest competitor would be Senator Gary Hart. Mondale outscored Hart by a three-to-one margin, but that was not the big news. The big news was that Hart's performance exceeded the expectations of even the most politically attentive. Hart was supposed to be an "also ran"—a candidate with a single digit or asterisk beside his name in the total column. However, his surprise finish made him the alternative to Mondale and media coverage quickly adapted to treat Hart accordingly. A week later, Hart defeated Mondale 37% to 28% in the New Hampshire primary and, though failing to win the nomination, dogged Mondale all the way to the Democratic convention.

Campaign organizations are fully aware of the potential effects of the mix that includes expected outcomes, real outcomes, "spin control," and media coverage. For this reason, campaigns will make every attempt to influence media treatment of their candidate's prospects for victory. One common form of "spin control" is for a campaign to publicly underestimate its candidate's expected vote share and to insist that the public polls are showing too much support for its candidate. If the candidate exceeds this depressed estimate, he or she has done better than expected or even "won."

It is interesting that such spin control has often given campaigns reason to be "ecstatic" with a 10% vote share. Also, if the candidate's performance meets the conservative estimates, the campaign does not have to face being wrong.

Another form of "spin control" is to downplay the importance of a particular event on the primary schedule. Senator Albert Gore ignored the Iowa caucuses and focused his attention on the Super Tuesday states in his home region. The rationale was that getting no support in Iowa was preferable to seriously competing and getting negligible support. The Bush campaign used the same rationale in the South Dakota primary. Certain to lose, Bush did not seriously compete in that state, with the hope that the results (Dole swamped Bush by a 55% to 18% margin) would not be treated with the same seriousness as the results from more pro-Bush states.

The spin game becomes much less important after the nomination process is over. At that point, there is no need for the nominees' campaigns to manage national media poll results on a day-to-day basis because, rather than being geared toward the primary of the week, the campaigns must focus on one final "poll" date—the election itself. Also, as each party's nominee can expect to receive a large majority of voters who identify with his or her party, the campaigns do not face the uncertainty and volatility inherent in the primary period.

Although the necessity of quickly reacting to public poll results diminishes after the nomination process, the results still have an effect on campaigns. First, although campaigns have their own internal polling, they can only afford to conduct a handful of expensive national polls, and available public polls provide a constant reality check. The Bush campaign knew that its candidate trailed Governor Dukakis by at least 10 points prior to the Republican convention, but the public data confirmed that Bush would have to campaign on more than the themes of peace and prosperity. Thus the public polls helped spur the Bush campaign to attack Dukakis.

Second, these media polls can profoundly affect the morale of candidates and campaigns. The Bush campaign was obviously not happy with the fact that Governor Dukakis held a double-digit lead over their candidate at the close of the Democratic National Convention. However, at that time, a deficit was not surprising for two reasons. First, Dukakis competed in contested primaries through the entire preconvention period while Bush, for all practical purposes, secured his own nomination in March. This gave the Democrats, and thus Dukakis, a significant media advantage. The second reason was that the Democratic National Convention gave Dukakis and his fellow Democrats numerous opportunities to promote their cause and attack Bush with little Republican interference.

Another glimmer of hope for the Bush organization was that there was a precedent for GOP nominees to gain back considerable ground after trailing badly in polls. Some Bush campaign operatives had witnessed Gerald Ford's narrow loss to Jimmy Carter in 1976 after trailing 29% to 62% during the Democratic convention of that year. Their man's 17-point deficit, put in a historic context, was not as ominous as the 33-point deficit that Ford faced. Bush's rapid rebound after the GOP convention, confirmed by a number of public polls, added a great deal of credibility to this optimism.

Although national preference poll results affected the Bush campaign's activities in only a few instances, polls conducted at a *statewide* level served a very important function. Because the presidency is ultimately decided by the electoral college, it was critical for the Bush organization to keep tabs on the pieces of the puzzle that would add to at least 270 electors. Because the campaign could not afford to conduct polls in all 50 states, public polls provided much of the necessary information. After discounting states with the highest probabilities of supporting Bush or Dukakis, the campaign was left with the true "battlegound" states to target.

Of course, historical patterns gave the campaign an indication of which states were safely Republican (Utah, Idaho, Indiana) and which states would probably support Dukakis (Massachusetts, Rhode Island, Minnesota). Nonetheless, the state-by-state polls were still critical for targeting decisions. First, these polls could give the Bush campaign clues as to which "reliable" states might stray from their historical pattern of supporting GOP presidential candidates. Second, the campaign could find a traditionally Democratic state that was not firmly in the Dukakis column. Having located the key competitive states, the Bush campaign could then conduct its own polls in each of them and learn how to pull these states into (or keep them in) the Republican column.

Effect of Media Polls on the Campaigns: The Subpresidential Level

Although media polls conducted during the general election campaign period need not be disastrous for presidential contenders, they might contribute to the unceremonious disposal of candidates who run for offices that appear lower on the ballot. One reason is that, while major party presidential candidates enjoy comparable financial resources, organization, and free and paid media, subpresidential races are often David versus Goliath matches (except David has no stones for his sling). The extent to which the media's use of poll data causes or exacerbates these tremendous disparities must be examined in future research.

The most likely negative impact is on the funding of candidates who challenge incumbents. Incumbency has numerous built-in advantages such as franked mail for communications and the privilege of distributing money and services. But, more important, incumbents generally have large advantages in name recognition among constituents. This gap in name recognition often translates into hefty leads in poll results. These leads, in turn, open the wallets of political action committees and other financial supporters who view contributions as investments. Therefore, with superior finances, the incumbent has superior campaign machinery and an advantage in paid media. Meanwhile, the challenger finds him- or herself in a catch-22 situation. Lacking good prospects for electoral success, the challenger is often denied the necessary tools for competing. For this reason, early media polls can become a self-fulfilling prophecy.

Experience, though, sometimes shows that challengers with seemingly hopeless candidacies were, in truth, formidable opponents. An excellent example is Jack Lousma, an unsuccessful challenger in the 1984 Michigan Senate contest. Late summer polls showed Lousma trailing incumbent Senator Carl Levin by 40 points. Polls released just one week before election day showed him trailing by 30 points. On election day, Lousma picked up 48% of the vote, an outstanding vote share given the prediction of a sound thrashing.

Future Use of Media Polling

The media's use of polling data in the past has often received unfair criticism. At the same time, the media have often misused poll results and have often managed to escape well-deserved condemnation. Although retroactive assessments are mixed, the media will continue to use polling information, as is their right. While the validity of this information will always be subject to the limits of methodology, it can be used to the benefit of the interested public, and its use can remain within the confines of responsible journalism.

Primary Polling

The main pitfall of the media reporting on a primary poll is that the poll's accuracy is dependent on correct answers to two questions. The first question asks who the surveyed individual supports. This question is usually easy to answer, as most Americans are willing to state a preference for a candidate. The second question—the question of who actually votes—presents the real hurdle. Unlike that for November, the composition and size of a primary electorate can vary widely because of mobilization efforts, weather, and other factors.

Pollsters have made a game effort to "scientifically" determine who will actually show up at the polls. Thus the population sampled is often composed of "likely" voters, "past primary" voters, "probable" voters, and so on. Regardless of the level of effort and good intentions, accuracy in primary polling can seldom match that of general election polling. Primary polls often provide more embarrassment than information. For this reason, the use of primary polling is inherently dangerous and results should always be treated as very soft indicators of what will actually take place.

General Election Polls:
The Subpresidential Level

As discussed earlier, subpresidential races have a special dynamic that a poll—a mere snapshot of the campaign process—cannot take into account. Nonetheless, polls for these races are conducted and interpreted in the same manner as a presidential poll. The results of such studies are often very different from the actual election day totals.

The best way to approach poll results for subpresidential races is to put the figures into two contexts—the context of campaign dynamics and the context of history. Journalists can put poll results into the context of campaign dynamics by asking the following questions:

- How does the name recognition of the challenger compare with that of the incumbent? Is there a disparity that would give one candidate a special advantage?
- Does the candidate with lower name recognition have an opportunity to improve it during the campaign? Does he or she have (or is there a possibility that he or she will receive) sufficient funds for advertising? To what extent, if any, will media coverage of debates, appearances, and so on help to make up for discrepancies?
- Prior to the poll's field dates, did one candidate buy a significant amount of advertising while the other candidate was not on the air? (Campaigns often try to time advertising to immediately precede public polls in the hope of boosting their candidates' standings.)
- What is the partisan distribution among the seat's constituents? Is there a potential for a large number of errant Republicans or Democrats to return to the fold?

The following questions might help put poll results into historical context:

- What is the best that a Democrat (or Republican) has done in past elections for this office? What is the worst? How do current poll results stack up against past results?
- Given the district's (state's, city's) partisan composition, are the poll results realistic?

Often, addressing these questions when interpreting poll results might lead journalists to conclude that the November reality might indeed match a poll's predictions. However, it is often the case that, in order to draw intelligent conclusions, the results must be put into perspective rather than taken at face value.

9

Journalism with Footnotes

Reporting the "Technical Details" of Polls

PETER V. MILLER
DANIEL M. MERKLE
PAUL WANG

An ambivalent closeness exists between the polls and the press. Polls provide the grist for much election reportage. Competition between media organizations for the "horse race" story is played out in tables, pie charts, and bar graphs in addition to the informal soundings of public wisdom garnered in taverns and on the street. And yet, there are, and always have been, misgivings about polling in the journalistic community.

The most vocal expression of second thoughts is heard when things go wrong. Events as long ago as Truman's "upset" victory in 1948 and as recent as the 1989 Dinkins and Wilder "close call" victories in New York and Virginia occasion soul-searching and recrimination. The press cannot live without polls, but—particularly in such instances—it finds it very difficult to live with them. Even when nothing untoward happens, the polls are sometimes resented for shaping election coverage. For example, Bill Kovach, curator of the Nieman Foundation at Harvard, recently decried the use of polls in promoting "horse race" journalism (Kovach, 1990).

One of the more obvious examples of the uncomfortable relationship between the press and the polls is the way polling methods are described in poll stories. That methodology is discussed at all is remarkable, because journalists rarely treat the process of news gathering as problematic. They are even less likely to suggest that they might have been mistaken in their fact gathering or to give the reader a "margin of error" for interpreting the story. But "proper" poll reporting requires just this sort of qualification. It is a unique kind of journalism with "footnotes," wherein certain facts about polling methods are appended to a discussion of poll findings.

The juxtaposition of public opinion "news" with methodological "fine print" exemplifies political journalism's close, but uneasy, relationship with the polls. In this chapter, we want to scrutinize the presentation of the "fine print"—its rationale, its parameters, and its utility. We will explore the dilemmas posed by the practice of disclosing information on poll methodology and various alternative ways of setting survey standards. The analysis will conclude with some recommendations for the treatment of methodology in poll reporting.

There is a long history to the practice of reporting poll methodology in poll stories. We begin with a review of this history and consider why explanation of polling methodology appears in polling stories at all. After reviewing the history and the rationale, we will examine the question of how much poll consumers should be told about polling methods and consider some dilemmas that journalists face in answering that query.

Standard Setting

Poll stories need footnotes because there are no generally accepted polling procedures. Unlike the accounting profession, which—under pressure from the federal government after the crash of 1929—adopted a voluminous code of correct practice and set up a bureaucracy to review, administer, and enforce the rules, pollsters have never been able to agree on how their work should be done. They have faced similar kinds of pressure, however, particularly following the 1948 election debacle. The American Association for Public Opinion Research (AAPOR) was formed a couple of years prior to that event, and, as Hollander (forthcoming) has noted, standard setting has always been a major theme in the organization's meetings. The Truman victory heightened the controversy, with some AAPOR members calling for a mechanism to censure and exclude incompetent and fraudulent pollsters.

But, despite the 1948 experience and repeated embarrassments due to poor correspondence between poll findings and election results, procedural and performance standards have never been adopted by the polling community. There are a number of reasons for this situation. A fundamental problem is that adopting any standard is a process of negotiation among various user interests. It is rare for any standard of measurement to show such an obvious connection to what is being measured that diverse interested parties automatically favor it. For example, length, weight, and temperature have been the subject of considerable controversy in measurement circles, as witnessed by the continuing presence of two widely used systems for measuring—the metric and the so-called English system. If such fundamental physical concepts do not engender measurement consensus, it is no wonder that the assessment of ephemeral opinions has not inspired a uniform method. The purposes for commissioning opinion surveys and the uses made of the results vary widely. A particular standard for data collection may be far too stringent or too lenient for a given purpose.

Economic and legal hurdles also stand in the way of the adoption of procedural or performance standards. If uniform polling procedure standards were adopted, pollsters who "cut corners" to offer a lower price would suffer the economic consequences of being perceived as unapproved or nonstandard. Absent a strong governmental interest or a "natural law" that determines the correct way to measure, and in view of the money to be won or lost depending on which standards are adopted, it is understandable for would-be standard-setters to take a catholic viewpoint. Standards that embrace a wide variety of procedures, or a completely laissez-faire approach, are probable outcomes. The threat of litigation against the standard-setting organization for restraint of trade is an additional disincentive to narrowly defined standards. The history of AAPOR attempts to set standards is replete with references to the need for liability insurance for the organization (Hollander, in press).

These considerations have led standard-setters in the survey business to focus on general, hortatory language in writing about procedures or performance and to be specific and directive only in the areas of safeguarding respondent confidentiality and disclosing information on survey methods. The AAPOR standards, for example, state that members "shall exercise due care" in their work, using only tools and methods suited to the research problem and making only those interpretations that are consistent with the data. The language does not specify what "due care" is; neither does it give examples of the misuse of tools or erroneous interpretations. The standards explicitly state that AAPOR does not purport to certify the professional competence of its members. Survey firms are forbidden to advertise that they adhere to AAPOR standards because of the fear that clients may interpret such ads as an AAPOR imprimatur for the firms' work.

Disclosure Standards

Rather than prescribing how to do the work, the polling community has set up guidelines for telling consumers of poll information how polls are conducted (AAPOR, 1986). Disclosure standards have the effect of shifting the responsibility for adequate measurement from the pollster to the data user. There is justification in this approach, given the multifarious uses to which polls can be put. As noted above, universal procedure or performance standards are difficult to establish because different users of polls have different demands for accuracy. Disclosure, while not as desirable as procedural or performance standards, limits the possibility of fraud (though does not eliminate it) and may, in the long term, serve to upgrade poll performance as users complain about behavior that departs from industry norms.

The AAPOR code for minimal disclosure reads as follows:

Good professional practice imposes the obligation upon all public opinion researchers to include, in any report of research results, or to make available when that report is released, certain essential information about how the research was conducted. At a minimum, the following items should be disclosed:

1. Who sponsored the survey and who conducted it.

2. The exact wording of questions asked, including the text of any preceding instruction or explanation to the interviewer or respondent that might reasonably be expected to affect the response.

3. A definition of the population under study, and a description of the sampling frame used to identify this population.

4. A description of the sample selection procedure, giving a clear indication of the method by which the respondents were selected by the researcher, or whether the respondents were entirely self-selected.

5. The size of the sample and, if applicable, completion rates and information on eligibility criteria and screening procedures.

6. A discussion of the precision of the findings, including, if appropriate, estimates of sampling error, and a description of any weighting or estimating procedures used.

7. Which results are based on parts of the sample, rather than the total sample.

8. Method, location, and dates of data collection. (AAPOR, 1986)

Let us consider more closely the kinds of information that this code says ought to be made available to poll data users. These aspects of poll methodology are conceived to have a bearing on survey accuracy; it make sense to tell people about polling methods that shape the results. The difficulty for journalists and for poll consumers is that, while these factors can greatly affect poll findings, for most of them, it is hard to specify how much they do so in given instances. This uncertainty contributes, we believe, to the changing nature of disclosure standards and to the highly variable disclosure practices adopted by news organizations.

Let us examine first those polling methods that are clearest in the nature and extent of their impact. Four of the eight categories deal with characteristics of the sample design and execution—the frame, selection procedure, size, and sampling error. Also relevant to this class of information are the population definition, screening criteria, completion rate, and weighting procedures.

It is obvious from this emphasis that sampling methods were viewed by the standards writers as a particularly important context for judging the validity of poll results. The body of statistical theory underlying the practice of probability sampling provides the foundation for this perspective. Because, according to the theory, one can form precise quantitative expectations about sampling error under specified conditions of sample selection procedure and sample size, informing data users about these matters makes good sense.

Users can only make judgments of a less precise nature about error when information on population definition, sampling frame, screening criteria, completion rate, and weighting procedures is known. If the frame appears to fail to cover elements in the population, for example, we can assume that the sample will produce biased estimates, but we don't know how biased. For example, if the sample for a poll is based on telephone contacts, we know that people without phones cannot be represented in the sample. Depending on the subject matter discussed in the questionnaire, this "coverage bias" may be great or small.

Similarly, if a poll achieves a low completion rate, we may suspect that opinion estimates are biased, but we know neither the magnitude of the bias nor the success with which the nonresponse error is corrected by weighting techniques. A low completion rate signals that there were many eligible poll respondents who refused to be interviewed or could not be contacted. Are their opinions different from the opinions of those who *were* interviewed? We may certainly suspect so, but we can never know how different the opinions are because these people can't or won't talk to us.

Finally, if a poll is not based on a probability sample at all (e.g., a quota sample, a convenience sample, or a "call-in" poll), we know that the opinion estimates are likely to be biased and that the degree of the bias is greater as the latitude for respondent self-selection increases. It is well known, for example, that people who "vote" in "call-in" polls are often very different from people at large on a variety of dimensions. Consequently, the opinion distributions reported in such exercises are different from polls that sample the general population.

To summarize, the information provided to users of poll data about sample design and execution may give very specific data about error or it may raise questions and suspicions that are difficult to quantify. Information about data collection procedures (items 1, 2, and 8 of the AAPOR code) also can raise serious questions about error in poll estimates, but we cannot be very specific about the nature or extent of the error. Research on question wording effects has provided convincing evidence that seemingly minor variations in wording can have large impacts on opinion distributions. In addition to the systematic work of Schuman and Presser (1981), Roper (1983) reports an instance in which a Roper poll and an NBC poll differed by some 35% on how many Americans favored ratification of the SALT II Treaty. The massive disparity appears to be largely or entirely due to question wording differences between the two polls.

Continuing with items covered by the AAPOR code, the mode of data collection (telephone, mail, in person) can have important implications for sampling and nonsampling error. For example, an exit poll in the 1989 Virginia governor's race was criticized for employing face-to-face data collection procedures instead of self-administered forms, which better preserve respondent anonymity. The location and dates of data collection are important for assessing the possibility of change in opinions since the poll was taken and for comparing multiple polls on the same topic—such as the presidential "horse race." Finally, the sponsorship of the survey and the organization conducting the fieldwork can affect the poll's perceived integrity and credibility. To the extent that the sponsor has a vested interest in the poll's outcome, and to the degree that the polling organization is not independent from the sponsor, questions can be raised about a poll's findings.

Even if an interested party's poll results are not fraudulent, they may be selectively released to achieve the most positive impact.

For the most part then, information provided about survey procedures and performance in response to the AAPOR guidelines enables the user of poll information to raise questions and suggest qualifications for interpreting poll data. In most cases, the questions that can be raised are of a general nature. We do not have theory or empirical evidence to allow data users to calculate the error contribution of particular survey practices, except in the case of sampling methods under the right conditions. We know that procedures *can* make a difference, but we don't know how much difference in any given case. Hence we typically are drawn to consider polling procedures post hoc, when a poll's findings seem wrong, in the search for causes of the error. When the findings seem right, we often ignore the procedures altogether.

Disclosure Dilemma I:
Too Little Information

Because we don't know how much difference it makes to employ different survey practices, the question of what to include in guidelines for disclosure is continually debated. The AAPOR code, for example, is currently under review, having been revised a number of times previously. It can be argued that any disclosure code is not inclusive enough or is too inclusive.

If any polling procedures or aspects of a poll's environment that *might* affect the findings should be mentioned, then the list of possible factors would quickly grow very long. The AAPOR code we just discussed is already quite lengthy, and a number of media polls (e.g., CBS) try only to comply with the shorter National Council on Public Polls' disclosure standards (NCPP, 1979). Nevertheless, at least in the case of preelection polls, there are some important things to consider when interpreting the findings that are not currently included in *any* list of disclosure guidelines.

Crespi's (1988) ground-breaking evaluation of preelection polling techniques provides a rare empirical base for judging whether a particular procedure merits inclusion in disclosure guidelines. For example, it is clear from his analysis that the treatment of "undecided" voters in estimates of candidate support affects the accuracy of preelection polls, but no set of disclosure guidelines addresses this factor. Some pollsters allocate undecideds evenly to each candidate, some treat them as nonvoters, and still others weight their likelihood of voting. Such decisions make a difference in the accuracy of preelection polls, Crespi discovered, when he compared the results of polls using these methods with actual vote totals. Poll consumers, however, are never informed about the pollsters' decisions.

Similarly, Crespi found that the type of election is a key predictor of poll accuracy, but this factor is not mentioned in any disclosure code. For most voters, primaries and caucuses are less salient events than general elections, and eligibility rules differ as well. The track record for preprimary polls is substantially worse than that for general elections. There are a variety of reasons for the failures of preprimary polls, prominent among which is the nature of preferences in these contests. A number of pollsters Crespi surveyed noted that voters may have no attitudes about candidates in primaries (and, in low-profile local elections, for that matter) and that their "vote intentions" merely reflect name recognition.

The "softness" or malleability of opinion in certain election contests is part of the "shoptalk" of pollsters, but none of our disclosure guidelines speak to the issue of how we should acknowledge the risks entailed in asking people for candidate preferences that may not exist. Polls form the basis for election outcome expectations published in the press. Those expectations set the context for interpreting the actual election results: Was there an "upset"? Did the winner win by the "expected" amount? What does the "unexpectedly" strong or weak showing portend for the candidate's future viability? Such questions follow the routine comparison of preprimary poll findings and actual vote totals.

But what if the expectations set by the preelection polls were illusory—based on uninformed or nonexistent opinions? We risk the early demise or the accelerated growth of budding candidacies because their primary vote totals failed to match the false expectations engendered by polls taken in a season of ignorance and volatility. Should we not have a way to disclose the possibility of "phantom" candidate preferences picked up in preprimary polls, assuming that we should do polls in these circumstances at all?

These are some of the factors that contribute to poll accuracy that are not treated in current disclosure guidelines. In other cases, disclosure guidelines are inclusive enough but they are routinely flouted by pollsters. For example, an important contributor to the accuracy of preelection polls is the estimation of the "probable electorate." Each pollster has his or her own recipe for creating the pool of likely voters, and the formulas are treated like trade secrets. So even though the AAPOR code calls for disclosure of respondent eligibility criteria and screening procedures, media reports of polls do not provide the information, except in the broadest terms.

Similarly, the AAPOR code asks for information about completion rates, but the issue of nonresponse is rarely or never treated in poll reports. Pollsters responding to Crespi's survey reported high refusal rates in telephone polls, and few reported having any procedure for trying to persuade those who refused to participate. Further, many polls attempt no callbacks when predesignated households are not reached on the first attempt. A large percentage of any random-digit dialing telephone sample can consist of people who initially refuse or cannot be reached. If no additional attempts are made to interview initial nonrespondents, the sample consists only of those who were easy to get. Are their opinions different from those who were not interviewed? Adam Clymer (personal communication) reports that the percentage of respondents favoring Dukakis in 1988 *New York Times* polls increased with successive callback waves. In other words, the Democratic supporters were harder to interview. Such results support the belief that pollsters ought to try harder to interview nonrespondents or at least to tell poll consumers that they only got the "easy" cases.

The tight time frame within which polls operate sometimes militates against extensive refusal conversion or callback attempts, but some sort of acknowledgment of response rate is important, given its bearing on poll accuracy. The tighter the polling deadline, the more likely that response rates will be low and the more effect of nonresponse that can be expected. Polls attempting to measure the immediate impact of major campaign events (e.g., debates) obviously are highly susceptible to response rate effects, but the possibility is never acknowledged in media accounts of poll findings.

If nonresponse is unmentioned in media accounts, how are other aspects of poll methodology treated in articles concerning poll results? Table 9.1 displays findings from a content analysis of preelection poll stories that we conducted during the 1988 primary elections.[1] We examined the disclosure of methodological information in *The New York Times*, *The Washington Post*, *The Wall Street Journal*, *Time* magazine, *Newsweek*, and *U.S. News and World Report*. The categories we examined were suggested by the AAPOR and NCPP codes discussed above. The majority of stories in this study included information about the population to be represented, eligibility criteria, the date the poll was conducted, and sample size. Sampling error was mentioned in 40% of the stories, while the organization that conducted the fieldwork, method of data collection, sample selection procedure, question wording, weighting procedures, nonsampling error, and sampling frame were mentioned less often. Response rate was not mentioned at all. This study points up the variation of reporting poll methods in major publications. There is a tendency for stories to report the more simple, nontechnical types of information

TABLE 9.1 Percentage of Stories Reporting Methodological Information

Disclosure Item	Percentage Reported
1. Date poll was conducted	67
2. Population	85
3. Eligibility criteria	80
4. Sampling frame	7
5. Sample size	58
6. Sample selection procedure	17
7. Sampling error	40
8. Exact question wording	15
9. Response rate	0
10. Weighting procedures	12
11. Method of data collection	29
12. Poll sponsorship	100[a]
13. Percentages upon which conclusions are based	100[a]
14. Who conducted the fieldwork	28
15. Nonsampling error	12
16. Sampling error for subgroup analysis	40[b]
17. Size of the subsample	60[b]

NOTE: N = 86. Percentages are rounded to the nearest percent.
a. These items have 100% disclosure because only stories that reported actual results from specific polls were included in the content analysis.
b. These percentages are based on N = 30, which is the number of stories reporting results for subgroups.

(population, eligibility criteria, date the poll was conducted, sample size), while the more ticklish areas (sample selection procedures, weighting procedures, nonsampling error, response rate) are virtually ignored.

It would seem in the best interests of the media to fully disclose those aspects of poll methodology and conditions that may lead to inaccuracy, because such disclosure can lower expectations about polls, give consumers appropriate caveats, and, incidentally, shield the press from criticism if their polls prove to be wrong. Pollsters commonly use language that puts limits on the inferences to be drawn from polls, and they encourage the press to follow suit. Bogart (1972), for example, wrote that public misunderstanding of polls would continue as long as the media "ignore or belittle their technical intricacies." Because consumers are the ultimate arbiters of poll quality, they should be inoculated against giving too much credence to polls. If they are forearmed with information on poll methods and conditions, they will not be totally disillusioned if poll findings are found to be in error.

Disclosure Dilemma II:
Too Much Information

We have discussed a few examples of preelection poll methods that affect poll accuracy and that are either unmentioned in disclosure codes or are not disclosed despite being mentioned. We also have argued that disclosure can, in theory, help give poll consumers appropriate expectations about poll accuracy and thus shield the polls from unwarranted criticism. On the basis of these considerations, a case can be made that current disclosure guidelines and media reports of polling methods are not inclusive enough.

Another disclosure dilemma, however, is that there are some grounds for arguing that the guidelines and the reporting are *too* inclusive. Media pollsters (e.g., CBS News) are prominent members of the National Council on Public Polls, a group that established an alternative to AAPOR's set of disclosure standards. A major impetus for the development of alternative guidelines was the belief on the part of the media pollsters that the AAPOR requirements demanded too much space or airtime in news reports. Naturally then, the NCPP code is substantially less specific than the AAPOR guidelines, which, we already have seen, omit some potentially important information.

Though much poll reporting today includes at least some reference to polling methods, disclosure presents the reporter and editor with uncomfortable options. As noted above, reporting of poll methods can be a rhetorical advantage, because it provides a line of defense against criticism if the poll is inaccurate. But, because time and space are scarce, and because polls represent a considerable monetary investment for the media organization, it is natural for journalists to want to highlight the findings and to keep the qualifications to a minimum. As noted above, disclosure standards call for information that is likely to constrain inferences and raise questions. If you tell poll consumers how questions are worded or how "likely voter" is defined, they can understand the limitations of the poll better and they may even argue with the methodological decisions.

Therefore, ambiguities, qualifications, and the like can blunt the impact of poll findings. Competition within the news organization and among competing news outlets motivates a positive, confident description of poll results—not a cautious or tentative approach. The more that poll findings are "couched," the more that consumers may wonder what the point of the poll is. They may even wonder why some polls have error and others appear not to have error. Following this reasoning, the less that need be said about polling methods, the better.

Polling practices and perceived reader understanding also contribute to the case for restricting, rather than expanding, the pool of disclosed information. Burns Roper, an AAPOR past president, has argued that the organization's disclosure guidelines should not include a statement of sampling error (the familiar "plus or minus × points" statement) because poll consumers do not understand how to interpret confidence intervals anyway, and they may interpret sampling error estimates as estimates of *total* survey error (Roper, 1983). Such arguments were important in the formulation of NCPP standards, which do not call for sampling error disclosure.

Actual poll consumer perceptions and understanding of poll methods reporting is relevant to deciding on disclosure policies, but there is relatively little research in this area. What research has been done supports Roper's view that the purpose of disclosure may be defeated by public ignorance of the meaning and significance of poll methods information. Polls conducted by Roper himself (1986) suggest that a large segment of the public does not understand the significance of sample size. Morin (1988) cites another Roper poll, which showed that nearly half of the respondents reported no understanding of sampling error. Lavrakas, Holley, and Miller, in another chapter in this volume, present findings from a national survey suggesting that a substantial portion of the sample were not subjectively or objectively knowledgeable about sampling error. Studies like these suggest that disclosure standards—which rely on poll consumers to police data quality—are simply wrongheaded. The public, as currently informed, is not equipped to handle the role envisioned for them. Information on poll methodology, if presented, is apt to be ignored or misinterpreted.

An Alternative Approach to Disclosure

We come to the end of our review of what we should know about how polls are done with two sharply different answers: disclose more information than is currently offered or disclose less or none. The goal of telling people that polls have error seems laudable—it puts poll information in perspective, it protects against unrealistic expectations, and, in addition, it is the truth. But, for disclosure to work, there must be well-defined disclosure criteria that are universally adhered to, and a knowledgeable, interested, user population.

It seems to us that the key to both goals is more leadership and involvement by journalists in the standard-setting and polling processes. Journalists should be able to decide best which aspects of polling methodology contribute most to the accuracy of their reports. They are responsible for the stories, so their judgment about what to say to poll consumers is most important. Outside organizations—such as AAPOR and NCPP—however well intentioned, cannot impose standards for disclosure on the press. Further, it is problematic whether news organizations *should* adhere to any standards set up by external bodies because of First Amendment concerns. Codes of behavior for journalists are always highly controversial because they may limit freedom of expression.

Journalists must take the lead themselves. They must decide, when reporting polls by outside groups or rival news organizations, what questions to ask about how the polls were done. Today, reports of such polls often treat the polls as sources to be quoted but not questioned. Reporters should show the same doggedness in gathering information about poll methodology that they use in investigating any other story. It is probably too much to expect journalists in rival organizations to sit down together to draw up common disclosure standards. But such standards could evolve through competition if journalists probe each other's polling methodology. We should note that such probing has little or no historical precedent and requires an important change of attitude on the part of poll reporters.

When reporting their own polls, journalists must take responsibility for explaining their work to poll consumers rather than relying on "boilerplate" methodological statements modeled on standards they did not establish (which, in many cases, they probably do not understand). When journalists do polls, they merely engage in news gathering by other means. Polls should not be treated as something the consultants do, but as *reporting*—the journalist's job. This attitude, accompanied by the requisite understanding of sampling, data collection, statistics, and so forth, can go a long way toward transforming the coverage of public opinion. Journalists who write poll stories should *be* pollsters, with all of the attendant "rights and responsibilities."

The AAPOR standards for disclosure provide a starting point for journalists in deciding how to report polls and how to scrutinize each other's work. But these rules, designed to cover a variety of surveys, are too broad to give specific guidance on what aspects of methodology to report concerning preelection polls, the subject of this volume. It seems to us that Crespi's (1988) book on factors that contribute to preelection poll accuracy may serve as a better guide. As noted above, he details a number of polling methods that make a difference in the correspondence between preelection polls and actual election results. The list of methodological factors he examines overlaps greatly with the AAPOR code, but he goes beyond the code to consider issues peculiar to preelection polls. We would like to see a universal set of standards evolve; this end is more likely to be achieved if we narrow the criteria to focus on one type of poll at a time.

A narrower set of methodological criteria, closely scrutinized and reported by knowledgeable journalists, could provide the foundation for more responsible poll reporting. Journalists can serve as the enlightened group of poll consumers that is necessary if the practice of disclosure of methodological information is to affect poll quality. As I. A. Lewis argues elsewhere in this volume, journalists are apt to be more affected by polling results than are members of the general public. The trick is to convince journalists that their interest in polls should be focused more on how polls are conducted and not just on the results.

The public at large can become involved in monitoring poll quality if journalists treat important methodological information as part of the poll story rather than as a technical appendix. Armed with information on factors that may affect poll accuracy, journalists can query their competitors and examine their own findings to get a more sophisticated view of voter preferences. Rather than simply reporting sampling error, reporters can discuss its significance in trial heats. Rather than a simple report of the percentages from a competitor's poll, the methodological and political context of the rival effort can be woven into the story. Rather than simply discussing who won the debate, reporters can examine the estimates from polls that attempted more or fewer callbacks. Rather than simply doing polls because everyone else is doing them, media organizations may marshal their resources for the most appropriate moments in the campaign.

If journalists treat polling methods as part of the story, they are more likely to pay close attention to how their own polls are done and to how their competitors do. The added scrutiny will do more to ameliorate polling practice and provide appropriate expectations for results than any long list of methodological factors printed in a box at the bottom of the story. Polling, to repeat, is news gathering. Journalistic skepticism and caution are as relevant here as in any other area of reporting. The rules for deciding whether to "go with the story" may be more complex, but they must be judgments of validity in the same sense as the judgment to publish, say, an investigative series based in part on anonymous sources.

Just as reporters become investigative experts, they must become polling experts. They must frame the inquiry and manage and participate in the process. They must understand the "technical details" intimately, because they are not merely "details" but journalism.

Note

1. This content analysis is based on stories that appeared in major publications during January and February of 1988 concerning primary elections. A *poll story* was defined as one that reported actual results from a specific poll. This increases the likelihood of compliance to disclosure guidelines given that it would be unlikely for stories referring to unspecified polls to disclose a significant amount of information. This selection procedure accounts for the fact that "poll sponsor" and "percentages upon which the conclusions are based" were reported 100% of the time. The number of usable stories for each publication included for analysis were as follows: (a) *The New York Times*, 31; (b) *Washington Post*, 37; (c) *The Wall Street Journal*, 6; (d) *Time* magazine, 10; (e) *Newsweek*, 1; and (f) *U.S. News and World Report*, 1. Each story was coded by four undergraduate students in a communication research class to ascertain the level of disclosure present in each and to permit intercoder variability analysis. The students received instruction in the meaning of the disclosure standards and also basic coding instructions. Discrepancies were resolved by the four students as a group. The consensus reached for each item in each story is the final measure of disclosure used in the analysis.

References

American Association for Public Opinion Research (AAPOR). (1986). *Certificate of Incorporation and By-Laws*. Princeton, NJ: Author.

Bogart, L. (1972). *Silent politics: Polls and the awareness of public opinion*. New York: Wiley-Interscience.

Crespi, I. (1988). *Pre-election polling: Sources of accuracy and error*. New York: Russell Sage.

Hollander, S. (forthcoming). Survey standards. In A. Gollin (Ed.), *AAPOR history*.

Kovach, W. (1990, May). Presentation at Plenary Session, Newspapers and Television as Election Pollsters: Do They Do Anything Right? Annual Meeting, American Association for Public Opinion Research, Lancaster, PA.

Morin, R. (1988, October 16). Behind the numbers: Confessions of a pollster. *Washington Post*, pp. C1, C4.

National Council on Public Polls (NCPP). (1979). *Principles of disclosure*. Princeton, NJ: Author.

Roper, B. W. (1983). Some things that concern me. *Public Opinion Quarterly*, *47*, 303-309.

Roper, B. W. (1986). Evaluating polls with poll data. *Public Opinion Quarterly*, *50*, 10-16.

Schuman, H., & Presser, S. (1981). *Questions and answers in attitude surveys: Experiments on question form, wording, and context*. New York: Academic Press.

10

The Press and Political Polling

JACK K. HOLLEY

The media focus too much attention on who is leading in the campaign and who is trailing, the so-called horse race aspects of the election. The media make news by conducting their own polls. Political polls have become increasingly more powerful components of the election process, and they interfere with that process.

These are among the criticisms leveled against the media and their use of political polls. This chapter discusses the media and these issues and is divided into three parts. They are as follows:

(1) The first part is a review of some of the criticisms and the findings of various academics and others: Much of this material may be familiar to academics and pollsters, but it is my judgment that many journalists are not familiar with some of the literature on the subject and do not have the time to go to the original sources. Thus the material is included in this chapter. It was selected, in part, because I feel these are issues that should be considered by the press.

(2) The second includes the findings from a national telephone survey conducted for this project on the number of newspapers involved in polling and how the surveys are handled. This section also includes some information from others on survey methods disclosures.

(3) The final part presents a discussion of the issues.

AUTHOR'S NOTE: I wish to acknowledge a grant from the Frank E. Gannett Urban Journalism Center at Northwestern University, which partially funded the study of polling practices. I also am grateful for the analytical and additional financial support provided by Paul J. Lavrakas and the Northwestern University Survey Laboratory, respectively.

Although this chapter talks primarily about newspapers and includes findings from a study about their polling practices, much of what is said could be applied to broadcasting and magazines.

The topic is significant not only because of the ongoing debate about polling, which escalated during the 1988 presidential campaign, and the implications of the criticisms, but also because four in ten American daily newspapers are involved directly in political polling, either conducting surveys in-house or contracting with an outside organization to have them done. This was among the findings from a 1989 survey of dailies that I conducted.[1]

Horse Races

The criticism that journalists too often focus on the horse race aspects of presidential and other campaigns has been voiced frequently (Asher, 1988, p. 89). It may have surfaced more often and more loudly during the 1988 races. For instance, at a three-day postmortem at Drake University in Des Moines, Iowa, titled, "From Iowa to the White House," several of the journalists and politicians participating said that "by Nov. 8 . . . campaign coverage had degenerated into almost nothing but the so-called 'horse race' kind of reporting" (Fitzgerald, 1988, pp. 14-15).

Some participants expressed the feeling that coverage had grown more shallow as the campaign progressed. *Boston Globe* national political reporter Tom Oliphant and others complained that the deep, analytical, and serious pieces discussing the candidates, their views, and their personalities were, by and large, written more than a year before the election.

" 'If there is a lesson in 1988, it takes the form of an appeal to editors,' " Oliphant said. " 'It's like, "Stop me before I kill again." We like to do the tactical pieces, the horse-race coverage. . . . Don't let us. Ruthlessly cut it out' " (Fitzgerald, 1988, pp. 14-15).

Horse race journalism is mentioned in several of the chapters in this book. I. A. Lewis, for instance, wishes journalists would focus more on the meaning of the campaign and less on the numbers. Another chapter author, Michael Kagay, makes a case that the horse race becomes the story near the end of the race. The Lavrakas-Holley-Miller survey showed that the media's use of horse race stories provided crucial information to the majority of the public. Nearly everyone knew that George Bush was leading. The study also concluded that the polls appeared to have an effect on some voters and nonvoters, a result some would consider to be negative. An argument against the horse race is that, while the journalist's energy and the newspaper's space and the television station's airtime are devoted to the story of who is ahead and who is behind, the issue stories do not get done.

"Three major features stand out . . . during the 1968, 1972, 1976 and 1980 presidential campaigns," political scientist Doris Graber writes.

> First and most significantly, the media devoted the bulk of their stories to campaign hoopla and the horse race aspects of the contests. They slighted political, social and economic problems facing the country and said little about the merits of the solutions proposed, unless these issues could be made exciting and visually dramatic. (Graber, 1989, pp. 215-216)

In the media coverage, Graber says, "winning and losing are presented as all-important, rather than what winning and losing mean in terms of the political direction of the country in general or the observer's personal situation in particular" (Graber, 1989, p. 221).

Increase in Primaries

Horse race coverage may have increased over the years, as many have said, but I did not find a study on that point. A 1986 study by David P. Demers, a doctoral mass communications student at the University of Minnesota, replicated work done in 1978 by John N. Rippey (Demers, 1987, pp. 839-842). Demers reported that public opinion polling by newspapers increased sharply in the 1960s and 1970s. It apparently leveled off sometime in the late 1970s and remained stable between 1978 and 1986. The difference between 1978 and 1986 was in the subject matter of the polls. Newspapers were more likely to poll about primary elections and referenda issues in 1986 than they had been in 1978, and they were less likely to survey subjects involving pending legislation (Demers, 1988, p. 841). Although the Demers and Rippey studies were not done in a presidential election year, my experience as a practicing journalist for 21 years has been that the top-of-the-ballot, off-year elections also get "their share" of horse race treatment.

The Demers finding that polling had increased in the primary elections should be alarming to those who say that the timing of polls does the greatest harm. The argument is made that the citizens surveyed before the primary are responding almost wholly on name recognition, and thus lesser-known candidates begin to be frozen out. If contributors and political workers are affected by who is leading in the polls, as many argue they are, then the whole process is hastened by the primary polls. The poll shows Joe Well-Known leading significantly and the money and potential workers for Sam Unknown dry up, the argument goes. The possible effects of primary polling are discussed again later in this chapter and also in the Hickman and McBride chapters in this book.

Another criticism has been that by conducting their own polls, the media leave the traditional role of reporting the news and enter the arena of making the news (Asher, 1988, p. 89). Columnist Nicholas Von Hoffman has written: "The big news organizations, therefore, are making their own news and flacking it as though it were an event they were reporting on over which they had no control, like an earthquake or a traffic accident" (Von Hoffman, 1980, p. 573).

Von Hoffman argued in the 1980 article that the frequent use of off-year polls pairing likely contenders had given the "news companies the power to make every day election day." Albert E. Gollin of the National Advertising Bureau notes: " 'Public opinion,' whatever that phrase once meant, now is taken by most people most of the time to mean poll findings" (Gollin, 1980, p. 448).

Deceive and Inform

Mark Miller and Robert Hurd, a journalism professor and survey researcher, respectively, wrote that a most fundamental criticismof

> polls is that they can deceive as well as inform. Pollsters know that survey results can be altered by subtle changes in question wording, by differences in interview method or by sampling different populations. But the public might accept "scientific" survey results without asking if the questions were loaded or the samples biased." (Miller & Hurd, 1982, p. 243)

Another cautionary note has been that, as other elements in the election process have weakened—such as in the diminished role of political parties—the polls have become a more powerful ingredient in the stew. This is not always voiced as a criticism of the media but as a statement of change in our society and as an area of potential harm.

According to Gollin (1980, p. 446),

> The changing structure of American politics—a consequence (among other factors) of party reforms, demographic shifts, volatile economic conditions and the impact of events (Vietnam, Watergate)—has progressively loosened the grip of power brokers on presidential candidate selection, and polls and the news media have stepped in to fill the vacuum.

Political scientist Graber says, "The advent of television and its ready availability in every home, the spread and improvement of public opinion polling and the use of computers in election data analysis have vastly enhanced the role of the mass media in elections" (Graber, 1989, p. 196).

Media "Cast" Candidates

Noting the decline in party influence, Graber says the media decide who the presidential hopefuls are early on, which she calls "casting." It

> occurs early in the primaries when newspeople, on the basis of as yet slender evidence, must predict winners and losers in order to narrow the field of eligibles. Concentrating on the front-runners in public opinion polls makes newspeople's tasks more manageable, but it often forces trailing candidates out of the race prematurely. (Graber, 1989, p. 198)

She goes on to say that Carter's 1976

> handling of the media was astute. He managed to convince newspeople that his election successes were far greater than could be reasonably expected. Such expectations, which are media creations, are based on poll results, projections from past campaigns and more or less educated guesses.

Graber calls the media's preelection polls "yet another weapon in the arsenal for king-making." She notes the wide dissemination of the major polls and adds:

> These widely publicized poll results become bench marks for voters, telling them who the winners and losers are and what issues should be deemed crucial to the campaign. Depending on the nature and format of the questions asked by the pollsters and the political contest in which the story becomes embedded, the responses spell fortune or misfortune for the candidates. (Graber, 1989, p. 201)

In another statement from which the media can learn, Graber reminds us that polls may determine who decides to run and who decides to bow out. She says that Ronald Reagan was "encouraged to enter the 1976 presidential race because President Gerald Ford's poll ratings were low prior to the Republican presidential nominating convention of that year."

Graber also notes that "media coverage and public opinion polls tend to move in tandem, especially in the early months of a campaign. Candidates who receive ample media coverage usually do well in the polls. Good poll ratings bring more media coverage" (Graber, 1989, p. 199).

A Positive Spin

Journalism educator and media researcher Philip Meyer put a positive spin on the polling power of the press. He argues that "representative government in the United States has always involved tension among competing factions. . . . George Gallup, the pioneer American pollster, thought of his poll as a continuous referendum by which majority will could be made known" (Meyer, 1989, p. 195)

Meyer argues that the "referendum model is much too simple" today and we now are governed by "temporary coalitions." The process of forming these coalitions is changing. One tool in that change is "precision journalism," the title of Meyer's 1973 book, which frequently is hailed as the vehicle that launched the use of social and behavioral science research in journalism.

Meyer says the motive for the press getting so intensely involved in polling was "simple competitiveness. The most interesting fact about an election is who wins. If you can find out ahead of time, that's news by definition" (Meyer, 1989, p. 196).

As one might expect with such a "good thing," its use has grown. Twenty years ago, we focused "chiefly on the two nationally syndicated newspapers polls, those of George Gallup and Louis Harris." But, by 1988, Meyer adds,

> there were 10 national polling organizations in the field, and a new poll was reported every second day on average during the final months of the campaign. Neither the public nor the press corps were accustomed to this density of polling data. Because the presidential selection process was itself in an era of change, some associated the undesirable and worrisome aspects of change with the polls and began to blame the polls. (Meyer, 1989, p. 196)

Regarding the frequent complaint that polls often are wrongly interpreted, he says that the media have made "considerable progress in understanding and interpreting election polls" in the last 20 years. Michael B. Salwen, a communication professor, says studies have shown that there has been marked improvement in reporting of public opinion poll stories in newspapers over the years (Salwen, 1987, pp. 813-819).

Swaying Voters

The complaint that probably is heard the most, Meyer writes, is that "polls affect the outcome of the election." Until recently, he writes, the polling fraternity dismissed the effects complaint, saying there either wasn't any effect or, if there was one, it was negligible. Meyer says that position no longer can be sustained, "particularly as researchers look at indirect effects through political contributors, campaign volunteers and endorsers." (See the Hickman and the Lavrakas, Holley, and Miller chapters for more about effects.)

Don't curb the polls, Meyer argues. Instead, "the democratic solution, of course, is . . . to teach those who use them to make decisions to do so rationally." Meyer goes on to argue that, although direct effects on voters are often so slight as to lack statistical significance, "that does not mean they lack substantive importance. In a close election, there may be no such thing as a negligible effect. The presidential elections of 1960 and 1968 could have been tipped the other way by an number of normally inconsequential factors" (Meyer, 1989, p. 198).

The deluge of polling information, Meyer argues, could be good for the democratic process. It can help build coalitions, he says. It can help the citizen vote tactically. In other words, the voter finds out from the polls who is leading and then decides how to vote based on where he or she thinks the vote will count the most or decides whether it is worthwhile to vote.

Meyer notes an uneasiness in the media—a feeling of guilt—about their "new role" as providers of information based on polls they have conducted or sponsored. But, he says, the media "have no choice except to fulfill" this role, "just as the rank-and-file voters must accept new and heavier responsibility."

Another criticism of the media's use of polls comes from a study by sociologists Carol H. Weiss and Eleanor Singer (Weiss & Singer, 1988). They found that one of the most common problems was the media's tendency to report poll results as if they would hold up for all time, as if the findings were etched in granite, not to be altered by events or time.

A simple device used at the Omaha, Nebraska, *World-Herald,* where I was a managing editor, was to write all poll stories in the past tense, giving them less permanency. The newspaper also insisted that all polls be given feature headline play, toning down the hard news element.

Journalistic Constraints

Albert H. Cantril, former president of the National Council on Public Polls, says that the constraints of journalism place certain limitations on the handling of polls (Cantril, 1976). One of these is brevity, with most stories running no more than 1,000 words in print and taking no more than a minute in television or radio. The polls also must be topical and timely if they are to be deemed newsworthy by print and broadcast decision makers. Another constraint, according to Cantril, is that "the reading or viewing audience seldom has patience for a complex presentation." Polls also must have broad appeal, he says.

Certain consequences flow from these requirements. One of these is

the need to ask simple questions. Presidential popularity and candidate pairings are examples of simple, straightforward questions repeatedly asked. It is on the issues—many of which are complex and about which the public knows little—that problems arise. Often the intricacies of an issue must be spelled out before the respondent's opinion is solicited. However, this raises the danger of inadvertently loading the question one way or another. (Cantril, 1976, p. 47)

It follows that "a complex matter must be boiled down to simple yes-no, agree-disagree, favor-oppose alternatives." Cantril says this is all right most of the time, "but there is always the danger that the response alternatives available to the respondent will either be at such extremes that a choice is meaningless or pose an issue in terms that are alien. In all cases, however, percentages will be generated and usually reported" (Cantril, 1976, p. 47).

Sources of Error

Cantril also says that the task of the media "is to determine the validity of poll findings and what they mean" (Cantril, 1976, pp. 49-50). He notes that there are many sources of error in a poll.

The source of greatest possible error is the method used to determine who will be surveyed but, Cantril says,

> with modern probability methods of sampling . . . it is possible to measure just how good the sample is. . . .

> The greatest error in polling usually creeps in at later stages in the process: interviewer cheating, question wording, or tabulation and analysis. The competent pollster is careful to validate interviews, pretest for bias in questions, examine tabulations for internal consistency, and carry analysis only as far as the data will go. (Cantril, 1976, pp. 49-50)

Another source of bias is the wording of questions. Two considerations stand out at the analytical level, Cantril says, and "both deal with the question of when differences in opinion are meaningful: between two polls and between segments of the population." He points out that a specific number of percentage points must separate two candidates to result in a statistically significant finding. This will vary with the sample size, but statistical procedures allow for the determination of the figure. For instance, if the margin of error in a survey is four percentage points, plus or minus, and George Bush has 51 and Michael Dukakis has 49, there is no statistically significant difference between the two. Bush might be as high as 55 and as low as 47; Dukakis might have 53 or 45. Regarding the second point, Cantril notes:

> When it comes to differences between groups within the same sample (for example, Democrats and Republicans) the same principle generally applies, except that one is dealing with many fewer interviews with each group than for the entire sample. Therefore, many more percentage points (up to eight or 10 points) are needed to state with certainty that a real difference of opinion exists between two groups. (Cantril, 1976, pp. 50-51)

Weiss and Singer cite several shortcomings in the reporting of social science research (Weiss & Singer, 1988). They say these include oversimplification, exaggeration, fragmentation, and uncritical reporting.

Judging Quality

Weiss and Singer, whose book deals with the reporting of the whole gamut of social science research, not just political polls, found that reporters and editors paid little attention to "research quality." Rather than evaluating the quality of the research, reporters judged the research by the standards they applied to other sources: the position and reputation of the individual and the institution with which he or she was affiliated (Weiss & Singer, 1988, p. 52). Editors often left the judgment to the reporter. (The Miller, Merkle, and Wang chapter also talks about quality.)

Weiss and Singer also found that, generally, there were no social science beats in the media and thus stories were dispersed among the reporters, "few of whom have adequate opportunity to become thoroughly familiar with social science concepts, findings, norms, leading figures or institutions" (Weiss & Singer, 1988, p. 72). (A similar finding emerged in my study regarding the handling of political poll stories, which is reported later in this chapter.)

Weiss and Singer also found far less citing of sources in journalistic writing than is found in academic articles. They noted that some newspapers and magazines usually "do supply at least one reference in text for major articles. It usually consists of a statement such as 'in the latest issue of the New England Journal of Medicine.'"

The media rarely discuss the methodology in stories focusing on a piece of social science research. Newspapers were better about citing the method than were magazines or television, Weiss and Singer found. But only one out of three of the newspaper stories "gave any detail about methods. . . . Surveys of public opinion were considerably more likely than other types of social science studies to provide some information about the method used" (Weiss & Singer, 1988, pp. 238-239). Weiss and Singer's book contains specific information about how frequently such items as sample size were used in the media they analyzed.

Weiss and Singer found that it was rare for the media to put research findings in context, generally failing to report whether the findings agreed or disagreed with other studies, for instance. Depending on the medium, 15% or less of the stories in which the social science research was the focus of the story tried to place the findings in context (Weiss & Singer, 1988).

Summary of Criticisms

These then are the primary criticisms of the media's handling of the polls:

(1) Too much attention is given to the horse race aspects of the campaign, and polling about and coverage of issues are slighted.

(2) By conducting their own polls, the media are making news.

(3) Polls interfere with the election process and have become more powerful as other elements, such as the role of the political parties, have grown weaker. Even excluding polling, the media have become more powerful players in the campaigns.

(4) Citizens answering preprimary polls are responding to name recognition only. Thus lesser known candidates begin to be frozen out of the process, with workers and contributions drying up. Polls also may determine who decides to run and who decides to stay on the sidelines.

(5) Survey results can be altered by question wording, methodological differences, and sampling strategies, and the media are not well enough informed about polling practices to alert the public. Some evidence exists that the media are improving with regard to handling survey results.

(6) Polls affect the outcome of elections.

(7) The media report findings as if they would be true for all time rather than being a snapshot of opinion at one point in time.

(8) Constraints imposed by journalistic practices place certain limitations on the handling of the survey stories, including the following: The articles must be brief; they must be timely and have broad appeal; and questions may be simplistic.

(9) Journalists have a tendency to oversimplify, exaggerate, and fragment survey results and to "park" their critical facilities when reporting the findings. The methodology of the survey rarely is covered.

(10) Findings seldom are put in to context. The change between surveys or whether the latest survey agrees with previous studies often is ignored.

A Survey of Newspaper Practices

As stated earlier, four out of ten (40%) American dailies are directly involved in political polling, either conducting surveys in-house, contracting with an outside organization to have them done, or doing both, according to

TABLE 10.1 Percentage of Daily Newspapers Doing Political Polling
(by circulation size)

Circulation	< 25,000 (percentage)	25,000– 49,999 (percentage)	50,000– 99,999 (percentage)	100,000– 249,999 (percentage)	> 250,000 (percentage)
Conduct own	26	23	10	17	25
Both	0	8	10	0	19
Contract	9	23	31	66	44
Don't do polls	65	46	48	17	13

a study I have done. The study had a margin of error of nine percentage points, plus or minus, and a response rate of 85%.[1]

Many may suspect that this is an increase in polling, but I did not find a directly comparable study. The previously cited 1986 Demers study included all opinion polling, not just political surveys. He found that "slightly more than a third of the newspapers surveyed . . . 34.9 percent . . . reported they had 'conducted an opinion poll on which to gather information to base stories,' which was not significantly different than the 37.1 percent in 1978" (Demers, 1987, p. 840). Political polls may well make up the bulk of surveys in which the press is involved.

The 1986 and 1978 studies also found a correlation between newspaper circulation and having conducted a poll. Larger papers were more likely to have conducted polls (Demers, 1987, p. 840).

The 1989 Northwestern study had a similar finding. Of the smallest dailies, those with circulations of under 25,000, 65% were not involved in polling, whereas only 13% of the newspapers with more than 250,000 circulation were not involved.

Table 10.1 gives a breakdown of the newspapers by circulation and whether they were conducting their own political polls, contracting for them, doing both, or not involved in any polling.[2] The figures are percentages and have been rounded. Those papers involved in political polling also tended to be doing other types of surveys. Nearly half of them said they were involved in polling on life-style questions (49%) and such issues as abortion and gay rights (51%). Nearly three out of four of the dailies were involved in market research (73%).[3]

Although only 40% of the newspapers were directly involved in polling, slightly more than eight out of ten (81%) had access to political surveys.[4] The most often mentioned source was the Associated Press (68%), followed by *The New York Times* (15%), the *Washington Post* (12%), the *Los Angeles Times* (12%), United Press International (10%), and Gallup (5%).[5] Newspapers doing their own political polling were much less likely to get surveys from the wires or a polling organization, while almost all of the nonpolling papers (97%) said they received such services. The figure for the papers doing surveys was 57%.

Few with Guidelines

Only 4% of the newspapers surveyed said they had written guidelines for handling poll stories.[6] The guidelines generally were based on either those adopted by the American Association of Public Opinion Research or those of the National Council of Public Polls. None of the newspapers under 50,000 circulation had written guidelines. Almost all of the papers with written guidelines were those directly involved in polling.

Two other sources are worth citing on the issue of standards—a study by Miller and Hurd and a speech given by Warren J. Mitofsky. In their 1982 study on the use of standards, Miller and Hurd analyzed three newspapers, the *Chicago Tribune*, the *Los Angeles Times*, and the *Atlanta Constitution*. They found that conformity to AAPOR standards was

> highest in presidential election years, 1972 and 1976, and lowest in nonelection years. . . . Newspaper conformity to the standards apparently has not increased despite efforts to promote them, nor has it kept pace with the frequency of publishing poll results. (Miller & Hurd, 1982, p. 246)

They also found that

> conformity was significantly higher in election polls than nonelection polls for all standards except sample size and sponsorship. Spokesmen for the three papers . . . stated that election polls are handled more conscientiously because they are more important than other polls. (Miller & Hurd, 1982, pp. 246-247)

Miller and Hurd also reported that there was more conformity to standards when the poll was done for or by the paper as opposed to a poll provided by "outside sources."

"That's Too Bad"

> Editors of the papers agreed that the methodological information required by the AAPOR standards should generally be included in reports of public opinion polls. When asked about newspapers' tendency to omit such information, the Gallup spokesman echoed a common sentiment, stating: "That's too bad." (Miller & Hurd, 1982, p. 249)

But pollsters and their professional organizations also have a role to play in the disclosure area. The burden is not entirely with the media.

Mitofsky, a contributor to this book, said in his 1989 address as the outgoing president of AAPOR:

> It is not satisfactory, in my view, for the researcher just to disclose the items that are called for in AAPOR's "Standard for Minimal Disclosure." That information is not informative enough for most consumers of survey research, certainly not for most members of the news media and other members of the public. It is barely useful to trained survey researchers. What we have done with our minimal disclosure is to place the burden on our users for making sense of the limitations of our surveys. (Mitofsky, 1989, p. 451)

He said that this is wrong and added:

> It is the responsibility of the researcher to spell out the limitations of his or her own survey when there are limitations. . . . Along with reporting the items contained in the minimal disclosure section, the researcher should go further. If there are biases in the research design—for good reason or not—the researcher conducting the study will be the one to make these design flaws—and their consequences—known to the consumer of the research.

Mitofsky also said: "If polls are a public utility . . . then we owe it to the public as well as ourselves to raise the level of our performance. . . ."

In the 1989 Northwestern study, respondents were asked whether the persons handling the polling stories were given training. About one out of two (51%) of the newspapers conducting their own surveys said "yes."[7] A smaller percentage, 37%, of the newspapers contracting for their polls said someone had been trained to handle the surveys.[8] Training was more likely to have occurred at the larger papers conducting their own polls rather than at the smaller papers or at the papers contracting for surveys.

Asked to "briefly describe this training," the most common responses at the newspapers conducting their own polls were "academic experience/degree," "professional background/job," "college course(s)," and "workshops/seminars."

The same question was asked of those newspapers contracting for political surveys. The most common response was "workshops/seminars."

The smaller the newspaper conducting its own polls, the more likely it was that a top executive was named as being responsible for the surveys.[9] This responsibility was delegated down below the level of political editor in almost all of the papers in the 100,000 and above range.

If any pattern emerged at the newspapers contracting for polls, it was a tendency to keep the responsibility for working with the outside organization at a slightly higher level than at those papers conducting their own surveys.[10]

What About Writing and Editing?

How were the political polling stories handled at the writing and editing level? In only about one out of ten cases (12%) were the stories written most often by the political reporters.[11] Nearly three out of four (74%) of the respondents named someone other than the political writer. The title given most often was "reporter," which included general assignment reporter. The next most common was "statehouse reporter," followed by "city editor" and "wire editor." The remaining 14% of the respondents indicated that no political survey stories were being written in the newsroom. The newspapers in the two largest circulation categories were most likely to have the political reporter write the stories.

The newspapers also were asked whether "nonpolitical poll stories [were] assigned to the reporter whose beat is related to the particular subject matter." Seven out of ten (70%) said this was the case. Fewer than one out of ten (8%) answered "no." The rest indicated that no such stories were being written.

Editing the Stories

Of those papers saying the story was not assigned to the beat reporter,[12] one out of four (25%) said a general assignment reporter was given the job. The remaining 75% gave such responses as "political reporter," "any reporter," "editor," "copy editor," and "news editor."

Political polling stories were edited by one person in six out of ten of the newspapers (59%).[13] That means the stories were passed around at four in ten of the papers. What happened in more than eight out of ten of the latter cases (85%) was that the story went to whichever copy editor was available.[14]

Newspapers that did not conduct their own polls were twice as likely (69%) to have the survey stories edited by one person as were the papers doing their own polls (32%). The position named most often at those papers using one editor was the "news editor."

The significance of this group of findings is that it appears that polling stories, political and otherwise, are passed around the newsroom rather than being assigned to someone with expertise in handling them. The assigning editor's eye may be on whether the subject matter of the poll falls within a particular beat rather than on the reporter's polling literacy. And, in most cases, it is probably "the luck of the draw" as to who edits the story.

The 1989 Northwestern study did not explore the quality of what the newspapers were doing. But, in his 1986 study, Demers found what he considered to be an increasing professionalism in newspaper polling. The papers were more likely to seek help from outside consultants in developing questionnaires, gathering data, and analyzing the material than they had been in 1978 (Demers, 1987, p. 840).

Some Concluding Thoughts

The press always has tried to have an effect on society—and has hoped that it did have. The muckrakers were not just trying to report a story; they wanted to bring about change, as do today's investigative reporters. Many newspapers were founded to express a political point of view. Newspapers continue to take editorial positions today—hopefully confined to the editorial page. The mere reporting of a story may bring change. The selection of the detail used, of the sources contacted, and of the way the story is displayed can have an effect.

Developing the investigative piece is making news. Having the ability to publish or broadcast those findings is a power, and, obviously, it can be abused. It does not have to be mishandled, of course, and the media can learn what effect the polls have, and they can modify practices.

Clearly, reporters and editors have been "making news" for a long time. Perhaps one of the differences in the public mind between the investigative piece and the poll story is that the good of and the need for the piece about city hall corruption is apparent, whereas the good of the survey telling us which presidential candidate is leading is not. Perhaps there is an associated negative reaction to media polls as the public becomes more aware of the candidate surveys used to probe the public mind and the resulting manipulation of the candidate to fit that image.

The media cannot and should not back away from using the relatively new and evolving technology of political polling, but clearly there are ways to handle the device better. If someone says "we ought to return to the good old days," we should recall what reporters did before they had their own polls. What they often did was write stories about who was expected to win based on contacting a few of their sources, almost all of whom had the interests of one of the candidates at heart. And, in the early days of polling—and continuing today—a political camp often "leaked" or gave its own "polls" to a reporter. The reporter frequently had little or no information about the methodology used in that poll, the questions asked, or the answers to *all* the questions, not just the ones the politician had chosen to make available, for instance. Those stories were published or broadcast. Did they affect the outcome? Possibly.

In those days before the media conducted its own surveys, we may have "justified" the use of the political insider interview and his or her "polls" on the grounds that they provided the best and only information available. But better information is available today, assuming we have conducted our poll accurately and reported it properly.

Today's polls, both preelection and exit, are not important because they can give us an early handle on who is leading or who has "won." Quite the contrary: In the total scheme of things, that really isn't important and, perhaps, it may even be harmful if it helps distract us from making decisions on the basis of the issues, the merits of the candidates, and a voter's own values. But there is no question that who is leading is newsworthy. The media will not turn away from using this tool, the preelection poll. The media, however, could pay more attention to margin of error and quit trying to call a "leader" when there really isn't one.

Exit Polls to Continue

The press also will continue to use exit polls; the "why" of the victory or loss fits the definition of news. But, again, the media could be more sensitive to the feelings of the public, as shown in the Lavrakas, Holley, and Miller public opinion survey, and back off on those early projections of winners.

What will the public have lost by waiting a few hours to hear an election projection? What will the media lose by continuing to be insensitive to public opinion? As this is being written, Congress is considering adopting a uniform poll-closing law. Will more congressional controls follow?

The media also are unlikely to abandon the horse race stories. To expect that the press would is to ignore the way journalists and this country think. We always have been interested in who is winning. The newsworthiness of the horse race is a given, as Meyer has noted. That does not mean the media could not down play those aspects of the story, or watch the timing of those pieces, or be aware that the polls taken very early in the season may only register name recognition and thus either put the "unknowns" at a disadvantage or out of the race. The media could do fewer trial heat surveys and do those later.

A Special Obligation

The media need to become more sophisticated about polling and its effects. With the media creating news with the polls, they have a special obligation to consider any possible effects on the political process. (The Lavrakas, Holley, and Miller chapter in this book explored the question of the effect of political polls.) Given the media's deep involvement in the polls, it is in their best interest to consider more than such traditional "standards" as whether the information is newsworthy, whether it is accurate, and whether "I must do it because the competition does." The effect also should be considered, perhaps dictating that polls not be done at certain times.

If the media won't stop certain practices outright, such as horse race polling immediately after such major events as the conventions, they could at least put those results in context. They might, for example, note that perceptions are affected by such events. What has happened historically? How is the post-convention number different from the numbers Candidate X was getting during the course of the campaign? (The McBride chapter discusses these aspects.)

A two-pronged and ongoing educational effort is needed. That is an idea that is suggested at various times throughout this book. One thrust is with the public. The other is with the media itself. And, while journalists write to educate the public about polling and its effects, they also will be educating themselves. They will have to become more knowledgeable in order to write those explanatory stories.

Those "Little Boxes"

Some persons have argued for doing away with the "little boxes" of methodological information attached to stories, arguing that few read them and perhaps even fewer understand them, as Lavrakas, Holley, and Miller found with the margin of error experiment.

Better explanations need to be placed within the stories or the boxes, and more information needs to be shared about the conduct and accuracy of the poll. (The use of methodological information is discussed in the Miller, Merkle, and Wang chapter.) It may be unrealistic to expect that the media, both print and broadcasting, will do that when they report the polls of others. But can't they—shouldn't they—at least do it with the polls they sponsor? This information provides a check against the media itself. A knowledgeable reader just might call Ms. Editor or Mr. News Director and say, "Your poll was flawed." And the rest of the public may gain knowledge over time. One of the roles of the media has been to raise the knowledge level of the population—to be an educator.

How can the press educate itself? The findings of my survey regarding training indicate that the efforts currently used could and should be strengthened.

The findings regarding how stories are assigned and edited indicate that newspapers could improve the handling of the articles by having them written and edited by trained persons. Polling stories, as shown throughout this book and chapter, deserve special consideration. They are not just another accident story or city council item or routine political announcement. For one thing, the news organization is making the news with its own polls and, when it publishes the surveys of others, it is disseminating the news they are making.

Some training programs already exist. Others could be started. Corporate sponsorship could be found for universities wishing to undertake such training. Training could be provided in-house or at state and regional press meetings, for instance. At a minimum, a survey methodologist from the local university could be brought in for a brown-bag luncheon with the news staff.

Poll editors could be designated at each media outlet in order to have survey stories flow through one or two trained persons, at least as part of the prepublication, prebroadcasting process. Even the smallest organization could have at least one person in this role. A newspaper might have two reporters and two copy editors trained as well as two supervising editors. Having two trained at each level would take care of vacations and days off. This cadre of polling "experts" also could work with the pollster on the medium's own surveys.

"The Competition Has It"

Editors and news directors could stop allowing the dissemination of poll stories provided by politicians unless their reporters have full access to all of the information. The argument, used by the media over and over again in all sorts of situations—that we have to publish or broadcast the information "because the competition has it"—always has struck me as the most feeble of excuses. Doesn't the need to be responsible outweigh the "need" to be competitive—or, at least, shouldn't it?

Hickman says in his chapter that "one should expect polls to have the greatest impact in races below the presidential level and to have greater impact in primary, nonpartisan, or multicandidate elections at every level." That is something editors and news directors should take into consideration in assigning and editing stories about those "lesser" races.

Regarding the Weiss and Singer findings about sources, reporters and editors appear to have been following the normal practices of checking sources, as one would expect. That may not be enough. Journalists handling these stories either need to be so knowledgeable that they can assess the validity of the research themselves or they need to be skeptical enough to seek opinions on the work. They should develop research methodologists as sources, just as they cultivate experts in other fields.

The print and the electronic media need to adopt guidelines and use them. The 1989 Northwestern survey showed how few newspapers have such standards. The American Association of Public Opinion Research standards have been available for several years.[15] (The National Council on Public Polls, "which is composed of polling organizations, has the same standards as AAPOR's except that the council does not require reporting of sampling error" [Miller & Hurd, 1982, p. 244].)

Miller and Hurd write that "the standards are primarily guidelines for pollsters releasing survey results. However, it is obvious that they also were meant to sensitize journalists."

One might decide, based on the Miller-Hurd work and the 1989 Northwestern survey, that it is not easy to "sensitize" journalists. Miller and Hurd note that *Public Opinion Quarterly* sponsored conferences in 1971 and 1980 on "standards and pollster-journalist relations" as well as one in 1979 by the NCPP and the Kettering Foundation. We, educators and journalists, will have to keep plugging away with these kinds of meetings and others as well as taking the other steps previously mentioned.

"Calling 900"

Another area in which journalists could be sensitized is in the use of the call-in polls, those 900 numbers that were among I. A. Lewis's favorite targets. Do the media justify these polls on the basis of "well, they are just fun" and "no harm done"? How can they be justified when they are meaningless or, worse, deceptive? The responsible media wouldn't publish or broadcast other stories knowing that they were erroneous or misleading? Further, the call-in polls have the potential to detract from the validity of the scientific polling the media are engaged in as well as adding to the media's credibility problems.

Guidelines on handling public opinion surveys from outside sources could include discussion on what kinds of polls will be considered for publication or broadcasting. This could include various methodologies, such as mail and telephone, as well as the source of the polls that will be considered.

The guidelines also could state what standards will be used on the newspaper's or television station's own polls. What will be the timing? How will these stories be reported and played? What kind of disclosure information will they contain? The Miller, Merkle, and Wang chapter discusses the difficulty of adopting standards. But that shouldn't stop us from working on them, perhaps starting with standards for political polls and then undertaking some other area, such as life-style studies, following along with Miller's idea that no one set of standards may fit all kinds of poll subjects.

Two primary areas for consideration are presented here. Many other suggestions flow from these. The two are education and an enhanced partnership between the pollsters and the press. If the public and the media are better educated about the polls, the election process can be enhanced. And a solid partnership between the pollsters and the press could better ensure that those who are involved in the media are serving the public—and themselves—well.

Notes

1. A stratified random sample of 129 daily newspapers was drawn from the 1989 edition of the *Editor & Publisher International Yearbook*. Stratification was done across five circulation size categories: (a) under 25,000, (b) 25,000-49,999, (c) 50,000-99,999, (d) 100,000-249,000, and (e) 250,000 and above. Approximately 25 daily newspapers were sampled in

each of the five categories. Interviewing was conducted by telephone from the Northwestern University Survey Laboratory during the last week of August and the first week of September 1989. At each newspaper, interviewers tried to reach the person most knowledgeable about the paper's polling practices. Of the 129 sampled newspapers, 110 papers (85%) yielded completed interviews. At 11 papers (9%), the designated respondent were never available during the field period, and at 8 papers (6%), the designated respondent refused to participate. Results from the 110 completed surveys have been adjusted to reflect the actual distribution of newspapers by circulation size throughout the nation: that is, papers from the larger circulation categories have been down-weighted, whereas papers from the smaller categories have been up-weighted. The margin of error is nine percentage points, plus or minus.

2. The question asked: "Does your newspaper conduct its own political polls or contract with a polling organization to have them done?"

3. The question asked: "Do you conduct or have polls done on: Other issues, such as abortion and gay rights? Lifestyle questions? Market research for internal use?"

4. The question asked: "Do you subscribe to or receive any political polls on a wire service or in any other form?"

5. The results total more than 100% because respondents could name more than one source.

6. The question asked: "Do you have written guidelines for handling poll stories?" Those answering "yes" then were asked: "Are these guidelines based on those adopted by the American Association of Public Opinion Research and the National Council on Public Polls."

7. This category included newspapers that only conducted their own surveys as well as some that contracted for polls. The other category included papers that contracted only for their surveys.

8. Both categories were asked this question about the person with the primary responsibility for the political polls: "Was this individual given training on handling polls?"

9. The question asked: "What is the title of the person who has primary responsibility for the political polls your newspaper conducts?"

10. The question asked: "What is the title of the person at the newspaper who has the primary responsibility for working with the outside political polling organization?"

11. The question asked: "What is the title of the person who writes most of your political poll stories?"

12. The question asked: "If they are not assigned to the beat reporter, what is the title of the person responsible for writing those stories?"

13. The question asked: "Are all of these poll stories usually edited by one person, including the writing of the headline?"

14. The question asked of papers saying that no single editor edits polling stories: "Since they are not handled by just one person, are they edited by whichever copy editor happens to get the story?"

15. The AAPOR standards are (a) reporting the number of persons interviewed (sample size), (b) the sponsor of the survey, (c) the complete wording of the questions asked, (d) sampling error, (e) who was sampled—the population, such as adults over 18, (f) how the interviews were obtained, such as telephone, mail, in person, (g) when the interviews were conducted, and (h) the basis for results that use less than the total sample, according to Miller and Hurd (1982, p. 244).

References

Asher, H. (1988). *Polling and the public: What every citizen should know*. Washington, DC: CQ Press.

Cantril, A. H. (1976, September). The press and the pollster. *The Annals of the American Academy of Political and Social Science*.

Demers, D. P. (1987). Use of polls in reporting changes slightly since 1978. *Journalism Quarterly*, (Winter), 839-842.

Fitzgerald, M. (1988, December 8). Autopsy of 1988 campaign reporting: Journalists and politicians meet in Iowa to dissect coverage. *Editor & Publisher*, pp. 14-15.

Gollin, A. E. (1980). Exploring the liaison between polling and the press. *Public Opinion Quarterly, 44,* 455-461.

Graber, D. A. (1989). *Mass media and American politics* (3rd ed.). Washington, DC: CQ Press.

Meyer, P. (1989). Precision journalism and the 1988 U.S. elections. *International Journal of Public Opinion Research*, 1(3), 195-205.

Miller, M., & Hurd, R. (1982). Conformity to AAPOR standards in newspaper reporting of public opinion polls. *Public Opinion Quarterly, 46,* 243-249.

Mitofsky, W. J. (1989) Presidential address: Methods and standards: A challenge for change. *Public Opinion Quarterly, 53,* 446-453.

Salwen, M. B. (1987). Credibility of newspaper opinion polls: Source, source intent and precision. *Journalism Quarterly*, (Winter), 813-819.

Von Hoffman, N. (1980). Public opinion polls: Newspapers making their own news? *Public Opinion Quarterly, 44,* 572-573.

Weiss, C. H., & Singer, E. (1988). *Reporting of social science in the national media*.

Index

About the Authors

Harrison Hickman is a partner in Hickman-Maslin Research, Inc., a Washington, D.C.-based public opinion research and political consulting firm that works for Democratic candidates and officeholders nationwide. The firm was named "Best in the Business" by CNN's "Inside Politics" in 1988 and "Most Valuable Pollster" by *U.S. News and World Report* for the 1986 midterm elections. In addition, he is a Ph.D. candidate in political science at Tulane University and has served as an election consultant to CBS News since 1982.

Jack K. Holley, is News Editor at the *Press-Enterprise* in Riverside, California. At the time of the writing of the book he was Assistant Professor at the Medill School of Journalism at Northwestern University, Chicago, and Project Director of the school's Gannett Urban Journalism Center. He also has served as Medill's Director of Undergraduate Studies and as Director of Evanston programs. At the time he joined the faculty, he was Managing Editor for Administration at the *Omaha World-Herald*, a 230,000 circulation regional newspaper. His other newspaper positions have included Assistant to the Executive Editor, City Editor, Urban Affairs Reporter, and Copy Editor.

Michael R. Kagay is Editor of News Surveys at *The New York Times*. He heads the department that designs, conducts, and analyzes public opinion polls for *The Times* as well as *The Times*'s half of Times/CBS News polls. Prior to joining *The Times*, he was Vice President at Louis Harris and Associates, where for five years he directed large-scale surveys on public policy and social issues for the firm's foundation clients. Prior to joining Harris, he was a faculty member for 10 years at Princeton University, where he taught the university's courses on public opinion and polling. He earned his Ph.D. in political science at the University of Wisconsin in Madison. He was a National Science Foundation postdoctoral fellow at the University of Michigan's Institute for Social Research. He has served on the executive council of the American Association for Public Opinion Research and was the program chairman of its annual conference in 1990.

Paul J. Lavrakas is Associate Professor with the Medill School of Journalism at Northwestern University, where he has been employed since 1978. He also is the founder and director of the Northwestern University Survey Laboratory. He is the author of *Telephone Survey Methods: Sampling, Selection and Supervision* (Sage, 1987). He has an international reputation on citizens' reactions to crime based on his extensive research in that field from 1974 to the present. His primary research interest is the manner in which the news media use sample surveys for editorial and business purposes. Born in Cambridge, MA, he completed his doctoral studies in applied social psychology at Loyola University of Chicago in 1977. From 1968 to 1972, he taught fifth-grade in the innercity of Chicago.

I. A. (Bud) Lewis began his journalism career in Paris as "un speaker" (an announcer) and writer for Radio-Diffusion Francaise in 1948. In 1949, he worked in Germany as a civilian employee of the Armed Forces Network (AFN), first as a newswriter in Frankfurt, Bremen, and Berlin, and then in 1951 as bureau chief in Stuttgart. Back in the United States, he was employed as a newswriter by UPI in 1952 and 1953 and for Armed Forces Radio from 1954 to 1956, both in New York City. In 1956, he became a writer for David Garroway on NBC Radio and in 1957 on NBC television. After a stint as first a writer for and later an Associate Producer of the *Today Show*, he wrote television documentaries until 1964, when he joined the NBC Election Unit and became its Director of Polling in 1966 and Director of Elections in 1969. In 1976, he joined CBS News as director of polling for the CBS News/*New York Times* Poll. In 1977, he joined the Roper Organization as a partner. From 1979 unitil his death in 1990, he was director of the *Los Angeles Times* Poll. He graduated with honors from Princeton University. During the Second World War, he served in the China-Burma-India Theater with Air Force Intelligence.

Frank W. McBride is a Project Director with Yankelovich Clancy Shulman, a marketing and public opinion research firm in Westport, Connecticut. A public opinion specialist, he plays a major role in conducting polls for *Time* magazine and the Cable News Network. His other areas of interest include conducting public opinion research for public relations firms, pharmaceutical companies, and the media. During the 1988 election cycle, he was a Senior Research Analyst with George Bush's polling firm, Market Opinion

Research. In addition to serving as an analyst for the Bush campaign, he has served as an analyst and consultant for a number of senatorial and gubernatorial campaigns in a dozen states. He received a B.A. in Political Science from the University of Chicago and an M.A. in Political Science from the University of Michigan.

Daniel M. Merkle is a Ph.D. student in the Department of Communication Studies at Northwestern University. His research and teaching interests include mass communication theory, public opinion polling, and research methodology.

Peter V. Miller is Associate Professor of Communication Studies and Journalism at Northwestern University. He is Director of the Institute for Modern Communications at Northwestern. A former chair of the Standards Committee of the American Association for Public Opinion Research, he has written on survey methodology and mass communication effects.

Warren J. Mitofsky is Executive Director of Voter Research and Surveys, which is an association of ABC, CNN, CBS, and NBC for producing election projections and exit polls for all network broadcasts. He was Executive Director of the CBS News Election and Survey Unit and Executive Producer of primary and election broadcasts. In 1975, he founded the CBS News/*New York Times* Poll, and he has consulted on the interpretation of social research for CBS News broadcasts. He is a past President of the American Association for Public Opinion Research and the National Council on Public Polls. He is a Fellow of the American Statistical Association. He came to CBS News in 1967 from the Census Bureau, where he designed many surveys for the poverty program, for presidential commissions investigating the selective service system, and for the Watts riots and other demographic surveys. He and Joseph Waksberg developed a telephone sampling technique that has been widely adopted by other researchers. He did his doctoral work in mass communication at the University of Minnesota, where he became a Candidate in Philosophy.

Michael W. Traugott is Professor of Communication and Program Director in the Center for Political Studies of the Institute for Social Research at the University of Michigan. He directs the program in Media and Politics there. A political scientist by training, his research interests include media and politics, campaigns and elections, and survey research methods. He has served as a consultant to several media organizations for their election coverage, and, for several years, he conducted surveys and wrote a column for *The Detroit News*. During 1988, he was on leave from the university at the Gallup Organization, where he directed surveys for a project titled "The People, the Press & Politics," supported by the Times Mirror Company. He received his B.A. from Princeton University and his M.A. and Ph.D. from the University of Michigan.

Paul Wang is Assistant Professor of Advertising at the Medill School of Journalism at Northwestern University. He earned his Ph.D. in Communications Studies at Northwestern. His research interests mainly concern data base management, consumer perception, and methodological issues in consumer research.